Real
Estate
and
You

Real Estate and You

FRANK BATTINO, CHAIRMAN
Real Estate Department
Merritt College
Oakland, California

LOWELL ANDERSON
Real Estate Department
Cerritos College
Norwalk, California

This text-syllabus supports the telecourse by the same name, which was produced through the cooperative effort and investment of the Southern California Consortium for Community College Television, the Bay Area Community College Television Consortium, the Valley Consortium, and the California Department of Real Estate. The course involves faculty representation from about sixty of the California Community Colleges, and production facilities and support services of KOCE-TV, Channel 50, Huntington Beach, California.

JOHN WILEY & SONS
New York   Santa Barbara   London
Sydney   Toronto

THIS BOOK WAS PRINTED AND BOUND BY VAIL-BALLOU PRESS, INC.
IT WAS SET IN TIMES ROMAN BY VAIL-BALLOU PRESS, INC.
THE DESIGNER WAS EDWARD A. BUTLER.
THE DRAWINGS WERE DESIGNED AND EXECUTED BY JOHN BALBALIS
WITH THE ASSISTANCE OF THE WILEY ILLUSTRATION DEPARTMENT.

Library of Congress Cataloging in Publication Data

Battino, Frank.
  Real estate and you.

  Text-syllabus to be used in conjunction with the
telecourse of the same title.
  1. Real estate business.   I. Anderson, Lowell, joint
author.   II. Title.

HD1375.B325   333.3′3   76-20543
ISBN 0-471-01792-2

Printed in the United States of America

10 9 8 7 6 5 4 3 2 1

TO KÄREN, GINA, GREG, AND GIANCARLO BATTINO

TO BARBARA AND KATHY ANDERSON

PREFACE

INTRODUCTION

Every day you come in contact with real estate. The place where you live is real estate. The place where you work is real estate.

Real estate trends affect your city's growth and development. They also affect the economic well-being of your state and nation.

This text-syllabus, written in nontechnical, clear language, answers many questions that you may have about real estate. Each unit contains information that is to be used in conjunction with the telecourse also entitled "Real Estate and You." The telecourse consists of thirty 1-half-hour programs that relate to the thirty text-syllabus units.

HOW TO USE THIS TEXT-SYLLABUS

Each unit contains a brief overview that describes the content of the unit. This is followed by your assignment.

Performance objectives are listed to emphasize the most important points. These objectives are followed by a list of terms that you should know.

There is a brief summary at the end of each unit, followed by study questions. The study questions are based on the performance objectives. Answers to the study questions and a Glossary at the end of the book are provided for your convenience.

Read the appropriate unit before you watch the corresponding television program. By combining the two resources, you will find the answers to many of your real estate questions. Remember, however, that general real estate rules and laws are discussed rather than the exceptions. Although this text-syllabus provides general real estate information, the advice of experts is recommended in individual situations.

SPECIAL CONSIDERATIONS

This text-syllabus and the telecourse of which it is a part are both components of a larger instructional system. "Real Estate and You" is designed as a telecourse for the real estate consumer. Both this text-syllabus and the related television programs are intended to help the real estate consumer find answers to problems with regard to his or her real estate concerns. Although the book and the television program will provide the reader-viewer with *general* answers to a great many questions, persons who have problems of a special nature are advised to seek out professional counsel from specialists in their fields of concern.

It is important, also, that the reader note that real estate is a dynamic, changing field, and that the television student is encouraged to keep in contact with the on-campus teacher for the telecourse "Real Estate and You." Further, both the television programs and this text-syllabus are continuously appraised and evaluated for purposes of periodic revision to avoid obsolescence of information. Teachers and students are encouraged to submit their suggestions and recommendations for improvement to the Southern California Consortium for Community College Television, Office of the Los Angeles County Superintendent of Schools, 9300 East Imperial Highway, Downey, California 90242.

FRANK BATTINO
LOWELL ANDERSON

ACKNOWLEDG-MENTS

The authors offer sincere thanks to the following people for their assistance in the preparation of this syllabus. For assistance in the development of the original outline, offering suggestions, and supplying information for the publication:

Robert Bond, Los Angeles Valley College
John Chambers, Diablo Valley College
Homer Davey, Foothill College
Cecelia Hopkins, College of San Mateo
Maurie Krause, San Diego City College
Murray Lewis, Santa Monica College
Dennis McKenzie, College of the Redwoods
Robert Peters, Santa Ana College
Marjorie Reed, San Diego Evening College
Milton Vail, Contra Costa College

For technical assistance offered:

Dr. August DeJong
Robert A. Lehman, Southern California Consortium for Community College Television
Dr. George A. Willey, Bay Area Community College Television Consortium.

The authors are grateful, also, for the endorsement of this work by the membership of the Commissioners Real Estate Education and Research Advisory Committee (CREERAC) and by the Community College Real Estate Advisory Committee.

And, for permission to reprint various forms incorporated in this study guide:

Wolcotts, Inc., Los Angeles, California
The California Association of Realtors
Title Insurance and Trust Company, Los Angeles, California

ABOUT THE AUTHORS

Frank Battino is a real estate broker with more than ten years of active real estate experience. He is also a real estate academician. He is chairman of the Real Estate Department at Merritt College, Oakland, California, which offers one of the most extensive real estate curriculums in the nation. He is a past president of the Berkeley Board of Realtors and the only member in that board's seventy-five year history to have received both the "Salesman of the Year" and the "Realtor of the Year" awards. He is a specialist in investment properties and exchanges, and was the recipient of the "Best Real Estate Exchange in California" award presented by the California Association of Realtors in 1970. He is one of thirteen members of the California "Real Estate Commissioners Community College Real Estate Advisory Committee" and one of the three members of the "Real Estate Curriculum Editorial Board." He is the 1976 chairman of the California Association of Real Estate Teachers.

Lowell Anderson received his B.A. degree from the University of Utah and his M.B.A. from San Diego State University. For nine years he was Regional Supervisor of the Business Division of the California State Department of Education and, for fifteen years, he was a coordinator of instructors in business and real estate with Cerritos College, Norwalk, California. He has been a member of the California Community College Real Estate Advisory Committee for the past eleven years, as well as a member of CREERAC for the past nine years. He also served as an officer in the California Association of Real Estate Teachers over a period of nine years. With the recommendation of the Department of Real Estate, he has acted as a guest instructor in methods and techniques of teaching real estate at San Jose State University, Fullerton State University, and Los Angeles State University. With Frank Battino, he is one of the three members of the Real Estate Curriculum Review Board.

CONTENTS

Real Estate and You

IN WHAT WAYS DOES REAL ESTATE AFFECT YOUR LIFE?

Since time began, most of what we call material wealth has been embodied in the possession of property.

California property ownership has had a romantic and interesting history. This unit reviews this history and stresses the historical, legal, civic, and economic importance of real estate in your life.

Read this study guide (pages 2–6).
View TV program, number 1.

At the conclusion of this unit, you will be able to:

1 Explain the statement that "real estate has a historical, legal, civic, and economic meaning to the average citizen."

2 List two reasons why each of these important items should be of concern to students.
a Historical significance.
b Legal significance.
c Civic significance.
d Economic significance.

3 List four steps in the beginning of land ownership in California under the U.S. government.

property	tenant
owner	lessor
landlord	lessee

In the preamble to the Code of Ethics of the National Association of Realtors there is the following statement.

Under all is the land
Upon its wise utilization and widely allocated ownership depend the survival and growth of free institutions and of our civilization.

The Realtor is the instrumentality through which the land resource of the nation reaches its highest use and through which land ownership attains its widest distribution.

He is a creator of homes, a builder of cities, a developer of industries and productive farms.

This statement typifies the importance of real estate in your life and magnifies the importance placed on it by one of the largest groups of professional men and women in this world.

BACKGROUND AND STATISTICS

Even in Biblical times, most of what we call "material wealth" was embodied in the possession of *property* of some kind. Today, the portion of property known as real property (this term will be defined in the next unit) provides two-thirds of all of the national wealth and contributes one-half of all of the commerce in the United States.

Of almost 2.5 billion acres of land in the United States, nearly 100 million acres are right here in California, the state with the greatest population.

According to the U.S. Department of Commerce, Bureau of Census, the population in California is about 23 million now. With a projected increase of 250 to 300 million by the year 2000 on a nationwide basis, and with California absorbing 10 percent of the projected increase, 10 million people will be added.

These statistics are important only if they help you to become aware of the significance of real estate in your life.

HISTORICAL IMPORTANCE OF REAL ESTATE

California has perhaps the most interesting and romantic history of any state in the union. Tracing its development, particularly as it relates to real estate, can be helpful educationally, civically, legally, and economically.

In the early days of California, land was owned by the Spanish government. It established missions and made land grants in the form of ranchos. These grants were made to the favored ones who had fought to secure Spanish ownership of the state.

Mexico was the next primary owner of California until the United States took over at the conclusion of the Mexican war in 1848.

The treaty of Guadalupe Hidalgo ended this war, and the United States guaranteed protection of all property rights of Mexicans in California.

HOW DID OWNERSHIP OF REAL PROPERTY IN CALIFORNIA ORIGINATE?

The United States confirmed Mexican land grants to individuals and issued documents called patents (forerunner of deeds) as evidence.

The United States issued patents of pueblo lands to a city, and the city issued deeds to individuals.

The United States issued patents of public lands to individuals under numerous land laws. The major laws were:

1853	California received land grants for public schools and a university.
1862	Congress passed the Homestead Act.
1866	Congress passed a bill providing a land grant to railroads.
1866–1868	Congress passed laws protecting timberland, mines, and desert land.
1887	Title Insurance first appeared in California.

Congress granted lands to California for education, reclamation, and other purposes as well as tidal and submerged lands.

ECONOMIC IMPORTANCE OF REAL ESTATE

Do you realize that as a property owner, if this is your desire, you help to provide jobs for millions of people and supply them with millions of dollars of income?

Do you realize that through property taxes you help to provide millions of dollars in income to the government, which allows you to enjoy the many services provided by the government? For instance:

Police and fire protection.

Schools.

Communication.

Other vital services.

Do you realize that other great industries depend, to a great extent, on real estate investment? Some of them are:

Lumber.

Steel.

Cement.

Plumbing.

How can you explain this statement: "Real property is one of the best protections against inflation"?

Have you ever stopped to consider these factors?

The growth and development of real estate has a vital effect on employment, national growth, free enterprise, and prosperity throughout our state and nation.

The ownership of land and a home will provide comfort and security for you and your family and will give you a feeling of economic independence and happiness.

Good upkeep of your home, whether you are an owner or a *tenant* (a person residing in the home of the owner), is necessary to maintain and increase real property values.

REMEMBER

Taking care of your home is not only good citizenship but good business.

LEGAL IMPORTANCE OF REAL ESTATE

In early history, possessing a piece of property was the same as owning it. Today there is a difference between ownership and possession of lands.

If you own property, you are known as the *owner* and have the right, within existing laws, of determining its use and its management whether you live in it or not.

A person not owning the property but living on it is called a *tenant*. If you are the owner, you may lease your property to a tenant. In this event, you become the *lessor,* and the tenant becomes the *lessee*.

CIVIC IMPORTANCE OF REAL ESTATE

If all of the land in the United States were divided, there would be about 4 acres per person on which to live, produce food, work, shop, and play. This land also would be reserved for public agencies to provide necessary services such as sanitation, transportation, government, and the like.

In the early history of California, public lands were made available through the Homestead Acts.

Land was set aside for parks, monuments, and national forests.

As more people came to California, land began to be divided into smaller and smaller parcels. This trend will continue, and innovations in living, such as mobile homes and condominiums, will continue to offer opportunities for ownership.

Private ownership includes improvements on your real property, and they will generally grow in value.

Every taxpayer knows that a progressive community increases and improves the value of his own property.

If this is true, then here comes the $64 question:

If you feel that every homeowner or prospective homeowner has an important stake in good government, schools, parks, highways, sanitation services, utilities, and all other services in order to enjoy a productive, healthy, and happy way of life—*what are you personally doing about it, or what can you do about it?*

UNIT SUMMARY

In this unit you learned that California had an interesting and romantic beginning and that land ownership played a part in that beginning.

The rights that existed under Spanish and Mexican rule and the effects on land ownership today make up that historical beginning.

The economic value of real property included its importance as a basis for large and small industries.

The legal importance of real property, including rights enjoyed as a tenant or owner, was discussed, and the civic importance of real property, including private and government ownership, was reviewed.

REVIEWING YOUR UNDERSTANDING

TRUE OR FALSE

(   ) **1** In the early days of California, land was originally owned by the Spanish government.

(   ) **2** Under the Treaty of Guadalupe Hidalgo, the United States guaranteed complete protection of all property rights of Mexicans in California.

( ) **3** The first real clarification of land titles came under the U.S. government.

( ) **4** Congress granted no land to California for education, reclamation, or other purposes.

( ) **5** The growth and development of real estate has no appreciable effect on employment and national growth.

( ) **6** The terms *lessee* and *tenant* are synonymous.

( ) **7** If all of the land in the United States were divided, there would be about 8 acres per person on which to live.

( ) **8** In California's early history, public lands were made available through the Homestead Acts.

Review any American history book for additional information concerning the early history of land development.

SUGGESTED LEARNING ACTIVITIES
REVIEWING YOUR UNDERSTANDING—ANSWERS

TRUE OR FALSE

1 True	5 False
2 True	6 True
3 True	7 False
4 False	8 True

NOTES:

About 50% of Calif. land is privately owned; approp. 46% is owned by Federal govt., 4% by other public bodies.

YEAR	AVG. SALES PRICE OF HOMES	AVG. FAMILY INCOME	RATIO
1900	5,000	500	10
1930	7,200	1,400	5.1
1945	6,600	1,300	5.0
1975	39,300	14,000	2.8
1980	65,000 (est.)	20,000 (est.)	3.3

2

There are two main divisions of property—*real* and *personal*. In this unit we do not explain personal property or delineate its characteristics. We simply say—it is property that is *not* real property.

When you *buy, sell,* or *exchange* real property, you are dealing in real estate.

An individual purchasing or selling real property often will become confused about what is considered real property.

At the time of a sale or a purchase it is vitally important for you to know whether certain property is *real* and stays with the property or whether it is *personal* and can be taken by the seller when he or she leaves.

In this unit we help you to understand the difference between *real* and *personal* property so that you will not be faced with this same dilemma.

A portion of this unit is devoted to the tests that can be used to determine whether an item is attached to the property and, therefore, can or cannot be considered part of the term "land."

To help you to avoid future problems, the unit also explains the special characteristics of real estate. These characteristics include:

Real estate can be measured.

Real estate can be used.

Real estate can be owned.

Read this study guide (pages 8–14).
View TV program, number 2.

At the conclusion of this unit, you will be able to:

1 Distinguish between real and personal property.

2 List the four-part definition of real property.

3. Define the terms intention, method, and adaptability as they relate to the tests that are applied to determine the presence of a fixture.

4 Discuss the meaning of the phrase "bundle of rights" from a legal standpoint.

fixture	adaptability
appurtenant	emblements
intention	fee simple
method	

WHAT IS PROPERTY? The law defines *property* as "that which is the subject of ownership." It defines ownership as "the right to use, possess, enjoy, transfer, and dispose of a thing to the exclusion of others."

The test of property is *transferability*. If it is transferable, it is property.

All property is either *real* or *personal*.

WHAT IS REAL PROPERTY? Land.

Anything affixed thereto.

That which is appurtenant to the land.

That which is immovable by law.

Land—this is often interpreted to be "solid material of the earth—whether it is soil, rock, or other substance." This means either residential or agriculture; mountain or valley; rock or swamp. In addition to the surface soil, it also means:

The *airspace* above the land.

Yielding to the realities of the air and space age, modern courts permit the public use of the air above private land as a highway available to everyone as long as this does not unreasonably interfere with the landowner's enjoyment of his property.

An ancient legal maxim is:

"One owns to the skies and to the center of the earth."

How does this relate to the most modern real estate concepts, the condominium, or "own your own apartment plan"?

Land below the surface of the earth consists of minerals and substances that go to the center of the earth. The law has recognized the fluid and "fugitive" or moving nature of subsurface oil and gas. Since these substances cannot be identified, isolated, or confined strictly in a given space they are incapable of absolute ownership.

Water as part of "land."

Because of the great economic importance of water to the state of California, a great deal of legal stress has been placed on water (both underground and surface) and the legal rights to its use.

Anything affixed to the land.

Anything that is permanently affixed to the land so as to be regarded as a permanent part of the land. A building or things permanently attached to buildings.

Items may start out as personal property and, by virtue of changes taking place, may become real property and then again return to personal property.

EXAMPLE

An underground deposit of iron is clearly land. When removed, transported, and processed into steel girders, it is movable personal property. When used to construct a building, it reverts to its status of real property. Eventually, when the building is torn down, the salvage steel becomes personal property.

TESTS FOR FIXTURES There are tests devised to help to determine whether personal property is now considered a *fixture* and must remain with the real property.

Intention.

Method of attachment.

Adaptability.

Existence of an agreement.

Relationship between parties.

INTENTION If the material or device used to make the attachment is of such a nature as to make it *permanent,* an intention is shown to make the item a fixture. If the item is tailored to the property, it is a *fixture*.

EXAMPLES
Drapes, wall-to-wall carpeting.

CAUTION
If you are buying a home that has carpeting in some or all of the rooms, make certain it is actually tacked down, as is true of most wall-to-wall carpeting. This would make it part of the real estate. On the other hand, if the rug had simply been rolled out neatly right to the edge where the floor and wall come together but was loose and untacked to the floor, it is likely that the rugging would be considered personal property, and the seller would have the right to roll it up and take it with him.

METHOD OF ATTACHMENT This example leads to the second test of a fixture. What method was used to fasten it down? Was it nailed, screwed, or bolted down permanently? Will the real estate be damaged if the item is removed?

ADAPTABILITY If the personal property attached for ordinary use in connection with the land is well adapted, it is probably a fixture.

EXAMPLES
Shutters, window air coolers.

EXISTENCE OF AN AGREEMENT This is an agreement between parties involved as to the nature of the property affixed to the land. If the parties have displayed sufficient foresight and have properly anticipated the problem, there is no problem.

RELATIONSHIP BETWEEN PARTIES Courts will consider the relationship between the disputing parties: buyer and seller; landlord and tenant; and borrower and lender.

CAUTION
Courts have a tendency to favor the *buyer,* the *tenants,* and the *lenders*.

In answer to the question—what is a fixture?—the California legislature has responded, at least partially, by statute.

EXAMPLE

It had declared that a thing is affixed to the land when it is attached to it by roots, as in the case of trees, vines, or shrubs; imbedded in it, as in the case of walls; permanently resting on it, as in the case of buildings; or permanently attached to what is therefore permanent by means of cement, plaster, nails, bolts, or screws. (Under the code, industrial growing crops and things that, by agreement, are to be severed before the sale or under the contract of sale, shall be treated as personal property and are governed by the law of sale of goods.)

APPURTENANCES That which is incidental or appurtenant to the land. This includes anything that is by right used with the land for its benefit.

EXAMPLES

Water courses or easements (rights of way over adjoining lands, or even passages for light, air, or heat from or across the land of another).

Another common type of appurtenance is stock in a mutual water company.

That which is immovable by law; except, for purposes of sale, *emblements* (growing crops of vegetables, production of the soil, produced annually by labor and not spontaneously), industrial growing crops, and things attached to or forming part of the land.

WHAT IS PERSONAL PROPERTY? The things that are not *real property* are considered as *personal property*.

If an item cannot be classified as real property or a fixed part of real property, such as movable goods, it is personal property.

EXAMPLE

A portable washer and dryer are considered as *personal property*.

CAUTION

In distinguishing between real and personal property, keep in mind that there are borderline cases.

SOUND ADVICE

To avoid disputes, it is extremely important that you put in writing all property to be included in the sales transaction. If legal questions arise, consult an attorney.

SPECIAL CHARACTERISTICS OF REAL ESTATE It is measured.

Land is measured by federal and state governments by the use of baseline and prime meridians—surveys are made from these and are drawn in townships and sections. (This subject will be treated in the next unit.)

It is used.

In order to insure the "highest and best use of land," properties are zoned for residential, multiple-dwelling, commercial, or industrial use. (More information on this subject is given in subsequent units.)

It is owned.

Real property is owned by governments at all levels for use as forest reserves, parks, schools, streets, and sidewalks.

It is owned by organizations such as churches and other nonprofit establishments.

WHAT IS YOUR "BUNDLE OF RIGHTS?"

Ownership is a "bundle of rights." These rights can be divided.

If you own all of the rights to your real property, you own it in *fee simple* (full rights of ownership).

You will have some rights as a *tenant:*

Right of possession.

Right of use.

Right of complete control of the property under the terms of the lease.

You have rights as an *owner:*

Right to sell or not to sell.

Right to build or tear down your building subject to the government building codes of your community.

Ownership rights can be restricted by encumbrances that comprise public and private rights, such as:

PUBLIC	PRIVATE
zoning	easements
use	covenants
taxes	reservations
police power	rights of way
eminant domain	conditions
escheat	restrictions
easements	
loans—bonds and assessments	

Note. These rights will be discussed elsewhere in the syllabus.

THE RIGHT TO ACQUIRE PROPERTY

The most common method of acquiring or owning property is through purchase from the owner or his agent. Other means of acquiring property are used, and they all involve the use of a deed.

The other methods of acquiring property and the types of deeds involved will be discussed in a subsequent unit along with the subject of how to take title to property.

UNIT SUMMARY

In this unit we pointed out that all property is either real or personal. Real property is land; anything affixed thereto; that which is appurtenant to the land; and that which is immovable by law. All other property is personal.

The unit explains that the test of a fixture includes the intention; method of attachment; adaptability; existence of an agreement; and relationship between parties.

The unit contains an explanation of the special characteristics of real estate: it is measured; it is used; and it is owned.

The unit describes the rights of the tenant and the owner as contained in your "bundle of rights."

REVIEWING YOUR UNDERSTANDING

TRUE OR FALSE

(   ) **1** Personal property can become real property, but real property cannot become personal property.

(   ) **2** Transferability is a basic test of whether something is property.

(   ) **3** To avoid disputes over fixtures, all real estate purchase contracts should carefully itemize all property that is included in the sales price.

(   ) **4** Appurtenances are a form of real property.

(   ) **5** All of the following are considered real property: land, fencing, natural trees, mobile home in a mobile home park, a built-in dish washer, and right of way to the street.

(   ) **6** Anything designed to be movable is personal property.

7 List five tests used to determine whether an item is a fixture and therefore must remain on the real property.

    a

    b

    c

    d

    e

8 Study the diagram and answer the questions that follow.

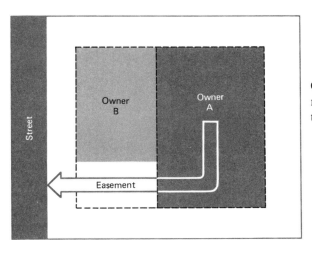

Owner A has easement right over B's land to the street.

a If owner A sells to X, will X have the right to cross over the land to the street? ( )

b If owner B sells to Z, will owner A still have the right to cross over the land to the street? ( )

c If owner A sells to Owner B, what happens to the easement? ( )

9 Describe what "bundle of rights" means.

Determine which items on your own real property can be classified as real property—or as personal property.

SUGGESTED LEARNING ACTIVITIES

REVIEWING YOUR UNDERSTANDING— ANSWERS

1 False

2 True

3 True

4 True

5 True

6 True

7 a Intention
  b Adaptability
  c Agreement between parties
  d Relationship between parties
  e Method attached

8 a Yes
  b Yes (appurtenant)
  c It is extinguished.

9 See page 12.

HOW IS REAL ESTATE
MEASURED AND
DESCRIBED?

In this unit we discuss land descriptions and why a study of them is important. The discussion includes the necessary requirements for recording descriptions, and a comparison of the methods used in California today for describing land with the ones used in early California.

The unit discusses in depth a type of description used when property is not completely described by a duly recorded map and is irregularly shaped.

A method of land description through government survey is also presented. The system and the mechanics used in this type of land description are discussed and directions for computing the area of a specific piece of property are given.

One of the most familiar types of land description, the lot and block system, is discussed.

At the end of the unit we explain the method by which land is mapped and how these maps are filed at the County Recorders Office.

Read this study guide (pages 16–26).
View TV program, number 3.

At the conclusion of this unit, you will be able to:

1 List at least three reasons for the study of land descriptions.

2 Using the metes and bounds system of description, locate a hypothetical piece of property.

3 Define the following terms:
a base lines and meridians
b range lines
c townships
d sections

4 Identify and locate the three principal California base lines and meridians.

5 Correctly number the sections within a township and locate a particular piece of property, calculating the area of that property.

6 List three reasons for using the lot and block system and locate a specific piece of property using this system.

vara	meridians
identification test	township
longitude	section
latitude	tier
metes and bounds	range
base lines	lot and block system

Figure 1 is representative of a land description found in early California. Such descriptions, often printed on parchment or on the skin of an animal, were a far cry from the deeds and land descriptions recognized as "legal" today.

QUESTIONS

1 Is the description given in Figure 1 "legal" today?

2 Would you be able to get title insurance on the basis of such a description?

3 What is wrong with such a description?

These questions will be answered as this unit develops.

HISTORICAL METHODS OF SURVEY

In one method of early land survey two men on horseback dragged each end of a cord or rawhide strip called a thong. This thong was usually about 100 varas in length, a *vara* being approximately 33 inches. One rider would remain stationary, while the other would ride past him when the length of the vara was reached. This would be repeated by the other rider until one of them arrived at the end of the property. The number of line lengths would then be counted.

Another method employed a wheel of a cart. The circumference of the wheel was measured. Then, a leather strip was tied to a spoke so that the revolutions could be counted and the exact distance recorded.

In contrast to these methods, modern surveyors establish exact directions and distances by transits and measuring tapes. Aerial photography is also used in modern mapping and its importance will increase in the future. Property surveys may even be conducted on the ocean floor where scientists foresee the construction of cities.

INTRODUCTION TO MODERN LAND DESCRIPTIONS

Land description is important for two reasons:

1 It is a means of identifying property.

2 It is a means of locating property.

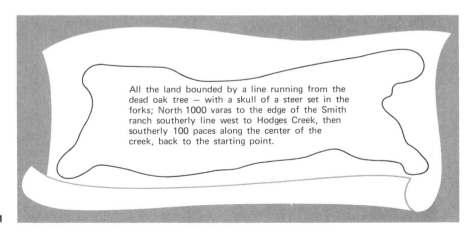

All the land bounded by a line running from the dead oak tree — with a skull of a steer set in the forks; North 1000 varas to the edge of the Smith ranch southerly line west to Hodges Creek, then southerly 100 paces along the center of the creek, back to the starting point.

FIGURE 1

It is important that you understand land description so that you can identify your property and minimize land disputes: without precise descriptions there would be considerably more disputes between neighborly owners.

Every parcel of land sold, leased, or mortgaged must be properly identified or described. These descriptions are often called "legal" descriptions. They are actually based on the field notes of a surveyor or civil engineer.

UNMISTAKABLE IDENTIFICATION TEST

The law insists that the description of land must identify with certainty the land being surveyed. The law stipulates that the land description must be complete within itself.

WHERE ON EARTH IS CALIFORNIA?

This is not a facetious question. I am referring to the longitudinal and latitudinal position of California.

This is an important question to anyone interested in real estate because it is the foundation upon which all land descriptions are based.

REMEMBER

No two pieces of property in this world have the same location and description.

What is meant by the terms *longitudinal* and *latitudinal?*

LONGITUDE AND LATITUDE

Longitudinal lines are imaginary lines circling the globe. They are located east or west of the prime meridian at Greenwich, England.

Latitudinal lines are lines running parallel at a given distance north or south of the equator.

WHERE IS CALIFORNIA?

The exact location of any piece of property, large or small, can be expressed in degrees, hours, minutes, or seconds.

The state of California is framed by *longitude* 125° W and 114° W and *latitude* 32° N and 42° N (Figure 2).

THREE METHODS OF LAND DESCRIPTION

There are three major methods of land description used today.

1 Metes and bounds

2 Section and township survey

3 Lot and block system

METES AND BOUNDS METHOD OF LAND DESCRIPTION   *Metes* refers to the measure of length, such as inches, feet, yards, rods, meters, or miles.

Bounds refers to the use of boundaries both natural and artificial, such as rivers, roads, fences, boulders, creeks, and iron pipes.

This type of description is one of the oldest used methods and is often found in legal descriptions.

FIGURE 2

WHY ARE METES AND BOUNDS USED?   This type of description is used when the property in question is not covered by a duly recorded map, or when its property is so irregular in shape that it is impractical to describe by section, township, and range.

HOW ARE METES AND BOUNDS USED?   In using this method of description, do the following:

1 Start at a fixed point of beginning.

CAUTION

> If a mistake is made at the point of beginning, the description is worthless.

2 Follow, in detail, the boundaries of the land described in courses and distances from one point to another.

3 Return to the point of beginning.

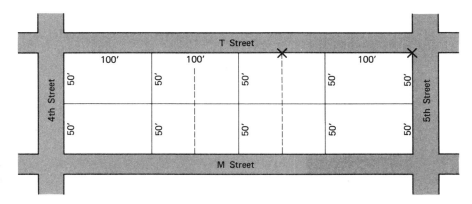

FIGURE 3
Sample metes and bounds description.

Here is an acceptable "legal" description of such property using the metes and bounds method of description.

Beginning at a point on the southerly line of "T" Street 150 feet westerly of the southwest corner of the intersection of "T" and fifth streets; running thence due south 100 feet to the northerly line of "M" street; thence westerly along the northerly line of "M" Street, 100 feet; thence northerly and parallel to the first course, 100 feet, to the southerly line of "T" Street; thence easterly along the southerly line of "T" Street 100 feet, to the point or place of beginning.

WEAKNESSES IN THE USE OF METES AND BOUNDS DESCRIPTION
Markers used have often ceased to exist.
Markers have been moved, or replaced.

CAUTION

> Use metes and bounds only when other means of description are not available and then only where every identifying feature is designated.

U.S. GOVERNMENT AND TOWNSHIP SYSTEM

This system originated with a survey of public lands made by the U.S. Surveyor General, who has jurisdiction over the surveys of all public lands.

It is used to describe agricultural or rural lots and may not be adapted to city lots.

Base lines and meridians are used in this type of description.

A *base line* is an imaginary line running East and West.

A *meridian* is an imaginary line running North and South.

In the state of California as in many other states, certain base lines and meridians are called by *local* names. Generally measurements are taken from them.

Figure 4 shows some base lines and meridians for California.

1 The Humboldt base line and meridian in the north.

2 The Mt. Diablo base line and meridian in the central area.

3 The San Bernardino base line and meridian in the south.

DIVISION OF THE LINES
Base lines are divided by lines running north and south, six miles apart.

Meridians are divided by lines running east and west, six miles apart.

TOWNSHIP DIVISIONS
The area between the intersections of the base line and meridian are called townships.

REMEMBER

> A standard township is six miles square and covers 36 square miles of land.

FIGURE 4

Base Lines
Principal Meridians
If all range and township lines
were drawn in this map, it would
show the state covered with small
squares (townships). They are
numbered east and west from the
principal meridians shown on the
map, and north and south from
the base lines. Thus each is
definitely located.
Dotted lines show where different numbering systems come together. If the state were square,
like New Mexico, only one base
line and principal meridian would
be needed.

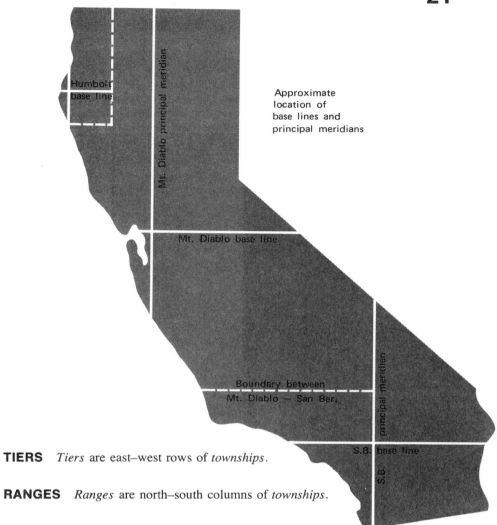

TIERS   *Tiers* are east–west rows of *townships*.

RANGES   *Ranges* are north–south columns of *townships*.

IDENTIFICATION BY
SECTION AND TOWNSHIP

To identify a piece of land through the section-and-township method a unique
method has been devised. Townships are given numerical identities in relation to
their position *above* or *below* the base line and *east* or *west* of the local meridian.

EXAMPLE

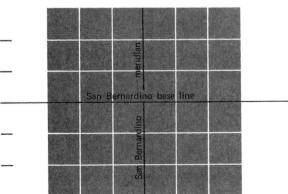

FIGURE 5

DESCRIPTION This is the wording used to describe the township marked with an X in Figure 5: "That township at the intersection of the third tier of townships, south of the San Bernardino base line, and the first range of townships west of the San Bernardino meridian."

SECTION Townships are divided into smaller units called *sections*.
There are 36 sections, six sections high by six sections wide in a township.
The numbering of sections in a township are *standardized*, as indicated in Figure 6.

1 The numbering starts in the northeast corner of the township.

2 Proceed west on the first row to section 6.

3 Immediately below section 6 on row two is section 7.

4 Proceed east on this row to section 12, then repeat the same procedure switching back and forth from one row to the next.

5 The numbering ends with section 36 in the southeast corner of the township.

DIVISIONS OF A SECTION Each section can be divided into halves, quarters, and even further.

EXAMPLE
This is section 22, divided into quarters, eights, and sixteenths. In Figure 7 these facts are given:

Each side of the section is one mile in length or 5280 feet.

Each quarter section is 160 acres.

One square mile = 640 acres.

Each quarter section is named according to the following directions:

The northeast quarter of section 22

The northwest quarter of section 22

North

6	5	4	3	2	1
7	8	9	10	11	12
18	17	16	15	14	13
19	20	21	22	23	24
30	29	28	27	26	25
31	32	33	34	35	36

West — East

South

FIGURE 6

FIGURE 7

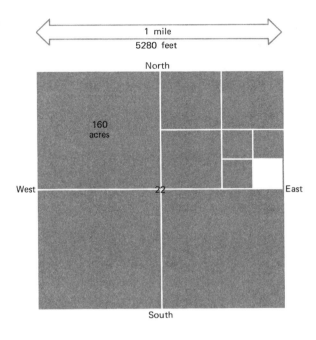

The southwest quarter of section 22
The southeast quarter of section 22

IDENTIFYING A SPECIFIC LOCATION   In Figure 7, the shaded area is located in the southeast quarter of the southeast quarter of the northeast quarter of section 22.

QUESTIONS   In the shaded area in Figure 7:

How many acres are included?   (10 acres)

How many square feet of land are included?   (435,600 sq feet)

LOCATING, READING, AND DESCRIBING A PLOT OF LAND   In locating a plot of land, read the entire description through to determine what numbered section is involved. Proceed in reverse, locating the next smaller parcel and continue until the actual parcel is identified.

EXAMPLE: FIGURE 8

East half of the southwest quarter of the northwest quarter of section 24.

Step 1 Start with section 24

Step 2 Then the northwest quarter of section 24

Step 3 Then the southwest quarter of the northwest quarter of section 24

Step 4 Finally, the east half of the southwest quarter of the northwest quarter of section 24.

OVERLAPPING SECTIONS   It is possible for a parcel of land to overlap more than one numbered section or more than one smaller division.

FIGURE 8

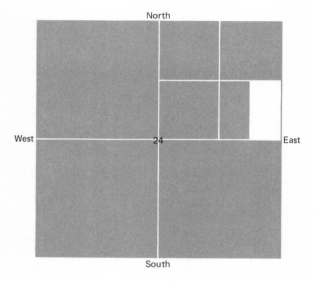

When stating such a description insert a semicolon between each separate entity.

EXAMPLE

Beginning at the northeast corner of the northwest quarter of section 18, thence running to the southeast corner of the southwest quarter of the southwest quarter; thence northwesterly to the southwest corner of the southeast quarter of the northeast quarter of section 39; thence one-quarter mile north; thence back to the beginning.

LOT AND BLOCK SYSTEM

The California Subdivision Map Act requires that all new subdivisions be either mapped or platted.

A map of such subdivision is recorded in the county recorder's office of the county in which the land is located.

This type of identification is most widely used today for residential or business property.

Specific property is located by lot, block and tract.

EXAMPLE

All of Lot 8 in Block 4 of Tract number 7024 in the city of Norwalk, Los Angeles County, California. As per map recorded in Book 65 page 42 of maps in the office of the Recorder of said County.

One of the characteristics of real property is that it is *unique*. This means there is only one piece of property in this world with its description and location.

Land can be given "unmistakable" identification through three methods: (1) metes and bounds, (2) government section and township system, and (3) map and block system.

California has three base line and meridians upon which township areas are based (1) Humboldt base line and meridian, (2) Mt. Diablo base line and meridian, (3) San Bernardino base line and meridian.

A township consists of 36 sections—1 mile square with 640 acres. Within the township a *standardized numbering* system is used, starting in the *northeast corner,* numbering from east to west and dropping down to the second line, then west to east following a serpentine course back and forth and ending in the southeast corner of the township.

Sections can be quartered *again,* and then *again* to account for small plots of land.

In locating a plot of land, *read the entire description* to determine what numbered section is involved; then, *proceeding in reverse,* locate the next smaller parcel; continue in this way until the actual parcel is identified.

The *lot* and *block system* is the most widely used today for residential and business property.

( ) 1 The angular distance on a global map east or west of the prime meridian is called (a) latitude, (b) lease line, (c) longitude, (d) meridian.

( ) 2 Adequate "legal" description of real property includes (a) lot and block system, (b) metes and bounds, (c) section and township system, (d) all of the above.

3 A base line runs _____ and _____.

4 A meridian runs _____ and _____.

5 The three base lines and meridians in California are known as:.

a _____

b _____

c _____

6 A township contains _____ square miles.

7 Townships are divided into _____ sections.

8 The _____ and _____ system is used in measuring residential and business property.

1 Check the deed to the property where you are now living and read the description given.

1 (c)

2 (d)

3 east; west

4 north; south

5 **a** Humboldt base line and meridian
  b Mt. Diablo base line and meridian
  c San Bernardino base line and meridian

6 36

7 36

8 lot and block

"Buying Land, Investigate Before You Invest"—
pamphlet from Calif. Dept. of R.E.

SHOULD YOU RENT?

4

This unit and Unit 5 discuss whether you should rent or buy. Unit 4 considers renting and Unit 5 considers buying.

Most Americans have been renters at one time or another. Many of them rent because they don't have the necessary initial investment to buy a home. They plan to accumulate the initial investment while they rent. Some prefer to continue renting because they enjoy the various advantages without the responsibilities of home ownership that renting affords.

Elderly persons sometimes decide to sell their homes and become renters after their children leave. They often want to be free to travel without the responsibility of home maintenance. Apartment units and homes are the most common types of dwelling rentals. Of the two, apartment rentals far outnumber home rentals. Therefore, we will concentrate our attention on apartment rentals in this unit. We will consider the advantages and disadvantages of renting.

Read this study guide (pages 28–34).
View TV program, number 4.

At the conclusion of this unit, you will be able to:

1 List 10 advantages of renting.

2 List at least 10 disadvantages of renting.

3 Give two advantages of a lease and two advantages of a month-to-month tenancy.

4 Give two disadvantages of a lease and two disadvantages of a month-to-month tenancy.

5 Explain in writing how inflation may affect a renter.

lease   lessee
rental agreement   escalation clause
lessor

28

ADVANTAGES OF RENTING

SMALL INITIAL OUTLAY   Only a small initial outlay of money is usually required to rent. Sometimes an owner will ask for the first and last month's rent. He may also ask for a cleaning or security deposit. Most often, however, he'll merely require the first month's rent in advance. It's much easier to raise that kind of money than trying to raise the down payment for a home purchase. If the apartment is furnished, no additional money is required to buy furniture.

NO RISK   Since your initial outlay is limited, you don't stand to lose much, even if you decide to move earlier than you had planned. If you're on a lease, however, you're responsible for the rent for the remaining term. But the owner (lessor) may find another tenant (lessee) soon. If he does, he probably won't hold you responsible for the remaining rent except for the period of vacancy.

FIXED COSTS   In the short run, your costs are fixed. You know exactly how much your rent will be each month. If you're on a lease the rent can't be increased until the lease expires, unless there's a special clause permitting an increase, which is called an escalation clause. You can budget accordingly. This means you don't have to worry about coming up with several hundred dollars to replace the furnace when it goes out. If you're on a month-to-month rental your rent could be increased next month.

LIQUIDITY   Let's say you manage to save a few thousand dollars. You put that money in the bank. You are earning interest on it. Since you're renting, you can keep it there earning interest. You don't have to withdraw it for a down payment. Aren't you in a better financial situation? Perhaps. Your investment is certainly more liquid. But are there other considerations?

MOBILITY   Suppose you decide to move. You're on a month-to-month tenancy. All that's required is a 30-day notice. If you're on a lease it's not that easy. But it can be worked out. If the unit is furnished you don't have to worry much about moving costs. If your unit is unfurnished it's a bit of a problem. But it's still not too bad.

LIMITED RESPONSIBILITY   What if you wanted to take a month-long trip? You won't have to worry about finding someone to water the lawn or look after the property. You can just go. That's a big advantage, and it's related to freedom from maintenance, our next advantage.

FREEDOM FROM MAINTENANCE   You don't have to get up on a ladder to paint. You don't have to worry about calling the plumber or the electrician; or watering, weeding, and fertilizing the lawn; or calling the roofer or a myriad of other repair men. That's the owner's responsibility, unless, of course, you have agreed to assume these responsibilities. You're free to spend your time as you wish. You don't have to face all these annoying problems.

SPECIAL FEATURES   Perhaps you'd like an apartment with a view. Or one with a swimming pool, sauna bath, or billiard room. Maybe you'd like one with a recreation room or one with a putting green and some open space. You're willing to pay a higher rent for these additional features. And, once again, you don't have to worry about maintenance.

CONVENIENCE   Apartment buildings are usually conveniently located. It's usually just a short walk to public transportation. You're only minutes from the grocery store or cleaners. Schools are probably close by. So are emergency facilities such as hospitals and police and fire stations.

EASY HOUSEKEEPING   Your unit may be relatively well designed. It's easy to keep it clean. You won't have to drag a vacuum cleaner very far. There aren't many places to dust. And you don't have to walk very far between the stove and refrigerator balancing things in your hands en route. You won't have to spend a whole day housekeeping. You can spend more of your free time on things you'd rather do instead.

SUMMARY OF ADVANTAGES   We've discussed several points that appear to be advantages to renting. The initial outlay is small. There is virtually no risk. In the short run, your costs are fixed and there are few surprises. You have a great degree of liquidity. Mobility is good. Your responsibilities are limited. You have few maintenance worries. You can select an apartment with special features (called amenities), if you wish to pay for them. The convenience factor is significant. But shouldn't we discuss some of the disadvantages of renting before we make a decision? It seems prudent to look at the other side, too. Maybe that will affect our decision.

DISADVANTAGES OF RENTING

LIMITED INVESTMENT FOR THE FUTURE   We saw that one advantage of renting was that there was a small initial outlay of money. However, with no capital investment, what are the prospects for your future financial security? Would you develop equity by reducing a loan balance? No. Would you share in any possible increase in the value or develop equity of your own, in the real estate? No.

NO TAX BENEFITS   As a renter you have no tax benefits. Some states have a special tax provision to provide tax relief for renters. However, it is extremely limited and provides very little actual tax savings.

RENT INCREASES   If you had a lease, we said that your rent was probably fixed unless there was an escalation clause. You wouldn't have to worry about a rent increase—in the short run. But what about the long run? And what about a month-to-month tenancy? Can you reasonably expect your rent to remain the same? Not really, because it is subject to some variables, such as vacancy rates.

The owner's cost are increasing all the time. His property taxes are going up each year. It costs him more to paint the building. When he calls the plumber or electrician, he finds that his bill is higher than it was last year. He usually has very little choice but to pass these increases on to you. This means that in the long run you'll be paying a higher rent when your original tenancy expires.

LACK OF PERMANENCE   The mobility factor that we discussed has certain advantages. It's difficult, however, to achieve a feeling of permanence and stability while renting. The owner could decide that your unit would be ideal for his son. Where does that leave you? What would happen if you couldn't afford a rent increase? It's difficult for you to "sink your roots" into the community when you're renting.

LACK OF INDEPENDENCE   Let's assume that you had an argument with the owner or with the tenant across the hall. How important is your psychological well-being? You could move. But that's an inconvenience. You might have to continue living in close contact in a relatively confined area with a disagreeable person.

CONFINED AREA   Few apartment units are large. Most of them are about 500 to 700 square feet. That doesn't leave too much room for each person. In a confined area, interpersonal relationships often suffer; and where do you go to work on your hobby or your sewing? What if one of you wants to watch television and the other wants to take a nap?

LIMITED PRIVACY   Limited privacy is closely related to the confined area aspect. Although construction methods have been improved recently, soundproofing is hardly ever satisfactory in an apartment. The tenant in the unit next door can often hear you; also, you can often hear them, usually at the wrong times. Overhearing discussions can often be extremely interesting and can enlighten an otherwise dull time. But what happens when the shoe is on the other foot?

LIMITED PRESTIGE   While it is unimportant to many, prestige is significant to others. Some look down on those who live in apartments. It's more difficult to entertain in an apartment because of the confined area. And there are certain restrictions on you if you want to have a party. Furthermore, it's difficult to sleep when the tenant above you is having a party that is still going strong at two o'clock in the morning.

RESTRICTIONS ON CHILDREN   Some owners, rightly or wrongly, will not rent to couples with children. They point out increased costs of maintenance and say that children will disturb other tenants. If you have children it will be more difficult for you to rent an apartment. And remember the confined area.

RESTRICTIONS ON PETS   Let's assume that you have a pet dog or cat. Do you think it will be harder to find an apartment? You'll encounter the same arguments as you would if you had children. Or, you may be required to put up a larger security deposit to defray possible damages.

MISCELLANEOUS DISADVANTAGES   Most apartment buildings have poor laundry facilities or none at all. Even if facilities are available, they usually work unsatisfactorily; and you often have to wait until another tenant is finished before doing your own laundry. What if you don't have the necessary change to operate the equipment, or if you find that you should run your clothes through one more drying cycle and you ran out of coins?

You'll generally find inadequate storage for your personal property. How would you feel if the antique piece that your grandmother left to you in her will was damaged by another tenant while moving in a case of motor oil?

Most buildings that are three stories or higher have an elevator. Some don't. Few buildings with two stories have elevators. That means you may have to climb stairs to get to your unit. If you're carrying groceries or other heavy items, that's an inconvenience.

Sometimes the heating is inadequate. You may still find floor furnaces, which are illegal in many communities. You may find no heating unit or register in the bedrooms. That can be uncomfortable.

Creditors often ask if you own or rent. Your credit rating is usually not as strong if you rent. Creditors look at permanence and stability. Renting is often a factor in their decision to extend credit.

You say you enjoy gardening? Your opportunities to use your "green-thumb" talents while living in an apartment are practically nonexistent. And there's not much room for hanging plants unless you have a balcony. But, even then, it might cause friction with the tenant below.

SUMMARY OF DISADVANTAGES   We've discussed several points that seem to be disadvantages of renting. We saw that there is a limited investment for the future. There are virtually no tax benefits. There is a lack of permanence. Another disadvantage is a lack of independence. Rent increases are a real probability. We found limited privacy. There is limited prestige for those who wish it. You can expect restrictions on children. There will be restrictions on pets. We also discussed some miscellaneous disadvantages that are very real and important: inadequate laundry facilities; inadequate storage; climbing stairs; inadequate heating; impairment of your credit standing; and no exercise of your "green-thumb" opportunities. Before deciding whether you'll be a renter, complete this unit and then consider the next one, "Should You Buy?"

CHECKLIST

ADVANTAGES AND DISADVANTAGES OF RENTING

ITEMS CONSIDERED	ADVANTAGE	DISADVANTAGE
Small initial outlay		
No risk		
Fixed costs		
Liquidity		
Mobility		
Responsibility		
Special features		
Convenience		
Housekeeping		
Future investment		
Equity buildup		
Tax benefits		
Permanency		
Independence		
Rent increases		
Confined area		
Privacy		
Prestige		
Children		
Pets		
Security		
Credit standing		
Heating		
Storage		

REVIEWING YOUR UNDERSTANDING

TRUE OR FALSE

( ) **1** In considering a rental the initial outlay is minimal.

( ) **2** If you had a lease you could move at your convenience.

( ) **3** Inflation has little effect on renters.

( ) **4** There are few problems in renting if you have children.

( ) **5** Burglaries are as common in apartments as in private homes.

FILL-INS

1 The required notice for vacating an apartment on a month-to-month tenancy is _____ days.

2 A clause in a lease stipulating that the rent may be increased is called an _____ clause.

REVIEWING YOUR UNDERSTANDING—ANSWERS

3 An owner might require a _____ if he permitted pets.

4 Your _____ standing might not be as good if you're a renter.

TRUE OR FALSE

1 True   4 False

2 False   5 False

3 False

FILL-INS

1 30 days (the notification period must be the same as the period of time for which the rent is paid)

2 escalation

3 security or damage deposit

4 credit

OPTIONAL LEARNING ACTIVITIES

1 Review your local newspaper. Find out how much rent is charged for different-sized units in different locations.

2 Talk to other renters and review with them your understanding of the advantages and disadvantages of renting.

3 Inspect some rental units to visualize if you would be comfortable living there for a prolonged period.

4 Read *Buy or Rent*, Greenwald Twayne Publishing Co., New York, $3.

SHOULD YOU BUY?

5

OVERVIEW

This unit concludes the question of renting versus buying. Here, we consider the advantages of buying, which are similar to the disadvantages of renting, already discussed. We also review the disadvantages of buying, many of which you will recognize as the advantages of renting from the previous unit. We conclude with an economic analysis of renting versus buying, which will help you in that all-important decision of whether you should rent or buy.

ASSIGNMENT

Read this study guide (pages 36–42).
View TV program, number 5.

PERFORMANCE OBJECTIVES

At the conclusion of this unit you will be able to:

1 List at least six advantages of buying.

2 List at least six disadvantages of buying.

3 List the effects that inflation has on renting.

4 List the effects that inflation has on buying.

5 Write, in your own words, what is meant by the statement. "All you have at the end of a year of renting are worthless rent receipts."

TERMS YOU SHOULD KNOW

initial investment   liquidity
total investment   variable rate mortgage
equity

ADVANTAGES OF BUYING

INVESTMENT FOR THE FUTURE   If you buy a home you'll have an investment for the future. Well-located properties usually increase in value. We call this appreciation. How much? That depends on a lot of factors. What is the demand for housing in your area? Is it high or low? What about the supply of homes? Are there many homes for sale or just a few? Good financing has a favorable impact on values. On the other hand, poor financing makes it more difficult to sell. Historically, values in California have tended to increase at an average of approximately 3 percent a year. In the last few years, increases have been substantially above that.

TAX BENEFITS   As a homeowner you'll enjoy income tax benefits that are not available to the renter. You'll be able to deduct your property taxes. You'll also deduct the interest payments on your real estate loan. These two items added together amount to a substantial deduction. This means actual money saved.

PERMANENCE   You'll feel secure in your own home. You won't have to worry about the owner asking you to leave because he wants his son and daughter-in-law to live there. You'll probably find yourself taking part in community affairs to a larger extent than when you were renting. You'll find yourself puttering around the yard. You'll be making repairs and improvements because you'll be proud of your home. Your children will feel a sense of permanence too. They'll form long-term relationships with the other children in the neighborhood. They won't have to change schools as often. You'll live in your home for several years until your circumstances change. Then you might need a larger home—or a smaller one.

INDEPENDENCE   You'll be independent in your home. You won't have to worry about the owner or the tenant across the hall. If you decide to entertain you won't have to worry about disturbing the tenant below. It's nice to be independent. It does marvelous things for the soul.

FIXED COSTS   Some of your costs are fixed. Your mortgage payments will remain the same; unless you have a variable rate mortgage that provides for an increase and decrease of your monthly payments depending on economic conditions.

It's true that your property taxes may increase but property taxes are tax deductible as we discussed. So the increase won't hurt as much. Your maintenance costs will also probably increase but most repairs last for a long time.

LARGER AREA   A home is almost always considerably larger than an apartment. You'll have several bedrooms, a living room, one or more baths, a kitchen, and maybe a dining room, breakfast room, and family room. The square footage of a home is usually at least twice as large as that of an apartment. Don't forget the yard. You'll probably have a lot that is about 5000 to 6500 square feet. You can have trees, bushes, and flowers. You might have a patio area and a barbeque. Children need room to play—in and out of the home. Your family won't feel confined in your own home.

PRIVACY   With more square footage and a yard, you'll have more privacy. The walls will be thicker and less conducive to sound. The separation of one home from another is an important factor. The trees, bushes, walls, and fences add a lot in this respect.

There's little question that because of the privacy involved, you'll feel better psychologically by owning your own home. You'll feel better entertaining your friends in a larger area.

FEWER RESTRICTIONS   There are very few restrictions placed on you in your own home. It's a good environment for the children. You can have pets if you wish. You can play the piano after 9:00 P.M. if you desire.

MISCELLANEOUS ADVANTAGES   You can have your own laundry facilities and not worry about waiting your turn. You'll have more storage space. It's amazing how many items you'll accumulate over the years that will have to be stored. The heating may be more efficient and comfortable. Your credit rating will be improved.

SUMMARY OF ADVANTAGES   Home ownership, as we have seen, offers many more advantages than renting. We saw that these translate to an investment for the future. There are tax benefits and permanency. Independence, fixed costs, a larger area, and privacy are important considerations. So are prestige and fewer restrictions. The miscellaneous advantages of ownership are not insignificant.

Now let's consider the disadvantages.

DISADVANTAGES OF HOME OWNERSHIP

LARGER INITIAL INVESTMENT   It's possible to buy a home with no initial investment (down payment). A GI loan will provide for no down payment if you qualify for the loan. An F.H.A. loan means a small down payment. Normally, however, you're talking about a down payment of 10 to 20 percent of the purchase price. If you're buying a $45,000 home, this means a down payment of between $4500 and $9000. Your closing costs will be between $1000 and $2000 in addition, depending on property tax prorations, and the like. If you buy a condominium unit, your initial costs will usually be less because the sales price is usually lower.

RISK   Whenever you invest money there is a risk that you might lose some or all of it. However, well located properties seldom lose value. Your investment is normally well protected.

INCREASE IN EXPENSES Although your mortgage payments will remain constant in most circumstances, other costs may increase. Property taxes have a habit of creeping upward. Maintenance costs will increase as the home ages. You'll have to weigh some of these increased costs against the advantages of ownership. Remember that your rent will increase too.

LACK OF LIQUIDITY Some say that they dislike home ownership because their investment is not liquid. While an investment in a home is not as liquid as having money in the bank, it's not all that bad. For example, if you need cash you could consider borrowing on the property by putting a second mortgage on the home. Or you could refinance the first mortgage once sufficient equity is developed. Or the home could be rented or sold. A property priced right will usually sell within 60 to 90 days.

RESTRICTED MOBILITY To a degree, you are less mobile once you've bought a home. However, as mentioned above, you could rent your home to a tenant. Or you could sell the house.

GREATER RESPONSIBILITY With an investment you have greater responsibilities. You'll have to properly maintain the property. You may climb a ladder to paint. Of course, you could call a painter and pay the bill. You'll be out watering and cutting the lawn; you'll want to protect your investment.

LESS CONVENIENCE You'll find that instead of walking to the grocery store, you may have to drive. That's an inconvenience.

MORE HOUSEKEEPING You'll have a larger area to keep clean. That means less free time. In fact, that's why many older persons decide to sell after the children have left. They sometimes decide to buy a condominium unit with its smaller area, or they may revert to being a renter.

SUMMARY OF DISADVANTAGES There are several disadvantages to home ownership. While there are exceptions, buying usually requires a relatively large initial investment. Some of your expenses, such as property taxes and maintenance costs, will probably increase. Your investment is not quite as liquid as you would wish it to be. You'll have somewhat less mobility and greater responsibility. You may find it less convenient from the standpoint of shopping. You'll have more area to keep clean. Before we go any further, let's consider an economic comparison of renting relative to buying.

AN ECONOMIC ANALYSIS— RENT OR BUY? Let's compare the economic benefits of ownership versus renting. Let's assume that a $40,000 home will be purchased. The initial investment will be $4000. The closing costs will be $1200 for a total initial investment of $5200. There will be a first deed of trust of $32,000 at 8.5 percent, 30-year amortization. There will be a second deed of trust of $4000 at 9 percent interest. The home will be sold after 10 years. Property taxes will be $1200 a year. Maintenance costs will be 1.5 percent of $40,000 per year.

We'll also assume that a comparable rental is $400 per month. (Don't make the mistake of comparing a seven-room home with a two-bedroom apartment renting for $200 per month.)

1 Total investment (purchase price) $40,000

2 First deed of trust   32,000

3 Second deed of trust   4,000

4 Initial investment (down payment) 4,000

5. Closing costs   1,200

6 Total investment and closing costs 5,200

7 Monthly payment for first deed of trust (principal and interest)   246

8 Monthly payment for second deed of trust (principal and interest)   40

9 Monthly property taxes   100

10 Monthly homeowner's insurance 20

11 Monthly maintenance costs estimate   50

12 Total monthly costs   456

13 Total monthly costs after second deed of trust is repaid   416

14 Principal payment on first deed of trust (first year)   232

15 Principal payment on second deed of trust (first year)   120

16 Total savings of principal (first year)   352

17 Interest deduction on first deed of trust (first year)   2,720

18 Interest deduction on second deed of trust (first year)   360

19 Real estate taxes deductible 1,200

20 Total deductible items (lines 17–19)   4,280

21 Tax refund assuming 25 percent tax bracket (4280 × .25)   1,070

22 Monthly tax savings (1070 ÷ 12)   89

23 Plus average monthly principal savings (line 16 ÷ 12) first year   29

24 Plus estimated monthly appreciation (4 percent × 40,000) ÷ 12   133

25 Less estimated costs of sale 10 years later (4500 ÷ 120 months)   38

26 Total monthly savings (lines 22, 23, 24, less line 25)   213

27 Net monthly cost of ownership—first year (line 12 less line 26)   243

28 Monthly cost of renting a comparable home   400

29 Net difference of monthly cost to rent (400 − 243)   157

30 Return on investment if owned (line 26) $213 × 12 months   2556

31 Percentage return on investment (line 30 ÷ line 6)   49%

32 Percentage return on investment ignoring appreciation (line 26 − line 24 = $80) × 12 months = 960 ÷ line 6   18%

As you can see from the analysis, the *economic* advantages of ownership are far superior to renting. It's been said that all you have to show after a year of renting is rent receipts. Some would say that the total initial investment of $5200 could be in the bank earning 6 percent interest if you were a renter. True. But what about inflation at even 4 percent? That would reduce the purchasing power of the interest to 2 percent. And interest is taxed as ordinary income. In the 25 percent tax bracket the 6 percent would lose 1.5 percent in taxes. So a loss of 4 percent purchasing power plus 1.5 percent taxes would leave a net return of 0.5 percent. Not too attractive in view of the economic advantages of ownership.

Also remember that on the sale of a personal residence the gain is taken at the more favorable capital gain rates. If a seller purchases another home within 18 months with an adjusted sales price that equals or exceeds that of the home sold within the prescribed period of time, the gain is deferred. There is also an exemption of the first $20,000 of the adjusted sales price for those of age 65 and over provided the taxpayer has owned and used the property as his principal personal residence for five out of the last eight years preceding the sale.

THE DECISION TO RENT OR BUY

As you can see from this unit and the previous unit, there are many considerations to be made when considering the question of renting versus buying. You have the facts. Remember that construction and land costs are going up each year. Quite possibly the $40,000 home of today will cost $44,000 next year. If you choose to buy, don't wait too long or it will cost you more. The decision is up to you.

ADVANTAGES AND DISADVANTAGES OF BUYING

ITEMS CONSIDERED	ADVANTAGES	DISADVANTAGES
Small initial outlay		
No risk		
Fixed costs		
Liquidity		
Mobility		
Responsibility		
Special features		
Convenience		
Housekeeping		
Future investment		
Tax benefits		
Pride of ownership		
Permanency		
Independence		
Rent increases		
Confined area		
Privacy		
Prestige		
Children		
Pets		
Security		
Credit standing		
Heating		
Storage		

TRUE OR FALSE

(   ) **1** Burglaries of homes are more common than burglaries of apartment units.

(   ) **2** The investment risk is greater in renting than in owning.

(   ) **3** Equity means the value of the home with a mortgage against it.

(   ) **4** The return on an investment is the purchase price divided by the down payment.

(   ) **5** The net monthly cost of home ownership is the mortgage payments and maintenance costs less the tax savings.

FILL-INS

1 The possibility that you might lose money on your investment is called _____.

2 _____ is the ability to quickly convert assets to cash.

3 An advantage of ownership that means you won't have to move for a long time is called _____.

4 An advantage of renting that means you can move quickly is called _____.

5 If a home is sold, the owner is taxed at _____ rates.

TRUE OR FALSE

1 False	**4** False
2 False	**5** False
3 False	

FILL-INS

1 risk	**4** mobility
2 liquidity	**5** capital gains
3 permanency	

1 Check some homes for sale. Find out what down payment is required.

2 Determine how long it will take you to save your down payment plus closing costs.

1 *The House for You to Build, Buy or Rent*, $6.75, Sleeper, Wiley, New York.

2 *Building or Buying a House: A Guide to Wise Investment.* $4.00, Johnstone et al. McGraw-Hill, New York.

3 *Your House—Here's How.* Prentice-Hall, New Jersey.

4 *Facts You Should Know About Buying a Home.* National Better Business Bureau, New York.

SHOULD YOU SEEK PROFESSIONAL HELP WHEN BUYING A HOME?

6

A great deal of technical knowledge is required to complete the purchase or sale of a home. Numerous pitfalls await anyone who is unknowledgeable in real estate. Some buyers deal directly with sellers without professional help. Most buyers and sellers, however, do seek professional assistance. It is recommended that you consider the services of a professional to protect your interests.

There are several professionals you should know about. A licensed real estate agent is involved in the largest percentage of real estate transactions. Here we discuss in detail the qualifications and requirements of the licensee and his responsibilities to the buyer and seller. He is usually able to handle the entire transaction himself because of his background and experience in virtually all phases of real estate. The licensee has sometimes been compared to a quarterback on a football team. He is a coordinator of various real estate specialties. He may call in other specialists in complicated transactions and coordinate their services.

These other professionals include appraisers, attorneys, building contractors, subcontractors, pest control operators, and escrow officers.

Read this study guide (pages 44–52).
View the TV program, number 6.

At the conclusion of this unit you will be able to:

1 List at least seven specialty areas of real estate with which the real estate licensee is familiar.

2 List six activities that require a real estate license if performed for compensation.

3 Name the two major categories of licenses issued by the Department of Real Estate and the requirements of each.

4 Give the definition of a realtor.

5 Give the definition of an appraiser.

6 State when the services of an attorney are beneficial.

7 List at least seven experts whose professional advice may be needed.

real estate salesman	agency
real estate broker	SRA, SREA, MAT
REALTOR®	CAR, NAR

THE REAL ESTATE LICENSEE

The real estate licensee is a professional career-oriented individual who is knowledgeable in virtually all phases of real estate. He is aware of the constantly changing trends that affect real estate. The licensee is a student of the many specialty areas within real estate. He must have a basic understanding of appraisal, law, finance, investments, economics, taxation, property managements, escrows, as well as many other areas.

The real estate license is issued by the California Department of Real Estate to applicants who have met the prescribed requirements. Without a license, one cannot collect a fee or commission for engaging in the following real estate activities.

1 Selling or offering to sell, buying or offering to buy, soliciting prospective sellers or purchasers of, soliciting or obtaining listings of, or negotiating the purchase, sale, or exchange of real property or a business opportunity.

2 Leasing or renting or offering to lease or rent, or placing for rent, or soliciting listings of places for rent, or soliciting for prospective tenants, or negotiating the sale, purchase, or exchanges of leases on real property, or on a business opportunity, or collecting rents from real property, or improvements thereon, or from business opportunities.

3 Assisting or offering to assist in filing an application for the purchase or lease of, or in locating or entering on, lands owned by the state or federal government.

4 Soliciting borrowers or lenders for or negotiating loans or collecting payments or performing services for borrowers or lenders or note owners in connection with loans secured directly or collaterally by liens on real property, or on a business opportunity.

5 Selling or offering to sell, buying or offering to buy, or exchanging or offering to exchange a real property sales contract, or a promissory note secured directly or collaterally by a lien on real property or on a business opportunity, and performing services for the holders thereof.

6 Selling, listing, or soliciting buyers of a mobile home for a fee if the mobile home has been registered for at least one year with the Department of Motor Vehicles.

If an individual acts as a licensee without being licensed, he is subject to a fine of up to $500 and/or imprisonment of up to six months. A corporation is subject to a $5000 fine. Any person who pays a fee to a nonlicensee for services that require a license is guilty of a misdemeanor and may be fined up to $50 for each offense.

Certain parties are exempt from the license requirement. They include: employees of lending institutions, lenders making loans guaranteed or insured by a federal government agency, certain agricultural associations, licensed personal property brokers, cemetery authorities, collectors of real property loans, clerical help, attorneys acting for their clients, and individuals buying and selling their own property.

There are two major categories of licenses currently issued by the Department of Real Estate: the broker license and the salesman license. There are many differences between them.

THE REAL ESTATE BROKER

To obtain a broker license, the applicant must:

1 Be at least 18 years old.

2 Have had the previous experience and education that is required by law.

3 Evidence his or her reputation for honesty, truthfulness, and integrity.

4 Pass the examination.

He or she must have been actively involved as a real estate salesman for at least two of the five years immediately preceding the application. An applicant's equivalent general real estate experience may be approved in lieu of the above requirement.

The broker applicant must have completed 18 semester units of college-level courses, including six 3-semester unit courses as follows: legal aspects of real estate, real estate practice, real estate finance, and real estate appraisal; *plus* one of the following two: real estate economics of accounting *plus* any one of the following real estate principles, business law, property management, real estate office administration, escrow, or any advanced course in legal aspects of real estate, real estate finance, or real estate appraisal.

All applicants must pass an intensive written examination that consists of a morning and afternoon session.

Once the applicant receives his broker license he can open his own office and employ salesmen. He is responsible for the supervision of his salesmen and is required, for example, to date and initial all of their sales contracts.

In 1966 the Department of Real Estate drafted a plan for the professionalization of the real estate business. This plan was revised in 1971 and was named the Plan for Professionalization. It had widespread industry support.

The Plan, which will be achieved in several stages, is to be completed in 1980. At that time all existing real estate brokers will be grandfathered into a new category known as "certified real property brokers." All new certified real property broker licensees after that date will have to meet a degree requirement or several alternate requirements that are similar to those of the certified public accountant program. They will include an AA degree plus supervised instruction in real estate and related business administration subjects equivalent to the baccalaureate degree.

THE REAL ESTATE SALESMAN

To obtain a real estate salesman license the applicant must:

1 Be at least 18 years old.

2 Have his application for a license signed by the licensed broker who is to employ him after he has passed the salesmen's examination.

3 Evidence good reputation for honesty, truthfulness, and integrity.

4 Pass an examination.

The real estate salesman cannot open his own office. He must be employed by a licensed broker. He cannot work for more than one broker (one company) at the same time. He must be paid for his services by his employing broker only.

REALTOR

Not all licensees are realtors. A Realtor is a licensed real estate broker who is a member of the National Association of Realtors (NAR) and who subscribes to a strict code of ethics. A realtor associate is a licensed salesman employed by a broker who is a realtor.

Realtors and realtor associates are also members of their local real estate boards and of the California Association of Realtors (CAR).

A realtor is subject to the rules and regulations of his local board in addition to those of CAR and NAR. The purposes of CAR are: (1) to unite its members; (2) to promote high standards; (3) to safeguard the land-buying public; (4) to foster legislation for the benefit and protection of the land-buying public; and (5) to cooperate in the economic growth and development of the state.

REALTIST   In 1947, a national organization of predominately black real estate brokers known as the National Association of Real Estate Brokers was formed in Miami, Florida, and in turn adopted the name Realtist. The organization now has local boards in the principal cities of forty states.

A Realtist must be a member of a local board as well as a member of the national organization. Both nationally and locally, Realtists are working for better housing in communities they serve.

In many cases, individuals are both Realtors and Realtists by virtue of voluntary dual membership.

CODE OF ETHICS   NATIONAL ASSOCIATION OF REALTORS®

As Approved by the
DELEGATE BODY OF THE ASSOCIATION
at its 67th Annual Convention
NOVEMBER 14, 1974

PREAMBLE . . .   Under all is the land. Upon its wise utilization and widely allocated ownership depend the survival and growth of free institutions and of our civilization. The REALTOR® should recognize that the interests of the nation and its citizens require the highest and best use of the land and the widest distribution of land ownership. They require the creation of adequate housing, the building of functioning cities, the development of productive industries and farms, and the preservation of a healthful environment.

Such interests impose obligations beyond those of ordinary commerce. They impose grave social responsibility and a patriotic duty to which the REALTOR® should dedicate himself, and for which he should be diligent in preparing himself. The REALTOR®, therefore, is zealous to maintain and improve the standards of his calling and shares with his fellow-REALTORS® a common responsibility for its integrity and honor. The term REALTOR® has come to connote competency, fairness, and high integrity resulting from adherence to a lofty ideal of moral conduct in business relations. No inducement of profit and no instruction from clients ever can justify departure from this ideal.

In the interpretation of his obligation, a REALTOR® can take no safer guide than that which has been handed down through the centuries, embodied in the Golden Rule, "Whatsoever ye would that men should do to you, do ye even so to them."

Accepting this standard as his own, every REALTOR® pledges himself to observe its spirit in all of his activities and to conduct his business in accordance with the tenets set forth below.

ARTICLE 1 The REALTOR® should keep himself informed on matters affecting real estate in his community, the state, and nation so that he may be able to contribute responsibly to public thinking on such matters.

ARTICLE 2 In justice to those who place their interests in his care, the REALTOR® should endeavor always to be informed regarding laws, proposed legislation, governmental regulations, public policies, and current market conditions in order to be in a position to advise his clients properly.

ARTICLE 3 It is the duty of the REALTOR® to protect the public against fraud, misrepresentation, and unethical practices in real estate transactions. He should endeavor to eliminate in his community any practices which could be damaging to the public or bring discredit to the real estate profession. The REALTOR® should assist the governmental agency charged with regulating the practices of brokers and salesmen in his state.

ARTICLE 4 The REALTOR® should seek no unfair advantage over other realtors® and should conduct his business so as to avoid controversies with other REALTORS®.

ARTICLE 5 In the best interests of society, of his associates, and his own business, the REALTOR® should willingly share with other REALTORS® the lessons of his experience and study for the benefit of the public, and should be loyal to the Board of REALTORS® of his community and active in its work.

ARTICLE 6 To prevent dissension and misunderstanding and to assure better service to the owner, the REALTOR® should urge the exclusive listing of property unless contrary to the best interest of the owner.

ARTICLE 7 In accepting employment as an agent, the REALTOR® pledges himself to protect and promote the interests of the client. This obligation of absolute fidelity to the client's interests is primary, but it does not relieve the REALTOR® of the obligation to treat fairly all parties to the transaction.

ARTICLE 8 The REALTOR® shall not accept compensation from more than one party, even if permitted by law, without the full knowledge of all parties to the transaction.

ARTICLE 9 The REALTOR® shall avoid exaggeration, misrepresentation, or concealment of pertinent facts. He has an affirmative obligation to discover adverse factors that a reasonably competent and diligent investigation would disclose.

ARTICLE 10 The REALTOR® shall not deny equal professional services to any person for reasons of race, creed, sex, or country of national origin. The REALTOR® shall not be a party to any plan or agreement to discriminate against a person or persons on the basis of race, creed, sex, or country of national origin.

ARTICLE 11   A REALTOR® is expected to provide a level of competent service in keeping with the Standards of Practice in those fields in which the REALTOR® customarily engages.

The REALTOR® shall not undertake to provide specialized professional services concerning a type of property or service that is outside his field of competence unless he engages the assistance of one who is competent on such types of property or service, or unless the facts are fully disclosed to the client. Any person engaged to provide such assistance shall be so identified to the client and his contribution to the assignment should be set forth.

The REALTOR® shall refer to the Standards of Practice of the National Association as to the degree of competence that a client has a right to expect the REALTOR® to possess, taking into consideration the complexity of the problem, the availability of expert assistance, and the opportunities for experience available to the REALTOR®.

ARTICLE 12   The REALTOR® shall not undertake to provide professional services concerning a property or its value where he has a present or contemplated interest unless such interest is specifically disclosed to all affected parties.

ARTICLE 13   The REALTOR® shall not acquire an interest in or buy for himself, any member of his immediate family, his firm or any member thereof, or any entity in which he has a substantial ownership interest, property listed with him, without making the true position known to the listing owner. In selling property owned by himself, or in which he has any interest, the REALTOR® shall reveal the facts of his ownership or interest to the purchaser.

ARTICLE 14   In the event of a controversy between REALTORS® associated with different firms, arising out of their relationship as REALTORS®, the REALTORS® shall submit the dispute to arbitration in accordance with the regulations of their board or boards rather than litigate the matter.

ARTICLE 15   If a REALTOR® is charged with unethical practice or is asked to present evidence in any disciplinary proceeding or investigation, he shall place all pertinent facts before the proper tribunal of the member board or affiliated institute, society, or council of which he is a member.

ARTICLE 16   When acting as agent, the REALTOR® shall not accept any commission, rebate, or profit on expenditures made for his principal-owner, without the principal's knowledge and consent.

ARTICLE 17 The REALTOR® shall not engage in activities that constitute the unauthorized practice of law and shall recommend that legal counsel be obtained when the interest of any party to the transaction requires it.

ARTICLE 18 The REALTOR® shall keep in a special account in an appropriate financial institution, separated from his own funds, monies coming into his possession in trust for other persons, such as escrows, trust funds, clients' monies, and other like items.

ARTICLE 19 The REALTOR® shall be careful at all times to present a true picture in his advertising and representations to the public. He shall neither advertise without disclosing his name nor permit any person associated with him to use individual names or telephone numbers, unless such person's connection with the REALTOR® is obvious in the advertisement.

ARTICLE 20 The REALTOR®, for the protection of all parties, shall see that financial obligations and commitments regarding real estate transactions are in writing, expressing the exact agreement of the parties. A copy of each agreement shall be furnished to each party upon his signing such agreement.

ARTICLE 21 The REALTOR® shall not engage in any practice or take any action inconsistent with the agency of another REALTOR®.

ARTICLE 22 In the sale of property which is exclusively listed with a REALTOR®, the REALTOR® shall utilize the services of other brokers upon mutually agreed upon terms when it is in the best interests of the client.

Negotiations concerning property which is listed exclusively shall be carried on with the listing broker, not with the owner, except with the consent of the listing broker.

ARTICLE 23 The REALTOR® shall not publicly disparage the business practice of a competitor nor volunteer an opinion of a competitor's transaction. If his opinion is sought and if the REALTOR® deems it appropriate to respond, such opinion shall be rendered with strict professional integrity and courtesy.

ARTICLE 24 The REALTOR® shall not directly or indirectly solicit the services or affiliation of an employee or independent contractor in the organization of another REALTOR® without prior notice to said REALTOR®.

Where the word REALTOR® is used in this Code and Preamble, it shall be deemed to include REALTOR®-ASSOCIATE. Pronouns shall be considered to include REALTORS® and REALTOR®-ASSOCIATES of both genders.

The Code of Ethics was adopted in 1913. Amended at the Annual Convention in 1924, 1928, 1950, 1951, 1952, 1955, 1956, 1961, 1962, and 1974.

The term REALTOR® is copyrighted, and nonmembers who use it are in violation of the Real Estate Law.

A broker is under no compulsion to join a trade association. His rights under the law are neither added to, nor detracted from, by his decision.

AGENCY The licensee acts as an agent for his client and owes loyalty to him. He is prohibited from personally profiting because of his agency. The agent is bound by law to exercise the utmost good faith, loyalty, and integrity. He must not deliberately withhold material facts from the buyer. His obligation is to deal honestly with both the buyer and seller.

HOW TO SELECT AN AGENT You should select an agent in the same way that you would choose any other professional. The recommendation of friends or associates is a guide. You should obtain several names and interview each applicant. You should select one on the basis of a proven record and reputation and your ability to work with the person.

An agent's fee is normally paid by the seller. It is usually a negotiable percentage of the sales price of the property.

OTHER PROFESSIONALS There are many other professionals whose expert advice is sometimes required when buying or selling a home. They include the appraiser, the attorney, contractors, engineers, and title officers.

THE APPRAISER The independent fee appraiser will give an estimate of the value of the property that you are buying or selling. This estimate should be impartial, since an appraiser has no personal interest in the transaction. Appraisers are not licensed by any agency of the state.

The appraiser will rely on data that he has collected to assist him in the valuation of the property. He considers both its exterior and interior. He also considers the location of the property, and its convenience to schools, transportation, stores, taxes, zoning and any other factors that may affect value.

To select an appraiser, you should solicit recommendations from friends and associates. You may wish to consider an appraiser with a professional designation. Examples are: senior residential appraiser (SRA) and senior real estate appraiser (SREA), both designations awarded by the Society of Real Estate Appraisers. An MAI is a Member of the Appraisers Institute, which is affiliated with the NAR.

THE ATTORNEY An attorney is sometimes consulted to review the purchase agreement.

In complex transactions the attorney may draft the purchase agreement and give other legal advice.

Some attorneys are specialists in real estate law and real estate transactions. It is recommended that a specialist of this kind be used when you are considering the services of an attorney for a real estate transaction.

An attorney may be selected from recommendations of friends or associates. A list of attorneys can be obtained from the Bar Association.

MISCELLANEOUS PROFESSIONALS If you believe that a building has structural problems, you may wish to consult one or more of the following experts: a building contractor, a structural engineer, or a soil engineer. Subcontractors such as roofers, plumbers, or electricians should sometimes be consulted. It is recommended that a licensed pest control company inspect the property. An escrow officer will oversee the details of the escrow.

UNIT SUMMARY

In this unit we discussed the various experts who are available to provide professional real estate services. We examined the role of the real estate licensee, appraiser, attorney, and other experts.

You will usually require the services of one or more of them in your real estate transactions.

REVIEWING YOUR UNDERSTANDING

TRUE OR FALSE

( ) **1** It is not essential that the real estate licensee be familiar with financing.

( ) **2** A real estate license is required for an attorney handling real property for his client.

( ) **3** An MAI is a member of the Master Appraisal Institute.

( ) **4** An SREA is a senior real estate appraiser.

( ) **5** The majority of real estate transactions are handled by attorneys.

FILL-INS

1 A licensed real estate broker who is a member of NAR is a
_____.

2 When unstable earth conditions are suspected, the services of a
_____ are recommended.

3 When an extremely complicated transaction is involved, it is sometimes advisable to have an _____ draw up the documents.

REVIEWING YOUR UNDERSTANDING—ANSWERS

TRUE OR FALSE

1 False	4 True
2 False	5 False
3 False	

FILL-INS

1 realtor	3 attorney
2 soil engineer	

WHAT CAN YOU AFFORD?

7

This unit explains that you can receive a real property loan only if the lender is satisfied with the forms you are required to complete and is reasonably sure you are a good risk.

The unit emphasizes the three steps in the financing process; namely, (1) the application, (2) an analysis of the application, (3) the closing process and costs involved.

As the unit points out, the application is not standardized, but does include the loan request, borrower information, property information, credit analysis, and lender's action.

An analysis of the application includes an evaluation of the appraisal report and of the ability and willingness of the borrower to repay the loan.

The unit concludes with an explanation of the closing costs involved in completing the loan transaction.

Read this study guide (pages 54–64).
View TV program, number 7.

At the conclusion of this unit, you will be able to:

1 Distinguish between the various mortgage guarantee programs.

2 List the basic steps in the real property financing process.

3 Enumerate and discuss the basic steps the borrower must follow to obtain a loan.

4 Define the 3 Cs of credit and show how they apply to the obtaining of a real property loan.

5 List and explain the closing costs involved in a real property transaction.

promissory note	3 Cs of credit
equity investment	capacity
assets	escrow
liabilities	closing costs

INTRODUCTION   Most of you are unable to pay cash for the full amount of a home, duplex, ranch, or other real property. Fortunately, there are a number of lending agencies that will loan the amount you need to purchase real property, if you can qualify.

The type of real estate you can afford will depend on the amount you have for a down payment, the type of job you have, your total income, your past credit history, the amount of bills you owe, and the amount of your monthly payments.

Usually when you buy real property you make a down payment and sign a *promissory note* (a promise to pay the lender the amount borrowed, plus interest, before a specified date) for the balance.

The lender asks you for collateral as security for the loan. If you do not have other security, you can place the property you are buying as security for mortgage.

TYPES OF LOANS   Usually, the ownership of real property is financed by either land contracts, trust deeds, or mortgages. Under a land contract the seller and you, the purchaser, enter into a contract for the sale of real property, you make a down payment, and the contract is placed in escrow. Monthly payments of principal and interest are made on the contract, and when payments are completed, the deed is delivered.

Most sales of real property are financed by means of a trust deed or a mortgage. Various types of mortgages are available, including F.H.A. insured, V.A. guaranteed, Cal-Vet, and conventional (which will be explained in detail in Unit 10).

Under F.H.A. loans, the government insures the loan to lender for a fee paid by the borrower.

Under G.I. or V.A. administered loans, loans can be obtained without a down payment.

Under Cal-Vet, a California veteran can obtain a loan at a low interest rate.

Under a conventional loan, you are required to make a higher down payment and pay a higher interest rate than is required by a government-insured loan.

A number of sources for home loans are available to you; which one you should choose depends on your circumstances. Although most home loans are made through savings and loan associations, banks and mortgage companies are also sources of financing.

The way each of these sources operate will be detailed in Unit 10.

THE FINANCING PROCESS   The process of obtaining a loan has three steps.

1 The application.

2 The analysis of the application.

3 The closing process and costs.

APPLICATION FOR LOAN   Before a lending agency will accept your loan, the lending officer must assess the potential profitability of that loan. This assessment is based on a review of the risk factors involved, including the loan characteristics, the characteristics of you, the borrower, and the characteristics of the subject property.

LOAN CHARACTERISTICS Whether or not your loan will be considered a good risk will depend on the nature of the loan and economic conditions surrounding the transaction.

When real property prices and incomes are rising, the loan likely will be profitable for both lender and borrower.

New loans have a higher risk than older loans because the hidden defects have not been ironed out. The newer the loan, the less the reduction of the principal with each payment.

EQUITY INVESTMENT The lender will seek borrowers with enough equity (amount invested in the property) that they would want to continue their payments or will want to be assured that in the event of default the property could bring, at sale, more than the outstanding loan.

The lender may be concerned about the size of the down payment you are able to make. His concern may be that either because of a fall in the price level or physical depreciation or obsolescence of the property, the value of investment may decline faster than the outstanding principal of the loan.

The length of time the loan is to run will be a determining risk factor; however, an amortization of 20 years or less won't affect the risk to any great extent.

INTEREST PAID The interest charge may affect the risk of the loan. The lenders usually adjust the loan amount so that even with the higher interest rate, payments are not too high. As a matter of fact, statistics show that default is more common among loans of relatively low interest rates.

APPLICATION FORM The application form itself is not standardized, it varies from one lender to another. The only thing that is standard is the basic contents.

The application will consist of the loan request, borrower information, property or collateral information, credit analysis, and lender's action.

BUYERS CONFIDENTIAL FINANCIAL STATUS
CALIFORNIA REAL ESTATE ASSOCIATION STANDARD FORM

(1) Down Payment $_____   Date: _____

Property Address_____ Sales Price: $_____

Type Loan Req: _____ Loan Amount $ _____ Interest_____%, Years # _____

P.I. Mo.: _____Taxes: Ann (NV) $_____/mo. $_____, Ins.: Mo. $_____, PITI ±_____

Name: _____Wife's Name: _____

Age: _____ Date Married: _____   Age: _____

Number of Dependents: _____Ages of Dependents: _____

Present Address: _____City: _____ St: _____Phone:_____

　Own/Rent _____Length of Residence: _____

Former address (if not 3 years at present address): _____

FIGURE 1　　Length of residence: _____City: _____St: _____

FIGURE 1 (Continued) **EMPLOYMENT:** Must Cover Two Years

(2) APPLICANT:

Employer: _____

Address: _____

Type of Business: _____

Position: _____

Supervisor: _____

Length of Employment: _____

Former Employer: _____

Address: _____

Type of Business: _____

Position: _____

Supervisor: _____

Length of Employment: _____

Describe Second Job If Any: _____

WIFE:

Employer: _____

Address: _____

Type of Business: _____

Position: _____

Supervisor: _____

Length of Employment: _____

Former Employer: _____

Address: _____

Type of Business: _____

Position: _____

Supervisor: _____

Length of Employment: _____

(3) INCOME: (Monthly)

Base Pay (Gross) . . . . $_____

Overtime (Ann. Av./mo.) . . . . _____

Second Job (Ann. Av./mo.) . . . . . . _____

Wife's Base Pay (Gross) . . . . _____

Wife's Overtime (Ann. Av./mo.) . . _____

*Income from R.E. (Net) . . . . _____

Other Income . . . . _____

Total Income Monthly . . . . $_____

Annual: (Mo. × 12) . . . . $_____

(Buyer does not complete
this Section:)

Net Monthly Income $_____

PITI $_____ =

_____ (×) Factor

2½ × Annual Income $ _____

(4) ASSETS:

Cash on Hand . . . . $_____

Bank Accounts . . . . _____

Savings Bonds . . . . _____

Securities . . . . _____

Other: _____ _____

TOTAL . . . . $_____

Automobile: _____$_____

Automobile: _____ _____

Furniture . . . . _____

Personal Property . . . . _____

Other: _____ _____

TOTAL . . . . $_____

*Real Estate Owned:

(1) Value Estimate . . . . $_____

    Address: _____

(2) Value Estimate . . . . $_____

    Address: _____

    TOTAL ASSETS . . . .$_____

Have you ever filed bankruptcy? _____

Do you pay child support? _____

Do you recieve child support? _____

(5) LIABILITIES:

Installment Payments:

(1) To:_____Bal. $_____Mo. $_____

(2) To:_____Bal. $_____Mo. $_____

(3) To:_____Bal. $_____Mo. $_____

(4) To:_____Bal. $_____Mo. $_____

Number of months to go on above accounts:

(1) _____ (2) _____ (3) _____ (4) _____

Automobile Loan Bal. $_____mo. $_____

Automobile Loan Bal. $_____mo. $_____

Liens or Judgments:

    To:_____ Bal. $_____ mo. $_____

    To:_____ Bal. $_____ mo. $_____

    Total Current Monthly Payments: $___

*Mortgage Payments:

(1) Balance Owed $_____ mo. pay_____

(2) Balance Owed $_____ mo. pay_____

TOTAL LIABILITIES $_____Mo. $_____

Any current suits or judgments?_____

Do you pay alimony?_____

Do you receive alimony?_____

From what source will balance of funds come from if not shown above?_____

X_____
    (signature)

X_____
    (signature)

BCFS-11

THE LOAN REQUEST   The loan request is simply a written request by the borrower that includes his name, the terms and amount of the loan, the loan's purpose, and how it will be repaid.

BORROWER INFORMATION   This information is necessary so that the lender can determine the borrower's willingness and ability to pay the loan.

Although forms required will vary with each lender, the form developed by the California Association of Realtors is representative of the kind of information sought by lenders (pages 56–57). An explanation of each section is given here.

(1) This first section of the application serves as a loan request.

(2) The second section covers present and former employment. The assurance that the employment will continue is important. The length of time on the job is important. If the borrower is in a new job, the job may not work out, either because of lack of accomplishment, personality clash, or other reasons.

Has the potential borrower developed a record of "job hopping" without an increase in his income? The answers to these and other questions can be obtained from information in this section.

(3) The income of the candidate is perhaps the single most important item in determining loan risk.

Risks appear to be higher for lower-income families. In some cases, a family makes a habit of over-extending itself. The ratio of expenses to income is important in determining ability to repay the loan.

In analyzing section (3) certain broad guidelines have been set forth:

1 Gross income of at least four to five times the monthly loan payment.

2 A job tenure of 2 years.

Sometimes the family income is supplemented with a second job, overtime pay, or with the spouse working. These items are accounted for in this section.

(4) Although most home buyers, especially young couples, have not accumulated a great many assets, this section is important.

Such items as cash on hand and bank accounts will determine the liquidity of the individual. Possession of stocks, bonds, automobiles, and other real estate indicates prudent living and an ability to invest wisely and conserve a portion of income.

(5) This section relates to those charges and obligations already levied against the borrower's income and will largely determine his ability to meet a mortgage obligation.

The mortgage payment is usually limited to 20 to 25 percent of the applicant's effective income.

PROPERTY INFORMATION   This part of the application is intended to determine how much security for the loan is offered by the property.

Information requested includes:

1 Specific identification of the property—usually the legal description. The geographical location is vitally important because, as the economy develops, one area may decline while others grow. Other factors, such as the general attractiveness of the site and location with respect to essential services, are also important.

2 Preliminary title information is necessary information. The existence of all claims, encumbrances, liens, mortgages, and so on will affect the risk value.

3 A description of the land, including improvements (especially work done within the last 90 days) that might be subject to mechanic's liens—demands for payment by contractors and workers who have been employed.

4 Economic data, including taxes, zoning, assessments, and date of purchase. If the property is income-producing, economic data would include operating income and expenses over several years.

5 An appraisal is usually made by the lender after interviewing the borrower. The appraisal will include the present value and economic trends.

ANALYSIS OF APPLICATION

If the prospective borrower and the lender have accurately completed the "application and financial status" report form, it does much to facilitate the loan request and helps provide information on which sound judgments can be based.

The analysis of application includes a careful scrutiny of forms submitted and a personal interview.

The forms to be analyzed include the application, appraisal report, and the credit analysis.

PROCESSING THE APPLICATION   Most lenders regard a personal interview with the borrower as extremely important. The nature of the interview will depend largely on the amount of the lender's assets and his type of operation. The amount of the loan or the complexity of the loan process is directly proportional to the management level at which the interview and final negotiations take place.

Figure 2 (page 60) shows the routing of a real estate loan in a large company.

The loan officer doing the interviewing must obtain confidential information from the client without causing ill feelings, so he is usually a good public relations man and is proficient in analyzing the necessary paperwork.

The interview is important so that the loan officer may:

1 Determine the accuracy of the application. The interview gives him opportunity to clear up any misunderstandings and enables him to make a personal judgment of borrower's financial condition.

2 Determine if the loan is sound and workable. If it is not sound for the borrower it is not sound for the lender.

3 Review the collateral. The interview often helps to determine if the collateral is sound enough to secure the loan and if it will continue to be sound.

4 Explain the various loan costs. Often a prospective borrower does not realize the many hidden costs involved in obtaining a loan. (These costs will be explained later in this unit.)

THE APPRAISAL REPORT   The appraisal of property is concerned with establishing present value and the trend of future values. This procedure will be discussed in detail in Unit 14.

ROUTE OF REAL ESTATE LOANS

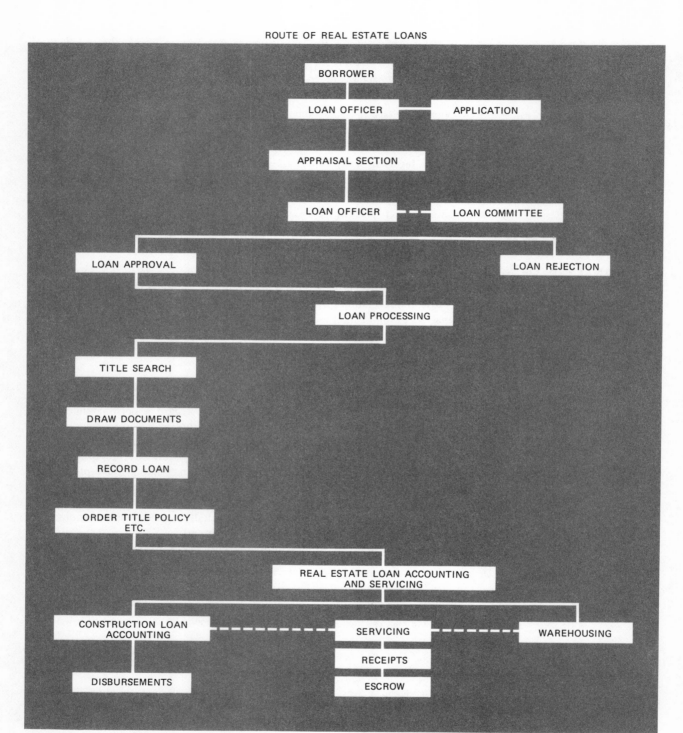

FIGURE 2

CREDIT ANALYSIS   The credit analysis is fundamentally a summary of the information supplied and the lender's judgment as to the ability and willingness of the borrower, or the ability of the property (in case of income property) to repay the requested loan.

To assist in this important phase of the application, many lenders will require the completion of an application for credit, in addition to the other forms required. This format will vary. A representative form is shown in Figure 3 (page 62).

In judging the risk, most lenders will adhere carefully to what is known as the 3Cs of credit. These are capacity, character, and capital.

Capacity refers to the borrower's ability to pay. Many lenders have established a standard formula to determine ability to repay. For example, some lenders use a standard that says that the borrower has the ability to pay if his fixed monthly expenses (car payments, installment loans, etc.) do not exceed 30 percent of his takehome pay.

Some instructions use the gross income multiplier. This states that the maximum price for a home purchased by the borrower should not exceed 2½ or 3 or 4 (the multiplier used varies) times the borrower's annual income from salary.

Character relates to the borrower's willingness to pay. A person of good character will usually prefer to pay his bill on time. A check of the borrower's habits in repaying others from whom he has received credit is helpful in determining his willingness to pay. In other words, does the prospective borrower pay his bills? Does he pay them on time?

Capital simply refers to a person's financial ability to pay as determined by declarations made in the original application and financial status report.

These three points, capacity, character and capital, are somewhat related, in that a person's willingness to pay a bill may result from his capacity to pay it, as measured by his income or the property he possesses.

CLOSING THE LOAN   We have covered the information needed to analyze a real property loan. After the borrower has been analyzed and the property appraised, the lender has the information necessary to accept or reject the loan application.

A neutral third party called the *escrow* (discussed in detail in Units 18 and 19) is charged with the responsibility of gathering the documents—properly executed and notarized—such as the promissory note, the security instrument (trust deed or mortgage), necessary to complete the loan transaction.

The escrow calculates the various charges to both parties and sees that required funds are deposited by each party. The closing costs include the following where applicable:

Amount of installment including interest and principal.
Appraisal fees.
Escrow fees.
Costs of investigating or guaranteeing title.
Notary fees.
Recording fees
Credit investigation fees (if any needed).
Prepaid taxes.
Prepaid insurance.

At the conclusion of escrow, the loan file is turned over to the lender or his representative for the administration of the loan. This process is called *loan servicing*.

FIGURE 3

APPLICATION FOR CREDIT
Answer All Questions Fully

Acct. No. _____ 84160 _____ Lot No. _____ Tract No. _____ Date _____

Name _____ Age _____ Wife's Name _____ Age _____ How Long Married? _____
      Last   First   Middle

Street Address _____ City & State _____ Phone _____

No. of Dependents _____ Age of Dependents _____

Length of Residence _____ Own or Rent _____ Amount Monthly Rental _____ Landlord _____

Former Address _____ How long there _____

WHAT EMPLOYMENT AND INCOME DO YOU HAVE?

Present Employer _____ Previous Employer _____

Address _____ Address _____

Phone _____ Position _____ Phone _____ Position _____

How long _____ Income _____ How long _____ Income _____

Period of Military Service _____ Other annual Income _____ Amount per year $ _____ Source _____

Wife's Employer _____ Address _____ Phone _____

Position _____ How Long _____ Income _____

WHAT ASSETS DO YOU OWN?

                Amount   Amount

Down Payment on Current Deal _____ Automobile (_____) _____
                                                  Make & Model

Cash in Bank _____ Furniture Value of _____

Bonds & Stocks _____ Real Estate Owned _____ (List on Reverse Side)

Life Insurance(_____) Other Assets _____
                 Cash Value

WHAT AMOUNTS DO YOU OWE?
(Include Mortgage if any and Payments)

	Amount	Name	Address
1	_____	_____	_____
2	_____	_____	_____
3	_____	_____	_____
4	_____	_____	_____

WHAT BANK ACCOUNTS DO YOU HAVE?

Bank _____ Branch & Address _____

_____ _____

Type Account _____ _____ Balances _____

FIGURE 3 (*Continued*)   WHAT ACCOUNTS (NOW PAID) HAVE YOU HAD? (Include Loans, Auto, or Appliances Financed)

	Name	Address
1	_____	_____
2	_____	_____
3	_____	_____
4	_____	_____

Signed _____

Use reverse side for additional information and references:
also for list of real estate owned.

UNIT SUMMARY

This unit has described a promissory note and showed its relationship to a mortgage transaction. Four types of guaranteed loans—F.H.A., V.A. or G.I., Cal-Vet, and conventional—were briefly explained.

The first step in the financing process, the application for loan was pointed out. The application should include the loan request, borrower information, and property information. Forms were provided in the unit to better explain each of the facets involved in the process.

The processing and analysis of the application were treated as the second step. This phase included an analysis of the application itself, the appraisal report, and the credit analysis.

The 3 Cs of credit, character, capacity, and capital, were discussed and their importance in a credit transaction revealed.

As a final step to the real property loan application, the closing costs were emphasized. These costs included such items as the amount of installment payment, appraisal, escrow and notary fees; costs of investigating title, prepaid insurance, and taxes.

REVIEWING YOUR UNDERSTANDING

MULTIPLE CHOICE

(   )   **1**   In evaluating a person's income for a loan, the least weight would be given to: (a) the spouse's income, (b) overtime earnings, (c) investment earnings, (d) earnings from a part-time job.

(   )   **2**   Most housing loans are made by: (a) banks, (b) savings and loan associations, (c) mortgage companies, (d) insurance companies.

(   )   **3**   The longer a loan: (a) the lower the interest, (b) the higher the interest, (c) the higher the payment, (d) the lower the payment.

(   )   **4**   Substantial down payments in real estate: (a) result in less danger of default, (b) help insure that the property will be well maintained, (c) result in better loan terms, (d) all of the above.

( ) **5** Which of the following terms is not one of the three Cs of credit? (a) cost (b) capacity, (c) capital, (d) character.

TRUE OR FALSE

( ) **1** The amount of investment equity is a determining factor in the processing of a real property loan.

( ) **2** The stability of income of the prospective borrower is the most important single item in determining loan risk.

( ) **3** Job tenure of at least 5 to 10 years is an essential factor in a property loan.

( ) **4** Most lenders feel that a personal interview with the borrower is superfluous.

( ) **5** The appraisal report of property is concerned with the present value of property and the trend of future values.

Analyze your own credit standing and prepare a report for purposes of obtaining a real property loan.

MULTIPLE CHOICE

1 (b)   4 (d)

2 (b)   5 (a)

3 (d)

TRUE OR FALSE

1 True   4 False

2 True   5 True

3 False

WHAT TYPE OF PROPERTY SHOULD YOU BUY?

In Unit 5, we discussed the advantages and disadvantages of buying your home. In this unit, our purpose is to help you to determine the type of property you should buy.

The pros and cons of purchasing a home will be discussed in detail in the next unit. A brief summary of the advantages and disadvantages of residential ownership will introduce this unit.

The advantages and disadvantages of purchasing a residence which gives you individual ownership of a single unit in a multiunit structure (condominium), along with pitfalls to avoid and the techniques that will assist you in making the right purchase, will be stressed.

The advisability of purchasing a vacation home and how to go about doing so will be covered.

The part a movable home now plays in our economy and the points of ownership of this type of real property are examined.

Undeveloped land for various purposes can provide a source of additional income when purchasing property. Factors to be considered when buying this type of real property are submitted to assist you in your investment choices.

Read this study guide (pages 66–75).
View TV program, number 8.

At the conclusion of this unit you will be able to:

1 List the advantages and disadvantages of making the following purchases:
a Condominium
b Vacation home
c Acreage and raw land
d Small investment property

2 Know how to go about purchasing each of these types of real property.

3 Determine the best property to purchase for investment purposes.

condominium	topography
mobile home	V.A.
F.T.C.	leverage
"fill" dirt	

SHOULD YOU BUY A HOME?

This question will be answered in detail in the next unit. However, the following are among the reasons for owning a *home*.

Peace of mind.

Pride.

Credit.

Convenience.

Forced savings.

Security.

Sense of independence.

Privacy.

Wide choice of neighborhood or location.

Safe investment.

Profit from sale if you move.

Greater personal enjoyment.

Permanency of location—roots in community.

Chance for involvement in civic affairs.

In addition to the personal reasons for owning a home, tax and other advantages accrue to the home owner. When you own your own home, you can deduct property taxes, interest paid on the mortgage, and you may even deduct a portion of your expenses if you use part of your house as an office. By owning a home, you are building an equity or ownership in the property; it's an ideal place for children to grow up; there is usually more room in a home than in an apartment; you can do what you want with it.

DISADVANTAGES OF OWNING A HOME

In the first place, buying a home can be an expensive undertaking, especially when you consider your down payment and other initial costs. When you take on this responsibility, you are assuming a heavy fixed monthly debt. You can't move easily if your finances fail or if you receive a job transfer. Other obligations must be assumed, such as taxes and insurance payments. Your asset depreciates daily and constant repairs along with painting, papering, and landscaping are your entire obligation. If you buy an older house, the maintenance cost, as well as the improvements and additions may increase your financial obligations.

SHOULD YOU BUY A CONDOMINIUM?

WHAT IS A CONDOMINIUM? Section 783 of the California Civil Code defines a condominium as

an estate in real property consisting of an undivided interest in common in a portion of a parcel of real property together with a separate interest in space in a residential, industrial or commercial building on such real property, such as an apartment house, office or store. It may include in addition, a separate interest in other portions of such property.

Perhaps a clearer definition is given by the Congressional Committee after a study made for F.H.A.

Individual ownership of single units in a multi-unit structure, with common ownership of halls, stairs, elevators, lobbies, driveways, recreation centers etc.

Each condominium unit may be bought, sold, mortgaged, and taxed separately from other units in the project.

ADVANTAGES OF BUYING A CONDOMINIUM

The advantages of buying a condominium are similar to those of purchasing a single-family dwelling. Some of these advantages are listed below.

You can sell your own unit as you would a residential home. Under the National Housing Act of 1961, F.H.A. was authorized to provide mortgage insurance to the condominium buyer. Insurance companies offer special packages for condominium owners for fire, accident, and damage insurance. A condominium combines the benefits of owning a house with the advantages of apartment living. You receive the same tax benefits as a home owner; in buying a condominium, you build an equity with each payment as you do in a home; there is little or no yard work to perform.

Common areas included in your ownership can include swimming pools, tennis courts, game rooms, and putting greens. Condominiums have become popular in recent years because they usually have large rooms, ample closet space, picture windows, pleasant views, wall-to-wall carpeting, modern kitchen equipment, air conditioning, and recreation centers. The law offers some protection to the owner; he can't be made to leave because of infractions of bylaws and regulations of the association.

DISADVANTAGES OF OWNING A CONDOMINIUM

As with a home, you are responsible for all building maintenance problems in your unit; you are assessed a fee to cover the costs of maintaining all common areas; there is a lack of state regulations regarding condominiums.

In some condominiums, the developer controls parking and recreation areas and may charge exhorbitant prices for their use. This is an exception, but a word to the wise should be sufficient. Some developers even control and dominate the management association set up as a governing board for the condominium development. Again this is an exception, but you should be aware that such problems exist.

There are some specific areas in condominium ownership that are protected by law. Some states have laws restricting the developer from controlling common areas or dominating management associations. Specifically the California Civil Code contains legal protection in the following sections:

cc 1353   States that condominium unit owner can decorate as he pleases.

cc 1353   An easement is granted to all unit owners in all common areas.

cc 1355   Provides a declaration of restrictions.

WHAT YOU SHOULD BE AWARE OF BEFORE BUYING

If you decide to purchase a condominium be sure to:

Check on the reputation of the builder.

Know and understand what you are doing and what your responsibilities are.

Read all legal documents carefully (consult an attorney if necessary).

Make sure management fees cover all contingencies.

Ask yourself these specific questions:

Is exterior and/or interior maintenance included in established fees?

Is there a warranty on equipment? If so, for how long?

Are there any restrictions on sale or lease?

Does the developer have reserve funds in case of an emergency?

Are you required to pay maintenance costs for unsold units?

CAUTION

> Be sure to read the operational budget in order to understand the extent of assessments and services.

ADDITIONAL POINTS OF INTEREST

It is estimated that one-half of the population will live in condominiums in 20 years.

Typical condominium buyers have been renters before. They are typically in two age groups:

45 to 64 years with grown families, seeking a smaller home.

25 to 34 years (young professionals).

Financing is on an individual-unit basis. Another's default does not endanger your interest.

LAST WORD

If you intend to buy a condominium look for one that has an attractive location and architectural styling and one that can be purchased on terms you are willing and able to meet.

SHOULD YOU BUY A SECOND OR VACATION HOME?

People have purchased single-family units, condominiums, mobile homes (described later in this unit), motor homes, and trailers for second homes. Statistics from a survey conducted by *Vacation Home and Leisure Living* magazine show:

An estimated two million people have second homes, increasing at the rate of 150,000 to 200,000 per year.

By 1980 $4 billion will be spent annually on second homes.

Two-thirds of vacation or second homes cost more than $10,000.

Nearly one-fourth cost at least $20,000.

More than 50 percent have two or more bathrooms.

Three-fourths have more than 1000 square feet of living space.

More than one-half are custom built and 40 percent are factory built prefabs.

57 percent are situated on or near a lake, river or seashore.

86 percent of the owners have incomes of $10,000 or more, while 54 percent have incomes of $15,000 or more.

One-half of the buyers are under 40 years of age and four-fifths of them are married.

Ask yourself this specific question, "What kind of a second home should I consider"?

Is it to be a cabin in the mountains?

Is it to be a cottage by the lake?

Is it to be a house on the beach?

Is it to be a chalet on a skiing slope?

Is it to be a hunting shack in the wilderness?

The decision you make will be influenced by a number of facts; for example, real estate property is a good investment; leisure time has increased; we all need a place where we can "just get away from it all."

YOUR SECOND HOME AS AN INVESTMENT

If you buy in a popular recreation area your purchase is likely to appreciate at 5 to 10 percent per year. If you live in this home only occasionally, the balance of the time you can rent it out for $200 and up per month. This provides a nice second income. Or you may wish to rent individual bedrooms, separately. If this is your primary reason for purchasing a second home, you must realize that top rentals are near beaches, lakes, rivers, or mountains.

If your second home is used as a business venture, you can use it as a tax write-off. If you can show an overall profit in 2 of 5 years, it is considered to be a business and you may deduct expenses for any year you lose money.

If you show no profit you might qualify for a tax write-off, but you must prove that you offered your place for rent at a reasonable fee—advertised it—and only occupied it for a portion of the time.

WHERE YOU BUY IS IMPORTANT

You should ask yourself these questions before you make your final decision regarding ownership of a second home:

Can I tolerate neighbors nearby or do I want complete privacy?

Do I want a place convenient to the conveniences of the city or one that is "out of sight and sound"?

Do I want a place I can reach in an hour or so, or one that takes a day's drive?

Depending upon the area chosen, is money a problem? If it is can I interest another family in a cooperative venture?

ADDITIONAL HELP AVAILABLE TO YOU

The Federal Trade Commission (F.T.C.), the U.S. Postal Service, and at least 39 states are regulating or investigating the practices of land developers (California is one of those states).

Before you commit yourself, the Better Business Bureau suggests that you resolve the following questions, and determine positive answers for each of these situations and conditions.

The promoter   Who is he and what has his performance record revealed?

Advertising   Are improvements specified in the advertising material completed or only planned? Are distances exaggerated or are they reported truthfully?

Location   Is clear access to the property assured? How far is the property from highway, towns, airport, shopping, schools, civic protection, and public utilities?

Value of land in the area   Is your property priced in keeping with current selling prices? Are homes well maintained and surroundings developed?

Improvements   What improvements exist, or are planned, for the future? Will tax assessments be forthcoming and who will be responsible for them?

Drainage   Is effective drainage possible or is land "high and dry"?

Sewers   Are sewers installed? If not, are septic tanks permissable and advisable?

Topography and soil   The topography is the description of the land. In addition, what does topsoil analysis reveal? Is the property "fill dirt" (dirt brought in to level the land)?

Status of Property   Who owns the property? Is the title clear? Are there any hidden liens, easements, or assessments?

Taxes   What is the present assessment rate? What does the future hold in store as improvements are made?

Zoning   Are there any zoning restrictions now or projected for the future?

Financing   How much are the closing costs? Are they included in the mortgage? Are arrangements for payment mutually agreeable?

THE RECOMMENDED FIRST STEP

One of the most economical ways to get started on that second home is to purchase a lot.

Be sure that you buy a large enough piece of land to assure privacy. Make sure you have ready access to your property, that a right-of-way exists or is possible.

Check the condition of roadway during inclement weather. Is it accessible in all weather conditions?

Be sure to check utilities. Are they available or must they be installed?

For answers to these and other questions check with a reliable real estate agent.

If you are planning on building, a one-, two-, or three-room house may be a good start (it can always be expanded).

There are a variety of designs to choose from—choose one that is compatible with the design in the area and fits your pocketbook.

CAUTION

> According to the U.S. Office of Interstate Land Sales there are unscrupulous land developers who:
> Misrepresent present and future values.
> Exaggerate promises of refunds.

ADVANTAGES OF PURCHASING A MOBILE HOME

Because of the rapid advancement in the mobile home industry, there are decided advantages to this type of purchase.

The best mobile home parks are small subdivisions that are landscaped and include other facilities. Mobile homes are generally less expensive than other housing; Most are less than $10,000, and over half are less than $25,000. Mobile homes (exclusive of land costs) complete with furniture, carpeting, draperies, major appliances, cost one-third to one-half less per square foot than conventional houses *without* furnishings and appliances.

Since the passage of the Veteran's Housing Act of 1970, the Veteran's Administration (V.A.) has guaranteed loans up to $17,500 for the purchase of mobile homes. The maximum guarantee for the home alone is $10,000; loans are made for 12 years and 32 days and if a veteran owns the site, he can borrow for improvements. If the loan is for a home and the lot, the maximum loan of $17,500 can be extended to 15 years and 32 days.

Another advantage of mobile home ownership is that the buyer can expect lower charges for insurance, utilities, taxes, and maintenance.

DISADVANTAGES OF PURCHASING A MOBILE HOME

There are many advantages to this type of living, but there are also some disadvantages. Among the disadvantages are: a high fire risk; lack of state and federal supervision; reluctance of local government to rezone to permit establishing mobile home parks.

Financing is also a distinct disadvantage. The terms of loans offered by banks and savings and loan associations are similar to those for buying a car. True interest rates are considerably higher than stated. Down payments of 20 to 30 percent are required, with from 5 to 25 years to pay compared to 20 to 30 years for a home.

Another distinct disadvantage is that mobile homes depreciate very rapidly. It runs about 20 percent for the first year, 10 percent for second and third years, and 5 percent depreciation for the balance of the life of the mobile home. At these rates, after 6½ years, the market value will be approximately half of the original price. A study by the First National City Bank of New York revealed that mobile homes go off the market after 15 years.

If your mobile home is located in a mobile park you may be required to buy these extras:

Steps with handrails

Skirting to conceal wheels

Supports or piers to provide foundation.

NOTE

> Most mobile homes are immobile and once established in a mobile park are considered to be permanent. This can mean that they are taxed as real rather than personal property.

LAST-MINUTE INSTRUCTIONS

If you're ready to purchase a mobile home, here are a few last-minute instructions and bits of information for you.

The site should be well drained; free from excessive slopes, rocky ground, swampy, or marshy areas.

Try to avoid a park in close proximity to a noisy industrial area.

The best parks have room and facilities for 50 lots—this ensures low maintenance costs.

Homes should take up no more than one-third of a lot. This means approximately 2800 square feet for a single-width home, and 4500 square feet for a double width.

The best parks group their homes around open spaces that contain recreational facilities or stagger the homes so that windows and doors do not face each other.

The current average price for a mobile home is about $8.50 per square foot, including furnishings and appliances.

The national average for original selling price is $7800 to $11,000; the average resale is $5000.

Over 400 firms produce mobile homes and there are many styles to choose from—make sure you choose the right one for you.

SHOULD YOU BUY ACREAGE OR RAW LAND?

WHAT IS RAW LAND?   Raw land is defined as any acreage that is not in use and for which no specific use has yet been determined. It is undeveloped and may not yet be zoned. Raw land offers the greatest potential for profit—but buying it is a speculative venture as the owner gambles on the *directional* growth of the population. It is usually cheaper than other forms of real property.

Raw land is usually purchased for one or more of these reasons:

To cultivate and sell crops for profit.

To use for mineral sources.

To use for residential, commercial, and industrial purposes.

If you purchase the land for agricultural purposes you will find that it can be a fairly inexpensive investment. Buying land for growing crops can be risky because farming itself is highly sophisticated and technical—expertise, patience, and handwork are inherent in this activity. However, you may buy land for farming, but hold onto it until the area is urbanized and the land will have increased in value. You may buy specifically to resell.

If you buy under a stressed sale, you might easily profit by a resale. Although the risk is high, there is also a large potential profit in subdividing.

USING RAW LAND AS A LEVERAGE

You may wish to purchase raw land with the express purpose of selling some of the property and developing the balance. This is known as *leverage*.

EXAMPLE

Mr. Green buys 30 acres of land at $400 per acre, a total of $12,000. He pays 25 percent down, or $3000.

The value of the land increases to $800 per acre. He sells 30 acres for $24,000, pays off the balance owed, $9000. This would leave $15,000. He would recover his $3000 and make $12,000 profit.

If you can afford to wait for the land to appreciate, you can deduct taxes, interest and carrying charges during the waiting period or, as previously mentioned, you might sell some of the property and develop the balance.

CAUTION

Sell the less desirable parcels and retain the better ones.

HOW MUCH SHOULD YOU PAY?

To determine whether the purchase price is reasonable, you should investigate previous transactions and determine whether or not adjacent land has changed hands and, if so, how frequently; consult with real estate brokers in the vicinity who specialize in raw land; calculate the *eventual* use value (as a rule of thumb, land must double in value every 7 years to warrant holding it).

WHAT RISKS SHOULD I LOOK FOR?

The cost of "carrying" the purchase may be burdensome because of mortgage payments, interest, taxes, and assessments.

Land could have legal or physical defects that might impede development.

Land may be overpriced through speculative transfers.

Land itself lacks liquidity.

Don't make this purchase your only operation. Don't place more than one-fourth to one-third of your total real estate in raw land.

If you've decided to purchase raw land, then look for the following: land that is high, dry, and flat; land that can be graded, filled, and/or has proper drainage; make sure you have plenty of road frontage; find the right location in the path of the city's growth, either residential, industrial, or commercial. (Through maps of 10-year growth periods you can ascertain trends.)

REMEMBER

> When you buy raw land you may have to hold it for 5 or maybe even 10 years before it will pay off.

UNIT SUMMARY

In this unit we have tried to help you select the right type of property to purchase.

The pros and cons in purchasing a home are discussed briefly (this subject is explored in detail in Unit 9).

The unit defines the term condominium and examines the advantages and disadvantages of buying this type of real property. The areas protected by law are discussed and instructions given as to what to look for and how to prepare for such a purchase.

The advisability of investing in a second home or vacation home is explored. Questions such as the following are posed so you will be in a position to make a wise choice. What kind of second home should I consider? In what area should I buy? What help is available to me before I make my decision? If I decide to buy what steps should I take?

Also discussed in detail is another type of real property—the mobile home. The advantages and disadvantages of purchasing a mobile home are explored. Specific instructions on how to go about this purchase transaction are given.

Should you invest in acreage or raw land? This question explores the advisability of such a move and advises how much you should plan to pay. Types of raw land and possible returns from refurbishing, reselling, holding for appreciation, and using as leverage are discussed.

REVIEWING YOUR UNDERSTANDING

TRUE OR FALSE

(   )   **1**   Greater personal enjoyment is undoubtedly one of the most important advantages of owning a home.

(   )   **2**   A person who lives in his own house may deduct depreciation of the home from his income for federal income tax purposes.

(   )   **3**   It is substantially cheaper to own a house than to rent, when all costs are considered.

(   )   **4**   A major disadvantage of renting a home rather than owning one is the lack of flexibility for the owner.

(   )   **5**   There are income tax advantages in renting rather than owning a house.

(   )   **6**   Although condominium owners can include the property taxes they pay among their itemized deductions, they cannot include the interest on their mortgages.

(   )   **7**   In condominiums, individuals are responsible only for mortgage indebtedness and taxes involving their own unit.

(   )   **8**   The most common type of mobile home is the single unit, usually 12 feet wide by 65 feet long.

(   )   **9**   In buying a mobile home, extras such as handrails for the outside door, skirting to conceal the wheels, and supports for foundation are usually part of the basic sales price.

(   )   **10**   Raw land is defined as any acreage that is not in use and for which no specific use has yet been determined.

SUGGESTED LEARNING ACTIVITIES

Visit a mobile home park and observe the layout of the park and the condition of the buildings and grounds.

REVIEWING YOUR UNDERSTANDING—ANSWERS

TRUE OR FALSE

1	True	**6**	False
2	False	**7**	True
3	False	**8**	True
4	True	**9**	False
5	False	**10**	True

WHAT SHOULD YOU LOOK
FOR IN A HOME?

OVERVIEW

There comes a time in everyone's life when they will become interested in buying or renting housing of some type. This unit describes in detail what should be considered before taking such a step.

The items that are important and that are explained in detail in this unit include the type of neighborhood you should look for, the size of the living quarters that will best satisfy your needs, whether or not you should look for a new or an old home, the structural aspects of the home that you must take into consideration, and the type of floor plan and design that best fits your tastes, desires, and "pocketbook."

Checklists and shopping lists will be provided to help you to do a better job of home selection.

ASSIGNMENT

Read the study guide (pages 78–88).
View TV program, number 9.

PERFORMANCE OBJECTIVES

At the conclusion of this unit you will be able to:

1 Select a place to live that combines such desirable characteristics as a neighborhood that is appreciating instead of depreciating, ready access to schools, shopping centers, employment and recreational facilities.

2 Make a list of factors that should be considered when choosing the floor plan and size of your house.

3 Distinguish between the advantages and disadvantages of a new versus an old home.

4 Construct a checklist of things to look for in checking the structural aspects of a home.

TERMS YOU SHOULD KNOW

traffic pattern
custom-built house
model

potable water supply
exposure

78

DECISIONS TO BE MADE

To rent or to buy? This is the first decision that you will have to make. In this unit we assume that you have made that decision and have decided to buy a home.

The second decision is whether your house will be new or old. Before you make this decision, you will have to consider location, floor plan and size of home, and structure and design.

CHOOSING A LOCATION

There are several factors to consider in choosing a location.

What about the neighborhood? Will it be easy to live in—a place where you and your family can, within your ability to pay, live a normal, happy, satisfying life? Do the neighbors appear to have the same interests and income and are they somewhat the same age? Having to curtail activities and expenditures normal to the rest of the neighborhood may be a setback to adults and a problem for family members.

Will the location of the property satisfy personal needs and desires such as:

Convenient location of schools.

Convenient shopping facilities.

Proximity to place of employment.

Convenient public transportation.

Play area for children.

Fire and police protection provided.

Absence of noise and unpleasant odors.

Safeguard of adequate zoning.

An important factor in location is nearby location of schools. If there are children in the family, you will want to know whether the house is close to an elementary school and junior and senior high schools. Consider the present school tax. If a new school will be needed, can you afford the tax increase?

A second factor is convenient shopping facilities. If your home is located near a local or a major shopping center, you will save much time and effort in shopping for daily necessities.

You may want to consider your place of employment. Of course, we all can't live within walking distance of our place of employment. However, when possible, the proximity of your employment is a factor to consider. Proximity to public transportation and freeway outlets can offset problems related to employment travel.

There are other factors to consider. When possible, it is helpful to be close to a hospital or medical service, recreational facilities and playground, church of your choice, post office, and other community activities.

REMEMBER

> *Each* mile from your employment, schools, shopping center, doctor, or other convenience is *two* miles when you make the trip and return—measure your distances from the above-mentioned conveniences in *minutes* rather than *miles*.

OTHER LOCATION FACTORS TO CONSIDER

Other factors for you to consider in choosing an exact location are how close the houses are to the street: are there trees and shrubs in the area (this may not be too important for new areas)? Do you want a house like everybody else's—or would you be happier with more individuality? Curved streets can be a consideration— they affect a street's appearance and slow traffic.

How can you best ascertain these and other facts? Visit the area at various times. Check at night—are streets well lighted? Locate and time your visits to the above-mentioned places. Talk to neighbors—you can get a "feel" for the area. Locate schools and pay a visit to meet the principal and ascertain the quality of education offered.

POINTS TO CHECK BEFORE YOU BUY

Here are 20 points to consider about any neighborhood. To compare two different houses or neighborhoods, rate one in column A, the other in column B in Figure 1. Use check marks, then figure the scores as indicated. Don't be discouraged if you don't have a lot of "good" checks—this is a tough test.

	House A	House B
"Good" checks × 3 =	_____	_____
"Fair" checks × 2 =	_____	_____
"Poor" checks × 1 =	_____	_____

Make comments on each item in the Good, Fair, and Poor columns in Figure 1, page 81, to help guide your future choice.

Ask yourself these questions before deciding what to buy:

1 What type of housing would best serve my needs?

2 How much can I afford to spend?

3 How can I be sure I am getting the most for my money?

In answering question 1, you should give careful thought to the advantages of owning a private home.

ADVANTAGES OF HOME OWNERSHIP

It gives you a sense of security.

It is a good investment for you.

There are tax advantages inherent in home ownership.

You are considered a better credit risk.

Your children should have a home to grow up in.

It gives you roots in the community.

It gives you a sense of pride and achievement.

SIZE AND SHAPE OF HOME

The size and shape of your home and property are vital points to consider as you choose the type of home that will fit your needs.

The size of your home depends on the size of your family. What you are already used to will also be a determining factor. Any special room requirements for

FIGURE 1

	Good	A	B	Fair	A	B	Poor	A	B
Shopping									
Churches-amusements									
Community pride									
Neighbors									
Police-fire protection									
Schools									
Playgrounds									
Trash-garbage disposal									
Street layout									
Transportation									
Growth trend									
Lay of land									
Trees									
Water									
Sewage									
Protection against encroachment									
Traffic									
Hazards									
Privacy									
Nuisances									
Add check marks									

hobbies, entertainment, and the like, as well as any projections and plans for the future also must be considered.

The space needed or "square footage" to look for depends on whether this is your first home or whether you are comparing it with your present living quarters.

ROOMS TO CONSIDER To help you in surveying your room needs, use the following "Room Shopping List":

ROOM SHOPPING LIST

You will need at least
_____ 2 bedrooms
_____ 3 bedrooms
_____ 4 bedrooms
_____ More than 4

You will need
_____ 1 bathroom
_____ 1½ bathroom
_____ 2 bathrooms

You will need a garage
_____ 1 car
_____ 2 cars

Special interests
_____ Study
_____ Office
_____ Music room
_____ Game room

Extra storage
_____ Boat
_____ Power tools
_____ Books

Social living
_____ Indoor entertainment
_____ Outdoor entertainment
_____ Both
_____ Neither

Other considerations besides the number of rooms needed are items like these:

Do you need a separate family room and living room?

Do you need a separate dining room or dinette in kitchen area?

Does the kitchen have adequate counter space, drawer space, and cupboard space?

Are the size of the rooms sufficient for their purpose?

Are there laundry facilities—space and outlet for washer and dryer?

Is there ironing board space, broom closet, a laundry tray, and garage storage space?

Is wall space sufficient to accommodate your furniture?

Are there stairs; if so, is there a bathroom upstairs as well as downstairs?

LOT ON WHICH HOUSE IS BUILT

You should think about the lot on which the house is built. The lot should be level or at least should provide sufficient drainage. It should be large enough to accommodate your needs for patio space, lawn, and shrubs or just plain "breathing room," as well as the required footage in the house itself.

The size of the front, rear, and side yards should be satisfactory for your likes and desires.

FLOOR PLAN OF THE HOUSE

A favorable *traffic pattern* for passage from room to room in the most accessible manner is important.

Visualize your furniture or the furniture you would like in this setting. Can you move throughout the rooms in comfort?

There should be more than one exit from rooms that will be heavily used.

The *exposure* or direction the house faces should be carefully considered. Avoid western exposure where youngsters go to bed early. Eastern exposure is best except for late risers.

Is there direct access to the bedrooms, bathroom, and kitchen without having to pass through other rooms?

Is there sufficient living space on the ground floor?

HOW MUCH CAN YOU AFFORD TO SPEND?

A rule of thumb in this regard is:

Don't pay more than two and a half to three times your annual income.

The annual housing costs, including payment on the principal, interest, taxes, and insurance, should not total more than one fourth of your yearly income.

Maintenance will run about 1.5 to 2 percent of the cost of the house per year.

The following table will give you an approximate amount to be spent according to the income received:

INCOME	MAXIMUM PRICE TO PAY FOR HOME
$10,000	$30,000
12,000	36,000
15,000	45,000
20,000	60,000
25,000	75,000

CAUTION

> Don't pay *more* than you can afford, but pay what you *can* afford.

In an existing house, you may want to remodel to suit your needs. These statistics will help guide you in this decision.

If the house is four or five years old, it may need painting. The approximate cost for this job is $1000 to $1500 (depending on its condition and size).

Check the roof; if new roofing is needed it will cost you approximately $40 to $70 per 100 square feet (for asphalt shingles $200 to $300).

Is the heating plan adequate? Are wiring changes needed? Are there cracks in basement walls? These items could easily total $200 to $1000.

What about the plumbing and pipes throughout the house? Are changes needed? This could run from $1500 to $3000.

Do you intend to upgrade the hardware, carpeting, garage, or fireplace? If so, it will add to your projected costs.

CUSTOM-BUILT HOUSE

Another major decision you must make is whether you want or can afford a *custom-built* house.

This, of course, is the dream of many of us: to design our own home to meet our own needs and specifications. These items must be considered:

You may have to hire an architect—he can give you expert advice on how to get the most for your money and how to select proper materials. However, "headaches" result from misunderstandings between architects and contractors.

The time element must be considered in building a house from personalized plans. Can you wait?

Your initial investment may be from three to four times more than normally required. Can you afford it?

Whether you design your own home or use a stock plan, you'll have to hire a contractor to build it. Selecting a contractor can be an added problem.

A NEW READY-BUILT HOUSE

Even though a new ready-built house is generally less expensive than a custom-built house, whether to buy the ready-built depends on several important facts.

Ready-built houses are designed for the "typical family." What is a typical family? A family with two children and two cars or three children and one car? A $15,000 income family or a $25,000 income family?

Then, too, it is more difficult to judge a new house than an old house for many reasons.

Many times you select from a *model*. (Remember, the builder will make sure that this model home, which you see on display, is perfect in every respect.) It will be on a good lot and it will be well landscaped.

The model is usually loaded with extras, such as expensive mirrors to make rooms appear larger. It may be fitted with small scale furniture, which also makes rooms look larger.

Appliances included in the model may be of better quality than those included in the new home.

BUYING A NEW HOUSE

In buying a home that has been lived in, consider its obsolescence and depreciation.

A zoning check is important. Is the area solely for single-family dwellings?

Important in the purchase of any home—but particularly applicable to the *used house*—are *structural considerations* relating to the interior and the exterior of the house. Because of the importance of this item, detailed instructions are included here.

STRUCTURAL CONSIDERATIONS

In the overall construction of the house, include the following items:

Make sure underpinnings of the house are free from dry rot and without soft spots in timbers.

Make sure floor joists, cross bracings and subflooring is in good condition.

Be sure structure is free of termites. (F.H.A. and V.A. loans require termite inspection.)

Make sure floors are level and walls are straight.

Rap on the wall boards—the sound should be firm and solid.

Check basement for wall cracks, stains, or flaking (usually an indication of excessive moisture).

The P.I.P.E. organization recommends that these plumbing items be checked:

Is there a *potable* water supply for drinking, cooking, bathing, and laundering?

How is the *hot-water* supply and distribution? The hot-water heater should hold 50 gallons for a family of four.

Are the pipes throughout steel or copper? (Copper pipes are free from corrosion.)

Check the pressure in the pipes by opening faucets throughout the house.

Are plumbing fixtures and appliances in good working order and appearance?

Are tubs, sinks, and basins cast iron or steel? (Cast iron is preferable.)

Test the drainage of sinks and drains—does the water run freely?

Does the water closet flush easily and drain quickly?

If laundry facilities are provided, a two-inch drain should be used.

Is the sanitation and drainage connected with the municipal or district sewer system? If a septic tank is used, how old is it?

SUGGESTION

> Include plumbing inspection with the termite inspection in the escrow procedure.

Electrical outlets should be checked.

1 Make sure each room has two or three outlets.

2 Check position of light switches. (Do you have to cross the room in the dark?)

3 Are there outlets adjacent to counter space?

4 Check lighting in the front and rear, outside.

5 Thermostats should be on the inside wall of house away from doorways or drafts.

CAUTION

> If many heavy appliances are to be used, make sure you have a three-wire, 220 volt, 100 ampere capacity in your electrical circuit.

Certain items on the outside of the house should be checked:

Test the driveway. Is it wide enough and free from cracks and bumps?

Are earth mounds in the lots properly banked?

Are the streets and walks paved and well lighted?

Are the sprinkler system or hose outlets adequate?

In conclusion it is recommended that the following checklist be used as an overall rating in helping you to make the proper decision in purchasing your house.

CHECKLIST TO RATE FEATURES

	GOOD	FAIR	POOR
Neighborhood			
Exterior of house			
Lawn sprinklers			
Hose bibs			
Outside cleanouts			
Electrical outlets			
Drainage			
Driveway			
Electrical			
Main switch			
Circuit breakers or fuse			
Convenient wall switches			
Light fixtures			

CHECKLIST TO RATE FEATURES

	GOOD	FAIR	POOR
Plumbing and piping			
Water shutoff valve			
Water supply lines			
Drainage and sewer lines			
Water heater			
Water softener piping			
Pressure regulator			
Kitchen			
Sink			
Disposal			
Dishwasher			
Gas line for stove and oven			
Kitchen ventilator			
Cupboards			
Laundry			
Laundry tray			
Drain piping			
Gas outlet for dryer			
Bathroom			
Wash basins			
Water closet			
Tub			
Shower			
Heating			
Structural			
Foundation			
Floor plan			
Wall space			
Windows			
Doors			
Closets			
Storage space			
Heating			
Air conditioning			

UNIT SUMMARY

This unit covered the decisions that you must make after you have decided to buy a house. Factors considered were location, size of home and lot, floor plan, a new or old home, structural consideration, and architectural design.

Items considered in choosing a location were the neighborhood and proximity and easy access to conveniences.

The advantages of owning your own home were explored.

What size home will best fit your needs was a primary consideration.

The floor plan and traffic flow within the house itself must fit the needs of the purchaser.

Consideration was given to the size, shape, and utility of the lot on which the house is built.

Measuring tables were provided to determine what the purchaser can afford in terms of his needs and desires.

The distinguishing features and the advantages and disadvantages of purchasing a custom-built house, a new ready-built house, or an older house were discussed.

Items to look for in an *older* house included detailed tips on structural considerations in such areas as overall construction, plumbing and pipes, electrical outlets, and the exterior of the house.

REVIEWING YOUR UNDERSTANDING

1 Name five locational factors to use in buying a home.

a _____

b _____

c _____

d _____

e _____

2 Measure your distances from various conveniences in _____ rather than miles.

3 A favorable _____ _____ from room to room in a convenient manner is important.

4 If your children go to bed early, avoid _____ exposure.

5 _____ exposure is best except for late risers.

6 Don't pay _____ than you can afford but pay what you _____ _____.

7 Having a _____-built house is the dream of many of us.

8 It is recommended that you include _____ inspection along with termite inspection in the escrow agreements.

SUGGESTED LEARNING ACTIVITIES

Make a list of the conveniences located within easy reach of your place of residence and rate them on a scale of 1 to 10 in importance as a locational factor.

REVIEWING YOUR UNDERSTANDING—ANSWERS

1 a schools
b shopping
c churches
d public transportation
e recreational activities

2 minutes

3 traffic pattern

4 western

5 eastern

6 more, can afford

7 custom

8 plumbing

10

Few buyers can afford to pay all cash for a home. Consequently, financing becomes an important consideration to the home buyer.

In this unit we discuss the characteristics of the various lenders. There are three categories of lenders: conventional lenders, government lenders, and other lenders.

You will learn what the lenders expect of the borrower and how you may qualify for the loan that seems to have the best terms for you. Our attention will be concentrated on home loans and where you can obtain them.

ASSIGNMENT

Read this study guide (pages 90–97).
View TV program, number 10.

PERFORMANCE OBJECTIVES

At the conclusion of this unit you will be able to:

1 List three conventional lenders and give four characteristics of each.

2 List the three government-backed lenders and give four characteristics of each.

3 List at least three other lenders.

4 Identify four ways in which government related lenders differ from conventional lenders.

5 Identify three lenders requiring the smallest down payment.

6 Identify two lenders requiring the largest down payment.

7 List five lenders who would usually charge a lower interest rate than the other lenders.

TERMS YOU SHOULD KNOW

points   conventional lenders
MMI   loan correspondent
impounds   agreement of sale

90

CONVENTIONAL LENDERS There are three main categories of conventional lenders: savings and loan associations, banks, and insurance companies. These conventional lenders assume all risks without any government guarantees against loss.

SAVINGS AND LOAN ASSOCIATIONS

Savings and loan associations provide the greatest number of home loans locally and nationally. They attract deposits from savers and lend the great majority of their money on homes. They provide funds for buying, building, improving, and refinancing real property.

What are the lending characteristics of savings and loan associations? They may be either federally or state chartered. Their loan term is quite long—usually 30 years, which keeps the monthly payments low. They permit a small down payment of as low as 10 percent of the purchase price. They allow a second deed of trust coupled with a small down payment. Their loan-to-value ratio is realistic. Although they can lend up to 90 percent of a property sold for $40,000, they normally lend 80 percent of the purchase price, or $32,000. The interest rates that savings and loan associations charge are often the highest in the market place. If secondary financing is involved, the interest rate on their first loan is generally ¼ to ½ percent higher than if the buyer would put down 20 percent in cash. Their loan fees are high and vary, depending on the supply of money available at any given time. Their primary security is the subject property.

BANKS

Commercial banks handle mainly checking accounts and demand deposits. They lend funds primarily to businesses and commercial customers on a short-term basis. However, a significant amount of their funds are lent for home purchases, construction, and refinancing. Their lending policies tend to be on the conservative side.

What are the lending characteristics of banks? Their loan terms are generally 25 years, although they can have a 30-year term. Their loan-to-value ratio is not as favorable as that of savings and loan associations. If a home sold for $40,000 they might value it at $36,000 and lend 75 percent of that, or $27,000. They usually do not permit secondary financing on a new loan although it is subsequently permissible. This means a large down payment—usually 20 to 30 percent. The interest rates charged are normally ¼ percent lower than a savings and loan association would charge. Their loan fee is usually somewhat less also. Banks want their borrowers to have an account with the bank. Banks want a strong borrower and a well-located property.

INSURANCE COMPANIES

Life insurance companies invest the money that they receive on policy premiums in many different areas. A portion of their funds are invested in real estate. Although they are prepared to invest in virtually all phases of real estate, they favor large loans for a long term on commercial and industrial properties. Typical projects on which they would lend would include office buildings and shopping centers. They generally prefer not to make home loans. The borrower need not be a policyholder. They place their loans mainly through mortgage companies and loan correspondents.

CHARACTERISTICS OF INSURANCE COMPANY HOME LOANS Insurance companies require a large down payment. Usually 25 percent down or more is required. They tend to loan 66⅔ to 75 percent of the market value of the property. The repayment period will vary depending on the market, but 20 to 25 years is typical. The interest rate charged is favorable as is the loan fee. They compare favorably with banks in this respect. Insurance companies will lend to a strong buyer with a large down payment on a well-located home.

Some companies do not allow the loan to be paid off within a certain period of years.

GOVERNMENT-BACKED LOANS

The federal and state governments instituted programs years ago to assist home and farm buyers. There are three categories that we will discuss: F.H.A., V.A., and Cal-Vet.

FEDERAL HOUSING ADMINISTRATION The Federal Housing Administration (F.H.A.) was created in 1934 by the National Housing Act. Its purposes are to encourage improvement in housing standards and conditions and to make home ownership available to lower- and middle-income borrowers.

The F.H.A. does not make loans. It insures loans made by supervised financial institutions. Banks, savings and loan associations, and mortgage companies typically make the loans insured by the F.H.A. This insurance is called mutual mortgage insurance, MMI for short. The borrower pays the necessary cost of the insurance that amounts to ½ percent, which in effect is added to the interest rate. The lender, because he is enjoying the added protection of insurance, is able to grant longer and more lenient terms.

There are nine different titles to the original National Housing Act, each specifying a different purpose for which a borrower might obtain an F.H.A. loan. Title I provides insured loans for housing repair, renovation, or modernization. Title II provides insured loans for construction and purchase of homes. Title III established the Federal National Mortgage Association (Fannie Mae). The purpose of Fannie Mae was to create a secondary money market where lenders could sell their loans. This money market expands the lenders' supply of capital to enable them to make more loans. Fannie Mae stock has been traded on the New York Stock Exchange since 1968. The Government National Mortgage Association (Ginnie Mae) was added in 1968.

What are the lending characteristics of the F.H.A.? The property must be inspected by an F.H.A. appraiser. The maximum loan for single family homes is currently $45,000. The loan amounts are:

LOAN AMOUNT

97 percent loan on first $25,000 appraisal value = $24,250
90 percent loan on the next $10,000 appraisal value = 9,000
80 percent on the remaining balance, not to exceed $45,000 on a single-family dwelling; $48,750 on two to three units (duplex and triplex), and $56,000 for four units (fourplex or quadruplex).
For *nonoccupants* the maximum is 85 percent of the above.

The *down payment* is small:

3 percent of the first $25,000	= $ 750
10 percent of the next $10,000	= 1,000

20 percent of the balance up to the maximum loan amount.

If the appraised value of a home was $40,000, the down payment would be $2750 and the loan amount would be $37,250.

The down payment on a new F.H.A. loan must be in cash or other assets. No secondary financing is permitted, although a second deed of trust may be subsequently placed on the property.

F.H.A. BORROWER QUALIFICATIONS

1 Your credit standing must be good.

2 Your monthly gross income after deducting major installment loan payments should be at least 4½ times the total monthly payment, which would include principal, interest, taxes, and insurance. Your spouse's income will normally be considered if it is a stable income.

3 Your income should be stable and sufficient. Your monthly housing payments should not exceed 25 to 30 percent of your take-home pay.

4 The property must meet minimum F.H.A. standards as determined by an F.H.A. appraiser.

VETERANS ADMINISTRATION LOANS V.A. or G.I. loans are made under the Serviceman's Readjustment Act (G.I. Bill) of 1944. This Act was enacted to assist veterans in making the necessary readjustment to civilian life. The Veterans Administration does not usually make the loan. The V.A. guarantees that the approved lender will be repaid up to 60 percent of the unpaid balance of the loan or $17,500, whichever is less, if the veteran borrower defaults on his loan payments. The lender will usually be a V.A.-approved savings and loan association, bank, or mortgage company.

The property must be appraised by a V.A. appraiser who will issue a Certificate of Reasonable Value, CRV for short. The V.A. will approve loans on one- to four-family dwellings, a new condominium unit, and on mobile homes and mobile home lots.

The veteran must occupy the home at the time it is being purchased. He may subsequently rent it.

Interest rates are set by Congress and are usually lower than those found in the market place.

The loan term is usually 30 years although, in some cases, it can be longer.

The loan origination fee to the buyer is set by law at 1 percent (1 point) of the loan amount (2½ percent on homes to be constructed). The seller must pay any additional points (discount points).

The monthly loan payment must include the following items: principal, interest, taxes, and insurance. If the monthly payment including principal and interest was $200 and the annual taxes were $1200 and annual insurance was $120, then the total monthly payment would be $310.

IMPOUND ACCOUNT As part of the closing costs the lender requires the borrower to provide a reserve for the payment of taxes and insurance. The amount would vary depending on the time of year when the escrow closed. The borrower would have any impound funds remaining returned to him when the property is sold.

F.H.A. loans for veterans are available under the 203(b) provision. To be eligible a person must have served 90 days of active duty under hazardous duty circumstances. These loans are made only to veterans who will own and occupy single-family homes. The loan amounts are:

100 percent loan on first $25,000 of appraisal value   = $25,000

90 percent loan on next $10,000 of appraisal value   =   9,000

85 percent loan on the balance, up to the maximum stated previously

There are many other types of F.H.A. loans, but the above are the most common.

There is no legal maximum loan amount set by the Veterans Administration. However, lenders set reasonable, prudent limits, usually not in excess of $75,000. A veteran may pay more than the Certificate of Reasonable Value if he agrees to pay the difference in cash.

If the purchase price does not exceed the Certificate of Reasonable Value there is no down payment required by the V.A., although the lender may require a down payment as a condition for granting a loan.

The maximum loan term is 30 years.

The interest rate is set by Congress. There is no fee to the veteran for the loan guarantee, and there is no mutual mortgage insurance required.

The monthly payment must include principal, interest, and one-twelfth of the annual taxes and insurance. There is an impound requirement as in an F.H.A. loan.

The loan origination fee to the borrower cannot exceed 1 percent.

The seller is required to pay any discount points.

BORROWER QUALIFICATION The borrower must have served at least 90 days on active duty during World War II or between June 27, 1950 and January 31, 1955 (Korean conflict). The 1966 G.I. Bill allowed veterans who served on active duty for more than 180 days, any part of which occurred after January 31, 1955, to become eligible. The veteran must have been discharged under circumstances other than dishonorable or because of a service-connected disability. A veteran who has served 181 days continuously will be eligible even if he has not met the above discharge or release provisions. Widows of veterans who would have qualified and certain U.S. citizens who served with allied governments during World War II are also eligible.

The combined monthly income of both spouses less major installment loan payments must be five times the monthly loan payment including taxes and insurance. The 5:1 ratio may be slightly lower for middle- and lower-income groups.

No secondary financing is permitted for a new loan. Secondary financing may be subsequently placed on the property.

CAL-VET LOANS The purpose of the California Farm and Home Purchase Program (Cal-Vet) is to assist qualified California veterans to acquire suitable farm or home property at a low financing cost.

Funds are obtained for these loans through state bond issue. The amount advanced by the state is repaid by the veteran through uniform monthly payments. These payments include all costs, such as bond issue, redemption, and interest to bond holders, and the cost of administering the program. Consequently, the program involves no expense to the taxpayer.

The loan limits are $35,000 for a home purchase and $80,000 for a farm purchase—these amounts subject to change. The loan may not exceed 95 percent of the V.A. home appraisal or 90 percent of the farm appraisal.

The veteran must pay the difference between the sales price and the loan in cash to the seller. Secondary financing is not permitted.

The minimum down payment is 5 percent on homes and 10 percent on farms.

The maximum loan term is 30 years but 25 years is normal.

The monthly loan payment includes principal, interest, taxes, and insurance.

The veteran must live in the property or agree that a member of his family will live in the property within 60 days of purchase.

The interest rate is set by the state and it changes periodically depending on the market circumstances. The interest rate has traditionally been very low.

The property must be of minimum standards (similar to F.H.A.) acceptable to the Department of Veterans Affairs. It must be a farm or single-family residence.

BORROWER QUALIFICATIONS The veteran must have been a bona fide resident of California when he entered the armed forces. He must have served at least 90 days in time of war or he must have participated in a military campaign or expedition for which a medal was authorized by the U.S. government.

The state actually buys the property from the seller. The state then resells the property to the veteran through an agreement of sale. The state retains ownership and gives a deed to the veteran only when the veteran has completely repaid the loan.

The veteran is required to purchase term life insurance for the amount of the loan plus a 20 percent cash payment. There is a double indemnity provision for accidental death as well as disability protection.

OTHER LENDERS In addition to conventional and government-backed lenders, other lenders include mortgage companies, pension funds, credit unions, and individuals.

MORTGAGE COMPANIES Mortgage companies act as correspondents or servicing agencies for blocks of money made available by savings and loan associations, insurance companies, and individuals and other groups. They charge a fee for their service (points) and often offer the same terms as available through the above lenders.

PENSION FUNDS Pension funds are becoming available in the mortgage market. Whereas they had previously been primarily invested in stocks, they are now becoming a more important factor in the mortgage market. They prefer to lend on large projects.

CREDIT UNIONS Many credit unions offer funds for first and second deeds of trust. The amount available for first loans is quite small, typically $10,000 to $15,000. They are a good source of secondary financing.

INDIVIDUALS Individuals provide a significant amount of first loans under $17,000. The seller frequently extends credit to the buyer taking a first deed of trust as security.

Individuals are the largest source of secondary financing.

UNIT SUMMARY

In this unit we discussed the various lenders and their lending characteristics.

Conventional lenders are savings and loan associations, banks, and insurance companies.

Government-backed lenders are the F.H.A., the V.A., and Cal-Vet.

Other lenders included mortgage companies, pension funds, credit unions, and individuals.

Your choice of a lender is made based on a number of factors. What is the current money supply? Under which of these lenders policies will I be eligible? Where can I get the best terms consistent with my needs?

REVIEWING YOUR UNDERSTANDING

TRUE OR FALSE

(   ) 1 Only one of the following loans normally requires a cash down payment: F.H.A. insured, G.I. guaranteed, and Cal-Vet.

(   ) 2 Secondary financing is never allowed for the life of an F.H.A.-insured loan.

(   ) 3 Effective interest rates on G.I.-backed loans are usually lower than the rates on F.H.A.-insured loans.

(   ) 4 Normally, the pay-back period on a Cal-Vet loan is longer than on a G.I. loan.

(   ) 5 A contract of sale gives the buyer possession and use of the property but does not deliver title until a later date.

MULTIPLE CHOICE

(   ) 1 If the sales price and appraised value of a home is $40,000, the amount of a nongovernment loan from a savings and loan association is:

a $33,000

b $36,000
c $32,000
d $30,000
( ) **2** Among lenders, the greatest percentage of home loans comes from:
a the F.H.A.
b savings and loan associations
c commercial banks
d none of these

REVIEWING YOUR UNDERSTANDING—ANSWERS

TRUE OR FALSE

1 True	**4** True
2 False	**5** True
3 False	

MULTIPLE CHOICE

1 c

2 b

OPTIONAL LEARNING ACTIVITIES

1 Call two different lenders and ask what the current interest rate is.

2 Determine how large a loan you can qualify for.

11

In the last unit you learned the basic characteristics of the various lenders and where to go for a loan.

In this unit we will concentrate on some finer points of real estate finance. We will learn why a lender charges points and who pays them, and the relationship between points and the annual percentage rate. We will discuss fixed interest rates and variable interest rates. We will explore the different types of notes, how they differ from each other, and which is best for you. We will also discuss deeds of trust, prepayment penalties, acceleration clauses, reconveyance deeds, and junior loans.

Read this study guide (pages 100–105).
View TV program, number 11.

At the conclusion of this unit, you will be able to:

1 Identify when points are charged to the buyer and when they are charged to the seller.

2 Identify the type of interest rate that is subject to change.

3 List two effects of a changing interest rate on you.

4 List three different types of notes.

5 Name the parties to a deed of trust and specify the responsibilities of each.

6 List the steps that could be taken by the lender if a loan is in default.

7 Distinguish between an acceleration clause and an alienation clause.

8 Identify the essential points of a prepayment penalty.

9 State the circumstances under which a junior lien might be used.

acceleration clause	trustor, trustee, beneficiary
alienation clause	power of sale
discount points	notice of default
yield	notice of sale
annual percentage rate	prepayment penalty
variable interest rate	reconveyance deed
straight note	junior loans
amortized note	request for notice of default
fully amortized note	

POINTS In the previous unit we briefly mentioned points. We said that 1 point is equal to 1 percent of the amount of the loan. On a $30,000 loan, 1 point would be $300. Two and one-half percent points would equal $750.

Why do lenders charge points in addition to charging interest? This is a fair question. A lender is in business to make a profit like any other businessman. A mortgage loan is made for a much longer period of time and at a lower interest rate than a consumer loan. In order to make a mortgage loan, the lender must receive a return that would be comparable to other investments. In other words, he must increase his yield on a mortgage loan. He does this by charging points. One point increases the yield to the lender by one-eighth of 1 percent. If the lender could receive 10 percent on a short-term consumer loan and 9 percent on a home mortgage, he would charge 8 points to make up the difference on the home loan. Points may be charged in two different ways—as loan origination fees and as discount points.

LOAN ORIGINATION FEE Although negotiable, on conventional mortgages the buyer almost always pays the loan origination fee (or loan fee). Depending on a number of factors, the fee usually varies from 1 to 3 points. The seller pays no loan fees.

On F.H.A. and V.A. mortgages we saw that the loan orgination fee to the buyer was limited by law to 1 point.

MORTGAGE DISCOUNT POINTS The interest rate on F.H.A. and V.A. mortgages is the same. The rate is set by Congress and is lower than the rate charged by conventional lenders.

To encourage lenders to make loans at a lower interest rate, F.H.A. and V.A. provide two major inducements. They allow the lenders to charge discount points to increase their yield and they insure or guarantee the lenders' losses up to a certain amount. The discount points must be paid by the seller.

Depending on the money market at any given time, the discount points could vary from 1 or 2 points up to 17 or 18 points or more. For example, on a $30,000 loan, 4 discount points would amount to $1200, which the seller would have to pay. Faced with this prospect, would the seller rather have the buyer obtain a conventional loan that would mean a savings of discount points to him? Yes, unless F.H.A. or V.A. financing was common in his area and the buyer expected this type of loan. Some sellers have increased the price of their homes to allow for this, but remember that the property must be appraised by an F.H.A. or V.A. appraiser to qualify for the government-backed loan.

ANNUAL PERCENTAGE RATE Under recent legislation, the lender must disclose to the buyer the annual percentage rate (APR) that the buyer is actually paying. The APR includes the interest rate plus loan fees charged to the borrower, amortized over the life of the loan.

INTEREST RATE—FIXED OR VARIABLE? In the past, mortgage loans in the United States have almost always been calculated as a fixed simple interest rate based on a declining balance. The interest rate and monthly payment were fixed.

Recently some lenders have been employing a variable interest rate. A variable interest rate could go up or down pegged to an economic indicator. It is usually limited as to how much it could increase or decrease in any given period. Under this system your monthly payment could change up or down. There are many arguments for and against the variable interest rate.

From your standpoint, you should always ask the lenders if they are employing a fixed or variable interest rate.

NOTES   If a lender is going to lend you money, he wants to know how and when the loan is going to be repaid. He will require you to sign a promissory note (trust note) specifying the terms of repayment. The trust note is the evidence of the debt. The borrower is called the maker of the note or the payer. The lender is called the payee or holder. There are three main types of notes: straight notes, amortized notes, and fully amortized notes.

STRAIGHT NOTES   A straight note calls for the payment of interest only during the term of the note. If you borrowed $10,000 at 9 percent interest on a straight note for 10 years, you would pay $900 per year interest. No payments are made on principal, and you are consequently not reducing the balance of the loan. After 10 years, when the note is due, you would still owe $10,000, even though you would have paid $9000 in interest.

AMORTIZED NOTE   An amortized note calls for the payment of both principal and interest during the term of the loan. The monthly interest is high at first and declines over the term of the loan. The principal portion of the monthly payment is low at the outset and increases over the term of the loan. An amortized note may not be fully paid off when the note is due, giving rise to a balloon payment. A balloon payment is a payment substantially larger than any of the previous payments. It is usually at least twice as large as the previous payments.

FULLY AMORTIZED NOTE   The only difference between a fully amortized note and an amortized note is that in a fully amortized note the entire loan will be paid off at the due date. There are no balloon payments. Most real estate first loans are fully amortized loans. A second deed of trust usually has a balloon payment.

DEED OF TRUST   In addition to requiring a trust note (secured note) on a real estate loan, the lender will require a deed of trust. A deed of trust is the security instrument for the debt and stipulates that the property can be sold to satisfy the debt if the borrower defaults on his payments.

The deed of trust is used almost exclusively in California, whereas the mortgage is chiefly used in eastern states. While there are significant differences in the two instruments, for purposes of this discussion we will often refer to deeds of trust as mortgages. Understand, however, that we mean deeds of trust in all instances.

PARTIES TO THE DEED OF TRUST   There are three parties to the deed of trust: the trustor, the trustee, and the beneficiary.

The trustor is the borrower (buyer). The trustor is said to hold the "real" title to the property. The trustee has a very limited function. He is said to hold the "legal" title to the property. He is authorized under the power of sale provision to sell the property at public auction when the trustor defaults on his payments. The beneficiary is the lender.

STEPS IN A SALE AFTER DEFAULT   Under the deed of trust, the beneficiary has the option of either foreclosing through the courts or selling under the power of sale provision at the trustee's sale. The property is almost always sold at the trustee's sale, since the time requirements are shorter. Foreclosure through the courts would be used only when the lender felt that the property would not bring enough at the trustee's sale to cover the balance of his mortgage. In that case the lender might try to obtain a deficiency judgment through foreclosure to enable him to recover the difference. It is not possible to obtain a deficiency judgment when the power of sale provision is used. If a home consists of one to four units, part or all of which is occupied by the owner, and there is a purchase money mortgage (extension of credit by the seller), there can be no deficiency judgment; however, there are some exceptions.

The beneficiary notifies the trustee that the borrower is in default. The trustee records a notice of default and sends a copy to the borrower. After 3 months the trustee posts a notice of sale on the property. The notice of sale must also be published in a newspaper for 3 weeks (at least once a week, not more than 7 days apart).

The trustor can reinstate his loan during the initial 3-month period by paying all past monthly payments, penalties, and fees. After the 3-month period and before the trustee's sale, the trustor must pay the entire amount of the loan plus penalties and fees, to retain the property.

After the trustee has advertised the sale for the necessary time period, the sale is conducted. The trustee's fees—which are nominal—are paid first. The beneficiary is then paid. If there is any money left, it goes to the trustor.

ACCELERATION CLAUSE   An acceleration clause in a note or deed of trust stipulates that on the occurrence of a certain event, the entire balance of the loan will become due and payable. The above discussion about how the entire balance of the loan would be payable if the borrower defaulted on his payments is an example of this. An acceleration clause must be clearly stated in both the note and deed of trust on 1 to 4 units if the lender wishes to exercise this right.

ALIENATION CLAUSE   An alienation clause is a special type of acceleration clause that specifies that the entire loan balance is payable if the property is sold or the ownership interest is transferred. This clause has the effect of disallowing a subsequent purchaser from assuming the present loan under the exact terms and conditions enjoyed by the original borrower. Under certain conditions relating to a contract of sale, the courts have held that the acceleration clause is not valid when the seller retains a substantial financial interest in the property. You should consult with an attorney if you have any questions concerning an alienation clause.

F.H.A. and V.A. loans have no alienation clauses. They can be transferred to a new buyer for only a minimal charge-of-record fee. Virtually all other loans will contain alienation clauses.

PREPAYMENT PENALTY   A prepayment clause in a note or deed of trust assesses a penalty to the borrower if the loan is repaid before its due date. Most loans will have an ''or more'' provision that allows the borrower to prepay up to 20 percent of the loan balance in any one year without penalty. Beyond that a penalty equivalent to 6 months' interest is usually charged. At this time, there is legislation pending to restrict conditions under which prepayment penalties may be charged.

F.H.A. and V.A. loans have no prepayment penalty provisions.

RECONVEYANCE   A loan will be recorded by the lender at the time it is placed on the property to protect the interest of the lender. This gives public notice that the lender has an interest in the property.

When the loan is repaid in full, the borrower should insist that a deed of reconveyance be recorded to show the public that the loan has been satisfied.

JUNIOR LOANS   Any loan placed on the property after the first deed of trust is called a junior or subordinate loan. A second deed of trust is an example of a junior loan.

Second deeds of trust can often be helpful in buying property. The buyer needs less cash as a down payment. The buyer should be able to handle the monthly payment and should be able to pay off the balloon payment when due.

Second deeds of trust also provide a source of borrowing on your equity after you have owned the property for a while.

A lender under a second deed of trust should record a request for a notice of default. The lender would then be advised if the borrower was in default on the first deed of trust. If that happened, the second holder could make the payments on the first deed of trust and foreclose on his second deed of trust.

UNIT SUMMARY

In this unit we discussed points. We made a distinction between loan origination fees and discount points and the effect of points with respect to consideration of the borrower's consideration of the annual percentage rate.

We discussed fixed and variable interest rates, the different types of notes, and the particulars of the deed of trust, including the parties and the steps followed by the lender and trustee in the event of default.

We also discussed acceleration clauses, alienation clauses, prepayment penalties, reconveyance, and junior loans.

You are now a more knowledgeable borrower or seller because you have a basic understanding of real estate finance.

REVIEWING YOUR UNDERSTANDING

TRUE OR FALSE

(   )   **1**   With an F.H.A. loan, the discount points may be paid by the buyer.

(   )   **2**   With a conventional loan, the seller usually pays the points.

(   )   **3**   An alienation clause is a type of acceleration clause.

(   )   **4**   Conventional loans usually have prepayment penalties.

(   )   **5**   Under a trustee's sale the lender could always obtain a deficiency judgment.

FILL-INS

1 A "due-on-sale" clause is an _____ clause.

2 A holder of a second deed of trust should record a _____ _____.

3 When a borrower has repaid the loan in full, he should have recorded a _____.

4 When the interest rate is not fixed, it is called a _____ interest rate.

5 A clause in a deed of trust that specifies that a charge will be assessed if the loan is paid prior to its due date is called a _____.

REVIEWING YOUR UNDERSTANDING—ANSWERS

TRUE OR FALSE

1 False   **4** True

2 False   **5** False

3 True

FILL-INS

1 alienation

2 request for notice of default

3 reconveyance deed

4 variable

5 prepayment penalty

OPTIONAL LEARNING ACTIVITIES

1 Look at your note and deed of trust (or ask to see your parents' or friend's) and see if you can find an acceleration clause.

2 Can you find an alienation clause or a prepayment penalty?

3 Ask your local lender or escrow company if you can have a sample of their note and deed of trust.

12

In this unit, we discuss the points that you must know regarding property taxes and assessments.

Subjects covered include the background of property taxes, who really pays property taxes, and what property tax procedures are. We will discuss property tax relief, when taxes are paid, the consequences of not paying taxes, and special assessments.

When you have concluded this unit, you will be able to answer these questions and be more informed concerning property taxes and assessments.

Read this study guide (pages 108–114).
View TV program, number 12.

At the conclusion of this unit, you will be able to:

1 Write the definition of "ad valorem" taxing.

2 Name three parties who pay taxes.

3 Identify the steps in the property tax procedure.

4 List three types of property tax relief.

5 Work problems concerning property taxes.

6 Identify four sources of authority for special assessment districts and the characteristics of each.

"ad valorem"   assessed value
assessor   tax rate
auditor   stamp sale
Board of Equalization

BACKGROUND   Property is taxed as a source of revenue by local governments. This practice evolved historically from the Middle Ages when the assumption was made that taxes should be assessed according to a man's ability to pay. At that time, agriculture was the chief economic force. The more land a person had, the more agricultural goods he could produce. Since his income was related to the land and production, he was therefore taxed according to his land holdings.

The practice of taxing property in the United States dates back to Colonial times—the colonists simply adopted the British practice of taxing land. The federal government subsequently turned to sales and excise taxes and left the property tax to state and local governments. By the beginning of the twentieth century, state governments replaced the property tax with other taxes, leaving the property tax to local governments who have retained it to this day. Property today is no longer taxed according to a person's ability to pay; it is now taxed according to its value. The Latin term for this practice of taxing according to value is called "ad valorem" taxing.

Why have the local governments retained the property tax? There are three main reasons. First, real estate is visible and immovable. It is easily assessable and difficult to conceal. Second, property taxes provide a stable source of revenue. This facilitates the budget-making decisions of city and county officials. Property taxes do not fluctuate widely with swings in the business cycle—income tax and sales taxes do. Third, if the property tax was discontinued, it would have to be replaced with some other method of collecting revenue. Any new tax proposal would encounter significant political and administrative problems.

It appears, therefore, that the property tax will be around for a long while despite significant opposition to it. Local governments will continue to use the property tax as their major source of revenue. Property owners will continue to pay the tax because the prospect of losing their property for nonpayment is too great.

WHO REALLY PAYS THE PROPERTY TAX?   Homeowners have no choice but to pay the taxes themselves. They cannot pass taxes on to others.

Owners of residential rental properties usually pass on tax increases to tenants in the form of increased rents. The strength of the rental market is significant in this respect. In a strong market in which there are few vacancies, the tenant will absorb all or most of the increase. In a "soft" market with substantial vacancies, the owner may not increase the rent or he may increase it only slightly.

Owners of commercial properties will usually pass on tax increases to the business tenants. Business tenants, depending on the market, will then usually pass the increase on to the consumer by charging a higher price for their products.

It should be noted that there are often escalation clauses in commercial leases that provide for increased rents if taxes are increased. Some leases require that the tenant pay the entire cost of taxes. In either event, the tax increase is usually passed on to the consumer ultimately.

THE PROPERTY TAX PROCEDURE   We said earlier that the purpose of the property tax was to produce revenue for local governments. The following explanation describes the various steps involved in the property taxing process.

109

DETERMINING EXPENSES The various governmental agencies determine what their expenses will be for the next fiscal year and submit budget requests. Involved are city and county schools, water districts, flood control districts, sanitation districts, mosquito abatement agencies, and numerous other city and county government agencies.

DETERMINING REVENUE FROM OTHER SOURCES After these expense budgets are established, sources of revenue other than property taxes are estimated and subtracted from the budget. Property taxes must defray all the other expenses.

DETERMINING PROPERTY TAX VALUE The assessor values all assessable property in the local jurisdiction by March 1. Property must be assessed at 25 percent of its full value. Full value means market value. If there is an increase in the assessment over the previous year, the owner must be notified of the increase by mail or by publication in a local newspaper.

WHAT IF YOU THINK THE ASSESSMENT IS TOO HIGH? If you feel your property has been assessed too high, you can appeal to the Assessment Appeals Board. In some counties, the County Board of Supervisors sit as a Board of Equalization to hear appeals.

Your appeal must be filed between July 1 and September 15. Many property owners find it advantageous to have an independent fee appraiser present their appeals. Current market data of comparable homes serves as the most convincing argument.

The appeal agency may decrease your assessment if your supporting data are reasonable and convincing. On the other hand, they may increase your assessment. You should carefully judge whether your argument is a sound one.

PROPERTY EXEMPT FROM TAXATION Some properties are wholly or partially not subject to taxation. Included are: federal, state, and local government property, property owned by nonprofit entities used exclusively for religious, charitable, or hospital purposes, churches, nonprofit private schools and colleges. There are other tax exempt properties, but these are the most significant.

THE TAX RATE Expenses and income from sources other than property taxes are analyzed. The remaining budget figure is divided by the value of the assessed property and a tax rate per $100 of assessed value is determined. The tax rate is set on or before September 1. The County Board of Supervisors sets the budget. The auditor maintains the tax rolls. The tax collector collects the taxes.

As an example, assume that a home is valued at $30,000 and the tax rate (T.R.) is $14 per $100 of assessed value.

$30,000 Full Value
×.25 (25%)
———————————
$ 7,500 Assessed Value (A.V.)

$7500 A.V. ÷ 100 = $75 × $14 tax rate = $1050 taxes for year

Note: This is an oversimplification, since many owners are entitled to certain specified exemptions that we will now discuss.

IS THERE ANY PROPERTY TAX RELIEF? There are three main exemptions for which a property owner may qualify, and thus pay a reduced tax.

HOMEOWNERS EXEMPTION An owner whose dwelling is his principal place of residence as of March 1 of each year is entitled to a $1750 homeowners exemption (H.O.E.) annually. The exemption is deducted from the assessed value.

$30,000 Full Value
×.25 (25%)
———————————
$ 7,500 A.V.
−1,750 H.O.E.
———————————
$ 5,750 Net

$5750 ÷ 100 = $57.50 × $14 T.R. = $805.00 taxes for year

This exemption applies to homes, mobile homes, condominium units, owner occupied rental units, or any other qualified dwelling.

The exemption does not apply to those not meeting the March 1 stipulation above, vacation or other second homes, those receiving veterans exemptions, or to those receiving property tax assistance from other governmental agencies.

CALIFORNIA VETERANS EXEMPTIONS A California veteran is entitled to a $1000 exemption if he has served in the armed forces during any of the following periods.

War with Spain	4-21-98 to 4-11-99
War with Philippines	4-11-99 to 7-04-02
World War I	4-06-17 to 11-11-18
World War II	12-07-41 to 1-01-47
Korean Conflict	6-27-50 to 1-31-55
Vietnam Conflict	8-05-64 to present

$30,000 Full Value
×.25 (25%)
———————————
$ 7,500 A.V.
−1,000 Vet's Exemption
———————————
$ 6,500

$6500 ÷ 100 = $65 × $14 T.R. = $910 taxes per year

If both spouses are veterans they may qualify for a $2000 exemption. You are not entitled to both a veterans exemption and a homeowners exemption on the same property, however. You may take the one exemption that benefits you the most.

The veterans exemption has certain other qualifications. A veteran is eligible only if his assessed value is $5000 or less ($20,000 full value) if single, or $10,000 or less ($40,000 full value) if married, or the widow of an eligible veteran. These figures include both real and personal property as of March 1.

SENIOR CITIZENS PROPERTY TAX RELIEF   Homeowners who are 62 or older are eligible for this tax relief if their incomes are $10,000 or less. The exact amount of the relief is scaled to the incomes of the spouses.

WHEN DO YOU PAY YOUR TAXES?

Secured property taxes become a lien against real property on March 1. The tax year extends from July 1 to June 30. In most counties, the tax year is divided into two installments for tax payments.

The first installment extends from July 1 to December 31. One-half of the yearly taxes is due on November 1 and becomes delinquent on December 10 at 5:00 P.M.

The second installment extends from January 1 to June 30. Taxes for this installment are due on February 1 and delinquent on April 10.

If December 10 or April 10 falls on a holiday or weekend, taxes can be paid on the next business day without penalty.

WHAT IF YOU DON'T PAY YOUR TAXES?

If taxes are unpaid by the delinquent dates, a 12 percent penalty is assessed on the amount of the unpaid tax.

Property taxes create an involuntary lien that takes precedence over other liens—both voluntary, such as mortgages, and involuntary, such as judgments. This is true even though other liens may predate the tax lien.

On or before June 8, the tax collector publishes a notice of intent to sell the real property on which the taxes remain unpaid. If the taxes remain unpaid by June 30, the property is sold to the state. This is called a stamp sale because the tax bill is marked with a rubber stamp. The effect of the sale is merely to begin a five year redemption period after which the property is deeded to the state unless redeemed. During the five year period, the owner retains possession and may redeem the property by paying all taxes, interest, costs, and redemption penalties.

SPECIAL ASSESSMENTS

Special assessments are made to cover the costs of specific local improvements such as streets, sewers, and irrigation.

The assessment districts issue their own bonds to finance improvements. To repay the bonds, these districts assess all properties within the district on an ad valorem basis. These liens can be foreclosed similar to a tax sale and they take precedence over private property interests. The following are the most important assessment acts relating to assessment districts.

VROOMAN STREET ACT The Vrooman Street Act gives authority to city councils to grade and finish streets, construct sewers, and so on. It provides the authority to issue bonds and to acquire public utilities.

STREET OPENING ACT OF 1903 This act provides for the opening, expansion, and straightening of streets by the county. Assessments must be paid within 30 days after notice.

STREET IMPROVEMENT ACT OF 1911 This act provides that bonds may be paid in equal installments along with the property taxes over a 15-year period or they can be repaid all at once. If the owner fails to pay within 30 days of completion, the city or county will determine the interest rate to be paid on the bonds. The bonds remain a lien on the property until fully paid.

STREET IMPROVEMENT ACT OF 1915 This act provides for series bonds for subdivision street improvements that also include sewers. Six percent interest is charged to the property owners, who repay through annual installments.

UNIT SUMMARY

In this unit, we discussed the background of property taxes. We made a distinction between the tax according to ability to pay and an ad valorem tax. We determined that taxes are paid by different parties depending on the type of property involved. We traced the property tax procedure including determination of expenses, revenue from other sources, determination of property tax value, properties exempt from taxation, the tax rate, the appeals process and property tax relief. We learned when property taxes are to be paid and what would happen if they were unpaid. We discussed special assessments and the authority for the special assessment districts.

REVIEWING YOUR UNDERSTANDING

TRUE OR FALSE

(   ) 1   The second installment of taxes is due on November 1.

(   ) 2   The penalty for not paying the taxes by the due date is 12 percent.

(   ) 3   Property is deeded to the state after five years, following June 30 delinquency.

(   ) 4   The three types of property tax relief are the homeowners exemption, veterans exemption, and senior citizens property tax relief.

(   ) 5   One authority for special assessment districts is the Street Improvement Act of 1915.

FILL-INS

1 The _____ sits as a board of equalization.

2 If a property had a value of $50,000, then $12,500 would be the
_____.

3 $15 per $100 of assessed value would be the _____.

4 There are said to be two tax sales. The first sale is called a _____.

5 The _____ provides that an owner can pay the entire amount within 30 days or pay the bonds over a 15 year period.

REVIEWING YOUR UNDERSTANDING—ANSWERS

TRUE OR FALSE

1 False   4 True

2 False   5 True

3 True

FILL-INS

1 County Board of Supervisors

2 assessed value

3 tax rate

4 stamp sale

5 Street Improvement Act of 1911

OPTIONAL LEARNING ACTIVITIES

1 Check your property tax bill. What is the assessed value? The tax rate?

2 Note the address of a property with a "for sale" sign on it. Call the assessor's office. Find out the assessor's full value. How much are the taxes?

13

A buyer does not have an unlimited interest in his property. He also does not have unlimited use of the property.

In this unit, we will discuss the different burdens that may arise on properties. We will be defining and discussing the different kinds of liens and restrictions and how they affect property.

Read this study guide (pages 116–121).
View TV program, number 13.

At the conclusion of this unit, you will be able to:

1 Specify the relationship between liens and encumbrances.

2 List the steps that must be followed before a trustee's sale can be held.

3 Distinguish between a voluntary lien and an involuntary lien and give at least two examples of each.

4 List the steps involved in the mechanic's lien process.

5 Give two examples of easements. State how they may be created and the manner in which they may be terminated.

encumbrance
lien
trustor, trustee, beneficiary
notice of default
deficiency judgment
contract of sale

notice of completion
notice of nonresponsibility
attachment
judgment
easement

ENCUMBRANCE   An encumbrance describes anything that imposes a burden or an obligation on property. There are two general types of encumbrances. The first type is a lien that is a financial claim against the property. The second type of encumbrance is a limitation or restriction on how the property can be used by the owner. You will note, therefore, that *all liens are encumbrances*. However, not all encumbrances are liens.

LIENS   Personal property and real property are the security for a debt or claim. Liens can be general or specific. A general lien is one that would apply to all of the real property owned by the debtor. A specific lien applies to only one particular parcel owned by the debtor.

VOLUNTARY LIENS   A voluntary lien is a financial lien created by owners by their own choice. Examples of voluntary liens are deeds of trust and contracts of sale.

DEEDS OF TRUST   A buyer can rarely afford to pay entirely in cash for the property being purchased. He usually has enough cash for a down payment (his equity), and the balance of the purchase price must be financed by some lender. In exchange for the loan, the buyer executes two documents. The first is the trust note (promissory note) that is the evidence of the debt. It stipulates the amount borrowed and from whom, the interest rate, the installment payments (usually monthly), to whom the payments are to be made, and the due date. The borrower is called the maker of the note or the payer. The lender is called the payee or the holder of the note. The second document is called a deed of trust, the security for the debt. It is prepared and signed at the same time as the trust note that then becomes a secured note.

There are three parties to the deed of trust. The trustor is the borrower. The beneficiary is the lender. The trustee is usually a corporation acting in the middle on behalf of both the borrower and the lender. The trustee is by law the "legal" owner, while the borrower is the "real," or equitable, owner. The borrower can reside on the property, borrow further against it, or rent it.

The beneficiary will have the deed of trust recorded to give public notice that he has an interest in the property.

If the trustor makes all his payments, he should have a reconveyance deed recorded to remove the obligation from the public records, thus releasing the beneficiary's interest in the property.

If the borrower fails to make his payments, the beneficiary has the option of either a judicial foreclosure or a sale at public auction under the power of sale clause contained in the deed of trust.

The value of the property normally exceeds the loan balance owed the beneficiary. Because of this and the simpler procedures involved, the lender almost always chooses to have the property sold at public auction (trustee's sale).

One of the few times when the beneficiary will choose judicial foreclosure is when the loan balance exceeds the value of the property that has lessened because of some factor. The beneficiary in such a case might seek a deficiency judgment to recover the difference between the loan owed him and the sales price at foreclosure. In such a case, the owner would have a one-year redemption period during which time he has the right to keep possession of the property. If the owner does not redeem the property during that year, the foreclosure sale buyer who has received a sheriff's deed can sue for the value of the use of the property. A deficiency judgment is not possible when the property consists of from one to four units and is owner occupied, wholly or in part.

There are a number of procedural steps involved in the trustee's sale. The first step is for the beneficiary to notify the trustee that the borrower is in default—which means that the trustor has not made his payments. The trustee then records a notice of default. He must mail a copy of the notice to the trustor. During the next three months, the trustor can make the missed payments to bring the loan current and pay the necessary penalties and fees. In such a case, the loan is reinstated or "cured," and no further legal proceedings will occur.

If the loan is not reinstated during the above period, the trustee must post a notice of sale on the property and also publish a notice of sale in a newspaper at least once a week for three weeks, not more than seven days apart. During this period of time, the trustor can retain his property by paying the entire loan balance plus penalties and fees. Once the process has gone this far, it is obvious that the trustor has all but lost his property.

After the necessary advertising requirement has passed, the trustee conducts the sale at public auction. The highest bidder must have all cash or its equivalent at the time of the sale. He acquires title from the trustee by a document known as a trustee's deed.

The proceeds of the sale are distributed as follows. The trustee is paid first. His fee is minimal, usually approximately one-half of 1 percent of the sale's price. The lienholders are then paid in order of priority. The trustor is entitled to any surplus. The sale is final and he has no redemption period as in judicial foreclosure.

CONTRACTS OF SALE   The second example of a voluntary lien is a contract of sale that is also called a land contract, an installment sales contract, or a number of other names all referring to the same situation.

A contract of sale is a document drawn to enable a buyer to purchase property. It differs from the normal sales transaction in that the buyer does not receive a grant deed at the close of escrow. Under a contract of sale, the buyer has possession of the property but does not receive his grant deed until after either the entire loan is paid off (as in a Cal-Vet loan) or a preagreed portion of the loan has been repaid. In the interim, he has equitable ownership.

INVOLUNTARY LIENS   An involuntary lien is a lien placed on the property by a party other than the property owner. The owner does not contractually or voluntarily place the obligation on the property. Examples of involuntary liens are: mechanic's liens, tax liens, special assessments, and attachments and judgments.

MECHANIC'S LIENS   A mechanic's lien is a lien placed on the property for nonpayment of labor performed on the property or for materials supplied to the property. Since improvements normally increase the value of the property, the assumption is that the lien should be placed on the property.

Often a secured loan will be necessary to finance improvements. Once a mechanic's lien is filed, it takes priority over any other lien, deed of trust, or encumbrance that may be attached after the work began or the materials were first furnished. For this reason, a lender is very careful to ascertain that no work is begun before his deed of trust is recorded to protect the priority of his lien over a mechanic's lien.

When an owner enters into an agreement with a contractor, he assumes that the contractor will pay suppliers for materials. However, this is not always done, and the owner will often require that the contractor post a bond to guarantee the payments of the materials to protect himself from a possible claim. Similarly, a contractor may employ subcontractors, such as roofers or plumbers, who would have a claim against the property if they were not paid by the contractor.

The procedure to be followed in mechanic's liens situations is quite specific according to law. A prelien notice—called a ''notice of intent to lien''—must be given by the potential claimant within twenty days of when the labor or services or materials are furnished to the job site. If the job is not completed due to work stoppage, strikes, Acts of God, and so on, a ''notice of cessation of labor'' may be filed. Within ten days after completion of the work, the owner should file a ''notice of completion'' with the county recorder.

An original contractor is one who contracts directly with the owner for his services. He can be a general contractor or a subcontractor but not someone dealing directly with materials. An original contractor may file a mechanic's lien within 60 days after the ''notice of completion'' is filed. Any other claimant may file the lien within 30 days of the ''notice of completion.'' If no ''notice of completion'' is filed, all claimants have 90 days after the completion of the work of improvement within which to file their lien claims.

The owner or any other person claiming an interest in the property may give a notice that he is not responsible for the work and consequently not subject to a lien. An example would be a tenant contracting for work unauthorized by the owner. This ''notice of nonresponsibility'' must be posted on the property and a copy must be recorded within 10 days of learning of the work.

A mechanic's lien may be discharged in a number of ways: if no foreclosure action on the lien is begun after 90 days; if a written release is obtained; if there is a satisfaction of the judgment lien against the debtor; if a prior lien is foreclosed; or if the court dismisses the action because the claim is invalid.

Tax liens and special assessments were covered in Unit 12.

ATTACHMENTS AND JUDGMENTS An attachment is a legal process wherein a defendant's real or personal property is legally seized and held as security pending the award of a possible judgment against him. In this manner, the claimant is assured that there will be something of value to satisfy his claim if the court awards in his favor. The attachment is a lien on the property for a three-year period, but may be extended beyond that period by a court order. Certain real and personal property is exempt wholly or partially from attachment.

A judgment is the final determination of the court concerning a claim. A judgment may be appealed. When a certified abstract of the judgment or decree of the court is recorded, it becomes a lien against all the property owned in that county by the debtor for a period of 10 years, and may be renewed for successive 10-year periods.

LIMITATIONS AND RESTRICTIONS

There are a number of encumbrances that are not liens but limit or restrict the use to which an owner can put his property.

EASEMENTS   An easement is the right of another person to enter and use the owner's property within certain specific limits. Examples of some types of easements include rights of way and water rights. When property is sold, the easements are passed on to the new buyers along with the property.

There are three principal ways in which easements arise. They may be expressly set forth in writing, as in a deed or a contract. They may arise by implication of law or by virtue of long use. An example is a parcel that has no access. Continuous and uninterrupted use for five years will create an easement by prescription under certain conditions. An easement can be terminated by an express written release or in a variety of other ways.

RESTRICTIONS   A restriction limits the use of the property owner. Restrictions are created by private owners or in general plans for entire subdivisions, referred to as "General Declarations of Restrictions." A restriction can be created by a deed for any legitimate purpose. Examples are restrictions that houses to be built must cost more than $30,000, specifications for location of structures such as side yard requirements and setbacks, and so forth.

Government or public agencies may regulate limitations also. Zoning laws can specify many restrictions.

An encroachment is the use of a portion of another person's land, such as a wall or building extending onto a neighbor's property.

UNIT SUMMARY

We discussed the various types of encumbrances and their effect on property. We saw that there are voluntary and involuntary liens. We learned that there are a number of restrictions and limitations on the use of property that you should be aware of.

REVIEWING YOUR UNDERSTANDING

TRUE OR FALSE

( ) **1** An easement is one of the most misunderstood types of liens.

( ) **2** A mechanic's lien is an involuntary lien.

( ) **3** A subcontractor has 60 days after the "notice of completion" has been filed to file a mechanic's lien.

( ) **4** A beneficiary is the borrower.

( ) **5** A trustee can collect 2 percent of the sales price for his services.

FILL-INS

1 A _____ lien is one that applies to all of the property owned by the debtor in the county.

2 A _____ is an example of a specific lien.

3 The process wherein a defendant's property is legally seized pending the court's decision is called _____.

4 Out of the proceeds of a trustee's sale, the _____ is paid second.

5 When your fence is discovered to be two feet on your neighbor's property, this is an example of _____.

REVIEWING YOUR UNDERSTANDING—ANSWERS

TRUE OR FALSE

1 False   4 False

2 True   5 False

3 False

FILL-INS

1 general

2 mechanic's lien

3 attachment

4 lienholder

5 encroachment

In this unit and Unit 15 we discuss valuation. Here we concentrate on the various principles affecting value. Then, in Unit 15, we consider the specific approaches to value. The concepts of value are different for different people. Here we discuss these value concepts and then learn how value is affected by the many different principles.

Read this study guide (pages 124–129).
View the TV program, number 14.

At the conclusion of this unit, you will be able to:

1 Define market value.
2 Compare market value with two other concepts of value.
3 List and define the four basic factors of value.
4 List and define at least 10 principles that affect value.
5 Give one example of each of the principles affecting value.
6 Define depreciation and appreciation.
7 Define and give an example of each of the three factors of depreciation.

scarcity, demand   depreciation
utility, transferability   appreciation
regression, progression

VALUE An appraisal is an estimate of value or an opinion of value. However, there are many different kinds of value. For appraisal purposes we are concerned primarily with the concept of value referred to as market value.

MARKET VALUE Market value is the price that a willing buyer will pay a willing seller, assuming that both parties are knowledgeable regarding the full usage of the property. Market value further assumes that the property is exposed to the market for a reasonable period of time. If a buyer were under pressure to buy quickly or if a seller were desperate to sell quickly, market value might be compromised. Similarly, if a buyer knew of some future event in the area that would increase prices and the seller were unaware of this, market value might be compromised. Appraisers have traditionally felt that if a property sells too quickly perhaps it may have been priced too low. However, another point of view suggests that when a property is priced closer to its eventual sales price, it will sell more quickly because a buyer will recognize the true value. Many buyers become discouraged viewing overpriced homes and will move very quickly when they find one that is priced fairly. Market value is often referred to as "objective" value, as distinguished from "subjective" value.

LOAN VALUE Loan value is the value that lenders will put on a property when they are considering the size of the loan to be extended. Loan value is often less than market value. For example, even though the buyer and seller agree to a sales price of $40,000, a bank may value the property at $36,000 and lend 75 percent of that amount.

ASSESSED VALUE Assessed value is discussed in Unit 12. It is 25 percent of full market value. Property taxes are based on assessed value after deduction for any exemption.

FACTORS OF VALUE There are four basic factors of value. They are scarcity, demand, utility, and transferability.

Scarcity and demand are related to supply and demand. If there are few homes available and a large number of buyers, price will increase. When there are many homes available and few buyers, the price will tend to drop.

Utility value is related to an appraisal concept known as the "highest and best use," which means the use that will give the greatest net return over a period of years. It may also reflect the property's usefulness to its owner, which may or may not be the same to a new buyer. Utility value is sometimes referred to as subjective value.

VALUATION PRINCIPLES Certain appraisal principles should be understood, since value is influenced by them.

PRINCIPLE OF REGRESSION   The principle of regression states that in a neighborhood of differing values a more valuable home will seek the level of less valuable homes. Assume that the average home in a new tract was worth $40,000 and an owner had a home built for $60,000. Also assume that one year later the $40,000 homes were selling for $43,000. The owner of the $60,000 home decides to sell. What could he sell the home for? There is a pretty fair chance that the home would sell for $50,000 to $55,000 because of the principle of regression. Another example would be the case of a buyer purchasing two lots and having one home built on the two lots to preclude the building of another home on the second lot. It is doubtful that the value of the extra lot could be recovered completely on resale. A new buyer would like the large yard but he probably would not be willing to pay that much extra for it. The principle of highest and best use would also be involved here.

PRINCIPLE OF PROGRESSION   The principle of progression is the opposite of regression. It contends that the value of a lower priced home in an area of predominantly higher priced homes would increase in value. The lower priced home would seek the level of the more valuable ones.

PRINCIPLE OF SUBSTITUTION   The principle of substitution contends that a buyer will not pay more for a home if he can buy basically the same home for less in an equally desirable location. If there were two homes for sale next door to each other which were basically the same, would you pay more for the one next door?

PRINCIPLE OF HIGHEST AND BEST USE   We have already touched on this principle. The most profitable use is the use that would produce the greatest net return over a given period of time. Assume that a duplex is situated on a lot zoned for eight units. Do you think that the highest and best use is represented by the duplex?

PRINCIPLE OF ANTICIPATION   The principle of anticipation suggests that some factor in the future will affect value beneficially. For example, a new rapid transit stop near a commercial area would add value.

PRINCIPLE OF CHANGE   Individual properties, neighborhoods, and cities are constantly changing. The first period of change is called the integration stage. During this stage, the property is constructed and development is rising. The second period is called the equilibrium or static stage. During this stage, the property increases to its maximum value because of a rise in demand. The third and final stage is called disintegration. During this stage, the property, neighborhood, or city decays and values decline.

PRINCIPLE OF SUPPLY AND DEMAND   When a commodity is scarce and the demand is high, its value increases. When there is an abundance of a commodity and a weak demand, its value tends to drop. Demand is affected by factors such as high or low interest rates, high or low taxes, and the like.

PRINCIPLE OF CONFORMITY   Appraisers point out that maximum values are achieved in areas where there is a great deal of similarity. As a general rule, the architectural styles, age, and condition of the homes should be similar. Likewise, it is beneficial if the residents are homogeneous or closely related in their economic, social, and educational backgrounds.

PRINCIPLE OF CONSISTENT USE   An underimproved structure on land is not unusual. When a triplex is situated on a lot zoned for 12 units, the triplex cannot increase the value of the land. Assume that the land would be valued at $60,000 if there were no improvements. The income from the triplex might justify a value of $45,000. A buyer would probably pay $60,000 for the property less the costs of demolition of the triplex if he planned to build 12 units.

PRINCIPLE OF COMPETITION   The possibility of good profits attracts competition. Excess profits will attract excess competition that, in many instances, destroys profits because the supply and demand relationship is adversely altered.

PRINCIPLE OF BALANCE   The principle of balance is also referred to as the principle of contribution or of increasing and decreasing returns. The principle contends that the balance of the four factors of production determines value. The four production factors are land, labor, capital, and management. Greater value can be achieved up to a maximum stage by introducing more of each of the four factors. This is called increasing returns. Any additional capital will not increase profits beyond that stage and, instead, there will be decreasing returns.

DEPRECIATION   As an improvement ages, it tends to lose value or to depreciate. Depreciation is a loss in value due to any cause. It should be pointed out that land is considered physically indestructible and, consequently, not normally depreciable. Depreciation is the opposite of appreciation, which is an increase in value due to any cause. Appreciation can occur as a result of inflation, which is a loss in the value of money or a shift in the supply and demand relationship in favor of demand. Three basic factors cause real estate improvements to depreciate. These are physical deterioration, functional obsolescence, and economic or social obsolescence.

PHYSICAL DETERIORATION   Physical deterioration is present in any improvement that is not new. It is caused by normal wear and tear. An example would be a home in need of new paint. Physical deterioration is said to be inherent within the property. This type of depreciation is less severe when a home is well maintained.

FUNCTIONAL OBSOLESCENCE This kind of depreciation results from poor floor plans, outdated fixtures, outdated architecture, and the like. Some of these causes are correctable.

ECONOMIC OR SOCIAL OBSOLESCENCE This is a loss in value due to forces extraneous to the property. Examples are neighbors who neglect their properties, high property taxes, or a garbage disposal site that has been located a block away.

UNIT SUMMARY

REVIEWING YOUR UNDERSTANDING

In this unit we discussed the different concepts of value and defined market value. We said that market value is the concept that we will be using in valuation. We discussed the various principles affecting value. We defined depreciation and examined the various types of depreciation. In the next unit we will concentrate on approaches to value.

TRUE OR FALSE

(   ) **1** A buyer from another state has been transferred by his employer. He flies to his new city the next weekend and pays $40,000 for a home that has been listed at $40,000 for nine months. This is a clear example of market value.

(   ) **2** A lender says he will lend 70 percent of $40,000. The home sold for $45,000. This is an example of loan value.

(   ) **3** The four basic factors of value are scarcity, demand, utility, and trusteeship.

(   ) **4** A home on a lot zoned for 4 units is an example of the principle of change.

(   ) **5** A large home in an area of smaller homes would tend to increase in value more than the others, since it is the most desirable home on the block.

FILL-INS

1 _____ is the purpose for which the owner is using the property.

2 A loss in value due to any cause is _____.

3 Massive cornices on a building are an example of _____
_____.

4 An increase in value due to any cause is called _____.

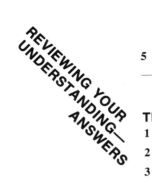

5 Active termite infestation, causing a lessening of value, is an example of

_____ .

TRUE OR FALSE

1 False	4 False
2 True	5 False
3 False	

FILL-INS

1 utility
2 depreciation
3 functional obsolescence
4 appreciation
5 physical deterioration

15

We discuss in this unit the different approaches to value that are used by the experts. By understanding what is involved in the various approaches, you will be able to ask meaningful questions of the experts—the real estate appraisers.

Read this study guide (pages 132–137).
View TV program, number 15.

At the conclusion of this unit, you will be able to:

1 List three ways of obtaining data for the market comparison approach.
2 Solve problems concerning transfer stamps.
3 Identify three disadvantages of using the market comparison approach.
4 Write a definition for the replacement cost approach.
5 Cite a weakness of the replacement cost approach.

subject property   "MLS"
"comparables"   accrued depreciation
documentary transfer tax   correlation

As a buyer, you should be sure that the price you pay for a home is reasonable.

You should pay no more than the market value, except in rare circumstances. Consequently, you should become familiar with the basic ways in which real estate licensees and appraisers determine market value. There are three basic approaches to value that appraisers use: the market comparison approach, the cost approach, and the income approach.

THE MARKET COMPARISON APPROACH

According to this approach, the property being appraised (the subject property) is compared to other comparable property that has recently been sold or is currently on the market. This is regarded as the most reliable way of estimating the market value of homes and vacant land, and it is widely used by real estate licensees and appraisers.

The properties used as comparables should have similar characteristics and there should be a market for them. The "principle of substitution" that we discussed in the previous unit is the foundation for this approach. A buyer should pay no more than the price of a similar substitute property.

HOW IS DATA OBTAINED?

The reliability of this approach depends on the accuracy of the data utilized. What sources do the experts have access to in order to collect the necessary data?

APPRAISAL FILES Over a period of years the appraiser develops files on a variety of properties. These are particularly good for properties that he has handled for past clients. He supplements his own files with data from other sources.

PUBLIC RECORDS The county assessor's office has records of all sales that have been recorded in the county in which the properties are located. Copies of deeds can be inspected to find useful information such as the names of the seller and the buyer and the legal description of the property. The amount of documentary transfer tax paid will appear either on the deed or on an accompanying document. Transfer taxes are required on all real property transferred for a consideration in excess of $100. The tax is $1.10 per $1000, $0.55 per $500 or portion thereof. It is based on the entire sales price of the property with one exception. When a loan is assumed or taken subject to the loan of record, it is based on the equity only. Let's work through two examples to make sure we understand the procedure.

Example 1 All cash paid or a *new* loan is obtained.

$$
\begin{array}{ll}
\$\ 40{,}000 & \text{price paid} \\
-\ 32{,}000 & \text{new loan obtained} \\
\hline
\$\ \ 8{,}000 & \text{equity}
\end{array}
$$

$40{,}000 \div 1{,}000 = 40$
1.10 per thousand $\times 40 = \$44$, amount of stamps

If you saw that $44 had been paid for the stamps you would calculate as follows:

$44 ÷ 0.00110 ($1.10 per thousand) = $40,000 sales price

$$\text{that is } \frac{\$44}{0.00110} = \$40,000$$

Example 2

$ 40,000 price paid
$\underline{- 30,500}$ loan assumed

$ 9,500 equity

$$9000 ÷ 1000 = 9$$

$1.10 × 9 = $ 9.90 (for $9,000)
$\underline{+ 0.55}$ (for the extra $500 of equity)

$10.45 required amount of stamps

In this case if you saw that only $10.45 had been paid, you would reason that a loan had been assumed, since $10.45 ÷ 0.00110 = $9500, which is obviously too low for the value of a property in that particular area. Also, if an existing loan is to remain on the property, that fact must be noted either on the deed or on a separate memorandum filed with the deed.

MULTIPLE LISTING SERVICES Local multiple listing services (MLS) are excellent sources available to appraisers. The MLS keeps detailed records of all past sales and current listings of properties marketed through the service.

CLASSIFIED ADS AND LISTINGS The addresses of properties listed for sale can be obtained from ads in local newspapers, various publications of banks and savings and loan associations, and other sources. List prices usually indicate the top market value; the prices offered normally indicate the lowest expected value. Nonetheless, the list price, although not as reliable as an actual sales price, provides a starting reference point.

HOW IS THE DATA USED? The data should be analyzed to determine how similar the properties are to the subject property with respect to the following characteristics: neighborhood location, size (number of rooms, baths, bedrooms, square footage, etc.) age, architectural style, and general price range.

Remember that a property in one location is worth considerably more than one in another location. Normally, you shouldn't compare a custom-designed home with a tract home. You should make adjustments for sales that are not current and for properties that have special features, such as views, trees, and so on. Try to get many comparisons; at least three current sales and three current listings are desirable.

Adjust the sales price of past comparable properties to reflect the changes in current prices. Adjust for the difference in locations. Adjust for the difference in properties due to physical features such as construction quality, condition, and obsolescence. An example follows:

Number	Date	Price	Time	Location	Property	Adjusted Value	Square Feet	Adjusted Rate Per Square Foot
1	October 3 last year	38,000	+3,000	+500	+1,000	42,500	1,700	25.00
2	April 17 this year	39,500	+1,500	0	0	41,000	1,650	24.85
3	October 1 this year	41,000	0	+1,000	+1,000	43,000	1,725	24.93

Find adjusted rate estimated at $24.90
Subject house contains 1750 square feet × $24.90 = $43,575

The advantages of using the market comparison approach are as follows. It is the approach most frequently used for home valuation by appraisers. It is the most reliable approach for appraising homes. And it is the easiest to compute and apply.

Some disadvantages to this approach are the following. It is sometimes difficult to make precise adjustments. It is difficult to determine the down payment and financing involved in the comparable sales that can affect the final estimate of market value.

Whenever possible, the comparable properties should be personally inspected to insure the reliability of the data.

THE REPLACEMENT COST APPROACH

The replacement cost approach seeks to put a value on a home based on today's cost to replace it. It should be noted that modern materials and labor are assumed and that an exact replica of the structure is not intended. The cost approach tends to set the upper limit of value, since a buyer would not ordinarily pay more for a property than it would cost to replace it.

The first step in using this approach is to determine the land value of the subject property as if it were vacant. The next step is to compute the gross square footage. The square footage is then multiplied by today's cost factor to determine the cost of replacing the structure new.

Cost figures are obtained from local contractors and appraisers and from certain cost guide publications.

Depreciation is deducted in the case of older homes. Site improvements are considered. All of the items are then considered together, resulting in the estimated replacement cost value.

Let's work through a simplified example of the cost approach. Let's assume that the land is 6000 square feet and comparable lots are selling for $1.50 per square foot. The basic structure is 1500 square feet. The garage is 400 square feet.

Land	6,000 square feet at $1.50 square foot =	$ 9,000
Living area	1,500 square feet at $23 square foot =	34,500
Garage	400 square feet at $10 square foot =	4,000
Site improvements	=	3,000
Total replacement cost		$50,500

Site improvements (landscaping, patios, fences, etc.) are valued at $3000. Let's also assume that we are actually building this home, and that depreciation consequently is not a factor.

Now let's assume that the property being appraised is 20 years old and that depreciation must consequently be considered. Let's assume that the property has an estimated economic life (period of time over which it can justify it's economic existence) of 50 years from the time it was new. This would mean that we should deduct 2 percent per year for depreciation of the structure. The site improvements should also be depreciated, but for simplicity in this example it will be ignored. Since the home is 20 years old we should take 40 percent accrued (past) depreciation (20 years × 2 percent per year = 40 percent).

Therefore, we should deduct 40 percent or $13,800 from the living area (40 percent × $34,500) and 40 percent from the garage or $1600 (40 percent × $4000).

A total of $15,400 is deducted from our replacement cost figure of $50,500, leaving a replacement value of $35,100.

It should be noted that most properties are well maintained; consequently, their rate of depreciation does not necessarily correspond to the age of the property. Also, many structures have a longer or shorter economic life than 50 years. Experience and good judgment are necessary for the appraiser to adjust properly for depreciation in older structures.

The cost approach is particularly useful when evaluating newer structures, where depreciation is of little concern.

THE INCOME APPROACH

The income approach is seldom used for appraising homes. We discuss this approach in some detail in Unit 26 in connection with investment properties.

CORRELATION

The wise appraiser or real estate licensee will use more than one approach to arrive at a reliable value. No single approach should be used exclusively. Both the market comparison approach and the replacement cost approach should be used when appraising homes, since each has something to contribute and each serves as a check on the other. Correlation is the process wherein the results of the different approaches are analyzed. More weight is given to the approach that is most reliable for appraising a particular property. Consequently, if the market comparison approach on a 10-year old home yields a value of $40,000 and the replacement cost approach yields a value of $44,000, more weight would be given to the $40,000 figure. An ultimate value might be given as $40,500 in this case. However, the two figures are not added together and divided by two.

UNIT SUMMARY

We discussed the three approaches to value and stated that the market comparison approach and the replacement cost approach were applicable to homes. The market comparison approach is the most reliable for appraising homes.

We saw how and when to use the various approaches and the advantages and disadvantages of each. We learned how to determine the ultimate market value through the process known as correlation.

REVIEWING YOUR UNDERSTANDING

TRUE OR FALSE

(   ) **1** Each of the following is a way of obtaining data for the market comparison approach: MLS, other experts, deeds.

(   ) **2** $33.55 in transfer stamps were paid on a property. No loan was assumed. The value of the property was $30,000.

(   ) **3** A disadvantage of the market comparison approach is its difficulty in determining depreciation.

(   ) **4** The chief advantage of the replacement cost approach is in its application to a new home.

(   ) **5** Generally the expert has limited access to appraisal data.

FILL-INS

1 You compare other sales to the _____ property.

2 The process of judging the final value after considering each of the approaches is called. _____.

3 The _____ tends to set the upper limit of value.

4 One of the best sources of appraisal data is the _____, which is available to REALTORS®.

5 Depreciation that has occurred in the past is referred to as _____ depreciation.

REVIEWING YOUR UNDERSTANDING—ANSWERS

TRUE OR FALSE

1 True   **4** True

2 False   **5** False

3 False

FILL-INS

1 subject

2 correlation

3 replacement cost approach

4 MLS

5 accrued

16

Many elements of basic contract law should be understood when the actual purchase agreement is discussed. In this unit we will discuss the legal requirements for an enforceable contract, the discharge of contracts, and the provisions in contracts. We then consider an example of the real estate purchase contract, which is also known as the deposit receipt.

Read this study guide (pages 140–146).
View TV program, number 16.

At the conclusion of this unit you will be able to:

1 List, at least, five situations that would be governed by the statute of frauds.

2 Identify and give an example of each of the essential elements of a contract.

3 Give, at least, eight examples of how contracts can be discharged.

4 List seven provisions that should be part of a real estate contract.

5 Define a deposit receipt.

6 Explain what is meant by each of the deposit receipt clauses.

statute of frauds	consideration
contract	discharge of contracts
mutual consent	enforceable

A deposite receipt is the form most often used to purchase real estate. It is a receipt for the money deposited when the offer is made. More importantly, it is also the contract for the transaction. A contract, simply defined, is an agreement to do or not to do a certain thing.

THE STATUTE OF FRAUDS

According to the Statute of Frauds, which has become a part of the California Civil Code, a real estate contract must be in writing to be enforceable in the courts. Similarly, any change from the original contract must also be in writing and dated and initialed by the parties involved. The purpose of the law is to prevent perjury, forgery, and dishonest conduct on the part of unscrupulous people in proving the existence and terms of certain important types of contracts. Practically speaking, a written understanding of the terms agreed on often eliminates ambiguities and misunderstanding at a later date.

The California Civil Code requires that the following contracts be in writing.

1 An agreement that by its terms is not to be performed within a year from the making thereof.

2 A special promise to answer for the debt, default, or miscarriage of another, except in the cases provided for in Section 2794.

3 An agreement made on consideration of marriage other than a mutual promise to marry.

4 An agreement for the leasing for a longer period than one year, or for the sale of real property, or of an interest therein; and such agreement, if made by an agent of the party sought to be charged is invalid, unless the authority of the agent is in writing, subscribed by the party sought to be charged.

5 An agreement authorizing or employing an agent, broker, or any other person, to purchase or sell real estate, or to lease real estate for a longer period than one year, or to procure, introduce, or find a purchaser or seller of real estate or a lessee or lessor of real estate where such lease is for a longer period than one year, for compensation or a commission.

6 An agreement that by its terms is not to be performed during the lifetime of the promisor, or an agreement to devise or to bequeath any property, or to make any provision for any reason by will.

7 An agreement by a purchaser of real property to pay an indebtedness secured by a mortgage or deed of trust on the property purchased, unless assumption of said indebtedness by the purchaser is specifically provided for in the conveyance of such property.

Any contract that does not comply with the above is not void but is unenforceable.

ESSENTIAL ELEMENTS OF A CONTRACT

According to the Civil Code, there are four essential elements of a contract. They are:

1 Parties capable of contracting.

2 Their consent.

3 Lawful object.

4 A sufficient consideration.

PARTIES CAPABLE OF CONTRACTING There must be at least two or more parties with at least a limited capacity to have a valid contract. As a general rule anyone is capable of contracting with some exceptions. A minor (under 18 years old) is incapable of contracting concerning real property. Incompetents who have been so determined by the courts cannot contract. Like minors, however, they may acquire title to real property by gift or by will. Aliens may hold and sell real property within California, according to state law. They are subject to certain federal restrictions, however. Partnerships and corporations are regarded as artificial beings, and may also hold and dispose of real property.

MUTUAL CONSENT The parties to the contract must mutually agree to be bound to the terms of the contract. This is exemplified by an offer by one party and an acceptance by the other. The offer must be definite and certain in its terms. The courts will not make the contracts for the parties nor will they fix the terms and conditions.

LAWFUL OBJECT A contract must have a lawful consideration and object. An object is what is required to be done or not to be done. A contract is void if there is a single object and it is unlawful or impossible to perform. If there are many lawful objects in the contract and one or more unlawful objects, usually only the unlawful objects will be void and the other objects will be valid.

SUFFICIENT CONSIDERATION Consideration can be a benefit conferred or agreed to be conferred on the person making the promise or on any other person, or a detriment suffered or agreed to be suffered. It can be the return of a promise. The consideration must have some value. Ordinarily it is money.

DISCHARGE OF CONTRACTS Contracts can be discharged in a number of ways. Full performance is the normal situation, wherein the parties accomplish what they set out to do in the contract. At the other extreme is a breach of the contract which means that one of the parties did not fulfill his agreement. In the case of a breach the injured party has a number of remedies available to him. There are several other methods of discharge:

1 By part performance.

2 By substantial performance.

3 By impossibility of performance.

4 By agreement between the parties.

5 By release.

6 By operation of law.

7 By acceptance of a breach of the contract.

PROVISIONS IN CONTRACTS The following provisions should be part of a real estate contract:

1 The date of the agreement.

2 The names and addresses of the parties to the contract.

3 A description of the property.

4 The consideration.

5 Reference to the creation of new mortgages or deeds of trust, if any, and the terms thereof; also the terms and conditions of existing mortgages, if any.

6 Any other provisions that may be required or requested by either of the parties.

7 The date and place of closing the contract.

THE DEPOSIT RECEIPT Many different purchase forms are available. Figure 1 shows the California Association of Realtors' standard form, which has been approved by both the California Association of Realtors and the California Bar Association.

Study this standard form and note the following, indicated by the corresponding numbers in boldface type on the form that follows:

BROKER'S COPY

CALIFORNIA ASSOCIATION OF REALTORS STANDARD FORM

REAL ESTATE PURCHASE CONTRACT AND RECEIPT FOR DEPOSIT

THIS IS MORE THAN A RECEIPT FOR MONEY. IT MAY BE A LEGALLY BINDING CONTRACT. READ IT CAREFULLY.

_____ (1) Willow Meadows _____, California, __September 1__, 19 76

Received from __(2) Jim Johnson and Barbara Johnson, husband and wife__ herein called Buyer,

the sum of (3) Five Hundred and no/100 _____ Dollars ($__500.00__)

evidenced by cash □, personal check ☒, cashier's check □, or _____ as deposit on account of

purchase price of (4) Forty Thousand and no/100 _____ Dollars, ($__40,000.00__)

for the purchase of property, situated in (5) Three Meadows _____, County of __Los Angeles__,

California, described as follows: (6) a single family residence known as 123 Elm Street, legally described as lot 7, block 13 of tract 149 recorded 1949 in Los Angeles County records book 51 of maps page 310.

(7) 1. Buyer will deposit in escrow with (7) a reliable escrow company the balance of purchase price as follows: _____

$ 4,000 cash down payment including the above deposit.

$32,000 new first deed of trust to be obtained. Monthly payments to be $270 or more including 9½% interest. 30 year due date. Loan fee to buyer not to exceed 1½ points.

(8) $ 4,000 Note and record deed of trust on subject property to be executed by purchasing in favor of seller. Monthly payments to be $40.00 or more including 9½% interest. 5 year due date. No loan fee. Stove and refrigerator are included in the above price. Standard terms to agreement attached and is a part of this agreement. The above offer is contingent on purchasor obtaining said loan. All appliances, plumbing and electricity to be in good working order.

Set forth above any terms and conditions of a factual nature applicable to this sale, such as financing, prior sale of other property, the matter of structural pest control inspection, repairs and personal property to be included in the sale.

2. Title is to be free of liens, encumbrances, easements, restrictions, rights and conditions of record or known to Seller, other than the following: current taxes and conditions, covenants, easements and restrictions.

Seller shall furnish to Buyer at _buyer's_ expense a standard California Land Title Association policy issued by _a reliable title_ Company, showing title vested in Buyer subject only to liens, encumbrances, easements, restrictions, rights and conditions of record as set forth above. If Seller fails to deliver title as herein provided, Buyer at his option may terminate this agreement and any

FIGURE 1 deposit shall thereupon be returned to him.

FIGURE 1 *(Continued)*

3. Property taxes, premiums on insurance acceptable to Buyer, rents, interest, and ----------
---------------------------------- [insert in blank any other items of income or expense to be prorated] shall be prorated as of (1) the date of recordation of deed or (2) ----------------------
[Strike (1) if (2) is used]. The amount of any bond or assessment which is a lien shall be ~~paid~~ assumed
[Strike one] by __buyer_____. Seller shall pay cost of documentary stamps on deed.

4. Possession shall be delivered to Buyer [Strike inapplicable alternatives] (a) on close of escrow, or (b) not later than _____ days after closing escrow, or (c)_____

5. Escrow instructions signed by Buyer and Seller shall be delivered to the escrow holder within __20__ days from the Seller's acceptance hereof and shall provide for closing within __30__ days from the Seller's acceptance hereof, subject to written extensions signed by Buyer and Seller.

6. Unless otherwise designated in the escrow instructions of Buyer, title shall vest as follows: ___
to be provided in escrow
[The manner of taking title may have significant legal and tax consequences. Therefore, give this matter serious consideration.]

7. If the improvements on the property are destroyed or materially damaged prior to close of escrow, then, on demand by Buyer, any deposit made by Buyer shall be returned to him and this contract thereupon shall terminate.

8. If Buyer fails to complete said purchase as herein provided by reason of any default of Buyer, Seller shall be released from his obligation to sell the property to Buyer and may proceed against Buyer upon any claim or remedy which he may have in law or equity; provided, however, that by placing their initials here Buyer: (J.J. B.J.) Seller: (T.S. M.S.) Buyer and Seller agree that it would be impractical or extremely difficult to fix actual damages in case of Buyer's default, that the amount of the deposit is a reasonable estimate of the damages and that Seller shall retain the deposit as his sole right to damages.

9. Buyer's signature hereon constitutes an offer to Seller to purchase the real estate described above. Unless acceptance hereof is signed by Seller and the signed copy delivered to Buyer, either in person or by mail to the address shown below, within __2__ days hereof, this offer shall be deemed revoked and the deposit shall be returned to Buyer.

10. Time is of the essence of this contract.

Real Estate Broker __XYZ Realtors_____ By __Gene Weston_____
Address __129 Grove Street, Five Meadows__ Telephone __273-5291_____

The undersigned Buyer offers and agrees to buy the above described property on the terms and conditions above stated and acknowledges receipt of a copy hereof.
Address _____1173 Spruce Street_____ Buyer __(9) Jim Johnson_____
Telephone__291-3764_____ Buyer _____Barbara Johnson_____

ACCEPTANCE

The undersigned Seller accepts the foregoing offer and agrees to sell the property described thereon on the terms and conditions therein set forth. The undersigned Seller has employed__Gene Weston_____as Broker(s) and for the Broker(s) services agrees to pay Broker(s) as a commission, the sum of_6% of sales price_Dollars ($_____) payable as follows: (a) On recordation of the deed or other evidence of title, or (b) if completion of sale is prevented by default of Seller, upon Seller's default, or (c) if completion of sale is prevented by default of Buyer only if and when Seller collects the damages from Buyer, by suit or otherwise, and then in an amount not to exceed one half that portion of the damages collected after first deducting title and escrow expenses and the expenses of collection, if any. The undersigned acknowledges receipt of a copy hereof and authorizes Broker(s) to deliver a signed copy of it to Buyer.

Dated: _9-2-76_____ Address __123 Elm Street___ Seller __Tom Seller (10)_____
Telephone__291-1432_____ Seller __Mary Seller_____
Broker(s) consent to the foregoing. Broker _XYZ Realtor_____ Broker _____
Dated: _9-2-76___ By _____Gene Weston_____ Dated: _____ By _____

A REAL ESTATE BROKER IS THE PERSON QUALIFIED TO ADVISE ON REAL ESTATE. IF YOU DESIRE LEGAL ADVICE CONSULT YOUR ATTORNEY.
THIS STANDARDIZED DOCUMENT FOR USE IN SIMPLE TRANSACTIONS HAS BEEN APPROVED BY THE CALIFORNIA ASSOCIATION OF REALTORS AND THE STATE BAR OF CALIFORNIA IN FORM ONLY. NO REPRESENTATION IS MADE AS TO THE LEGAL VALIDITY OF ANY PROVISION OR THE ADEQUACY OF ANY PROVISION IN ANY SPECIFIC TRANSACTION. IT SHOULD NOT BE USED IN COMPLEX TRANSACTIONS OR WITH EXTENSIVE RIDERS OR ADDITIONS.

FORM NO. NCR-D (Rev. 6-71)

1 The location where the deposit receipt is being prepared should appear here.

2 The names of all buyers should appear here with a designation of their legal status or relationship.

3 The amount of the deposit and the form that the deposit takes should be entered here.

4 The purchase price being offered should appear here both in writing and in numerals to avoid mistakes.

5 This is where the property is located.

6 It is considered good form to have both a common and legal description.

7 A particular escrow company can be agreed on during the escrow.

8 The terms of the offer should be clearly spelled out. In the case of new F.H.A. or G.I. financing the seller would pay the discount points. A limit should be placed on the amount of the discount points to be paid by the seller.

9 Each of the buyers should sign here.

10 Each of the sellers should sign here.

EXPERT ADVICE RECOMMENDED What is presented here is a simple set of circumstances. You should not attempt to fill out a deposit receipt by yourself. An expert should be consulted.

UNIT SUMMARY

REVIEWING YOUR UNDERSTANDING

In this unit you learned many of the basic elements of contract law. We defined a contract, discussed the statute of frauds, the essential elements of a contract, and the discharge of contracts. We also learned the provisions that should be part of a real estate contract and examined a simplified sample of a completed deposit receipt.

TRUE OR FALSE

(   )   **1**   A lease of nine months would not be required to be in writing.

(   )   **2**   A person aged 17 can legally contract if married.

(   )   **3**   If a fire severely damaged a home prior to close of escrow, the buyer would still have to complete the transaction.

(   )   **4**   A description of the property is not absolutely necessary for a valid contract.

(   )   **5**   A deposit accompanying the deposit receipt must be in some form of money.

FILL-INS

1 The _____ requires that most real estate contracts must be in writing.

2 Agreement of the parties is also known as _____.

REVIEWING YOUR UNDERSTANDING—ANSWERS

3 In order to have a valid _____, you must exchange a promise for a promise.

TRUE OR FALSE

1 True	**4** False
2 False	**5** False
3 False	

FILL-INS

1 statute of frauds

2 mutual consent

3 contract

HOW IS AN OFFER
TO PURCHASE MADE?

In the preceding unit, we discussed the deposit receipt and explained that this is the form on which most offers to purchase are made. In this unit we discuss the mechanics of presenting offers and counteroffers, including the legal requirements for offer and acceptance.

Presenting offers and counteroffers involves delicate negotiations. It is sometimes unwise to present your own offer personally.

Read study guide (pages 148–152).
View TV program, number 17.

At the conclusion of this unit you will be able to:

1 Point out, at least, two items of preparation that should be undertaken prior to the presentation of an offer.

2 List the steps involved in the sale of property, from offer to acceptance.

3 List the steps involved in a counteroffer.

offer   acceptance
offeror   counteroffer
offeree

BACKGROUND   Making an offer to buy real property, a home, in this case, is not a matter to be taken lightly. You are entering into what could become a legally binding transaction. Therefore, you should be reasonably certain that you really want to buy the home. If you have any doubts concerning the property, you or your agent should seek more information and the advice of specialized experts. If your doubts remain after further analysis, perhaps you should look for another home. Also, remember that you must submit a deposit along with your written offer to show good faith. This deposit is called an earnest money deposit, reflecting the fact that you should be making your offer in earnest. If the seller accepts your offer, he may, in some instances, be entitled to retain your deposit if you later decide not to complete the transaction. Let's assume that you are satisfied that the home is right for you after having analyzed the situation fully. The deposit receipt has been prepared under the terms that are agreeable to you, the offeror. You have signed the deposit receipt and have retained a copy of it. What is the next step?

PRESENTING THE OFFER   You or your agent should arrange for an appointment to present your offer to the seller, the offeree. Remember that this is a business transaction and that the situation should be handled accordingly. If at all possible, emotions should not enter into the negotiations. The written offer should be clear and detailed, and should be presented in a businesslike manner. It is in this connection that a real estate agent's professional services are of the utmost value. The agent has probably presented numerous offers and is therefore experienced in presenting them in a clear and knowledgeable manner. Also he is not emotionally involved.

After the usual greetings and informal pleasantries are completed, a copy of your offer is presented to the seller. The seller should be given adequate time to read the offer in its entirety. Understandably, he may raise questions concerning its terms. It is important that these questions be answered accurately, thoroughly, and in a professional manner. A wise businessman understands that the transaction should be viewed through the eyes of both parties. He knows that the seller has lived in the home for many years and has become emotionally attached to it. He appreciates the fact that the seller may have made costly improvements. However, he also knows that a built-in range that cost $300 originally is not worth $300 today because it has depreciated. He understands that an offer with a conventional loan means that the seller will not have to pay the F.H.A. or G.I. points. Consequently, the seller might accept a lower offer with conventional terms because he could net the same or more money than he could with an F.H.A. or G.I. sale. A list of recent comparable sales in the same area should always be part of the homework done prior to the actual presentation. The list could be made available to the seller in support of the offer.

Assuming that all the terms of the offer are acceptable to the seller, the deposit receipt is signed by him. A copy of it must be left with the seller. A completed copy of the accepted offer must then be delivered back to the buyer. Once these steps have been completed, you are on your way to owning your own home.

COUNTEROFFERS   If an offer is unrealistic, the seller may feel insulted and may totally reject it without any further action on his part.

However, the offer will frequently be realistic, but the seller will think some changes are necessary before he agrees to sell the home. In that case he might make a counteroffer to the buyer. A counteroffer is, in effect, simply an offer made by the seller to the buyer. It is recommended that a counteroffer be made on a special counteroffer form (see Figure 1), although a separate sheet of paper can be used to specify the changes. In the counteroffer, reference should be made to

COUNTER OFFER

CALIFORNIA ASSOCIATION OF REALTORS ® STANDARD FORM

This is a counter offer to the Real Estate Purchase Contract and Receipt for Deposit dated __September 1__, 19 _76_, in which ___John Buyer and Mary Buyer___ is referred to as buyer and ___John Seller and Mary Seller___ is referred to as seller.

The undersigned accepts the offer on the terms and conditions set forth in the above designated agreement with the following changes or amendments:
Purchase price is changed to $44,000. Stove and refrigerator are not included in the purchase price. First deed of trust to be obtained by buyer is to be increased to $35,200. Other terms of loan remain the same.

Seller reserves the right to accept any other offer prior to actual receipt of buyer's acceptance. This counter offer shall otherwise be deemed revoked on __September 3,__ 19_76_, at _12:00_ a.m./p.m.

Receipt of a copy hereof is hereby acknowledged.

DATED: _Sept. 1,_ 19 _76_   *John Seller*
TIME: _10:00 A.M_   *Mary Seller*   SELLER

SELLER

The undersigned buyer hereby accepts the above counter offer.

Receipt of a copy hereof is hereby acknowledged.

DATED: _Sept. 2_, 19_76_   *John Buyer*
TIME: _2:00 p.m._   *Mary Buyer*   BUYER

BUYER

Receipt of buyer's acceptance is hereby acknowledged.

DATED: _Sept. 2_ 19 _76_   *John Seller*
TIME: _4:00 P.M._   *Mary Seller*   SELLER

SELLER

FIGURE 1   CO-11   (7-1-74)

the original deposit receipt, its date, and the names of the buyer and the seller. There should be a statement that the seller accepts the offer referred to, and the changes or amendments should then be inserted. The counteroffer should be signed and dated by the seller and a copy should be left with him. The counteroffer is then presented to the buyer.

If the buyer rejects the counteroffer nothing further happens. However, the buyer may again counter the counteroffer, or may simply draw up a new deposit receipt and make another offer.

A buyer accepts the counteroffer by signing and dating it, and retaining a copy. Acceptance must be communicated back to the seller, and a completed copy must be given to him.

Counteroffers are most frequently made because the seller believes that changes should be made in price, down payment, closing date of escrow, possession date, personal property, or loan terms.

In the case of both an original offer and a counteroffer, communication of acceptance to the appropriate party is imperative. Until acceptance is received in writing, either party may withdraw the offer or counteroffer.

A buyer should view a counteroffer with proper perspective. Although his original offer, which represents perhaps an ideal situation for him, was not acceptable, it may still be advantageous to conclude the transaction under the terms of the counteroffer.

UNIT SUMMARY

REVIEWING YOUR UNDERSTANDING

An offer to purchase should be made only when the prospect is serious about buying the home. The offer or counteroffer should be prepared carefully and should be presented in an unemotional, businesslike manner. Copies of signed papers must be left with each of the parties. Acceptance must be communicated to the appropriate party. Presentation of offers and counteroffers involves delicate negotiations. The proper perspective is important.

TRUE OR FALSE

(   )   **1**   The buyer's deposit will always be returned if the buyer changes his mind after the seller's acceptance has been communicated back to him.

(   )   **2**   Little negotiation is required in most offers.

(   )   **3**   Most buyers have the necessary knowledge and diplomacy to present their own offers.

(   )   **4**   Inadequate price is one of the more important reasons for counteroffers.

(   )   **5**   The buyer is the party who accepts the counteroffer.

FILL-INS

1 The _____ is the seller (offeror/offeree?).

2 Acceptance must be _____ to the appropriate party.

3 An offer or counteroffer may be _____ prior to acceptance.

REVIEWING YOUR UNDERSTANDING—ANSWERS

TRUE OR FALSE

1 False

2 False

3 False

4 True

5 True

FILL-INS

1 offeree

2 communicated

3 withdrawn

18

ESCROW AND
TITLE INSURANCE—
WHAT ARE THEY?

Every real estate transaction must eventually go through an impartial third party. For this reason anyone contemplating the purchase or sale of real property should be familiar with the procedure and the forms and terms used.

In this unit we discuss the method and procedure for completing a real estate transaction. You will learn what forms are necessary and the role of a neutral third party in completing the transaction.

The unit will point out who may act as impartial third parties and what their responsibilities are.

Read this study guide (pages 154–160).
View the TV program, number 18.

At the conclusion of this unit, you will be able to:

1 Define such terms as escrow, conveyance fee, and title insurance.

2 List the requirements of a valid escrow.

3 Explain the functions of an escrow company.

4 Describe the activities of a title insurance company.

escrow	ALTA
title insurance	reconveyance fee
CLTA	chain of title

WHAT IS AN ESCROW?

It is the last major step in the real estate transaction.

Webster's Dictionary defines escrow as follows:

A deed, bond, or other written engagement, delivered to a third person, to be delivered by him to the grantee only upon the specific performance or fulfillment of some condition. The deposit of the *Escrow* places it beyond the control of the grantor; but no title passes until the fulfillment of the condition.

This definition has been somewhat changed for various reasons and the activities of an escrow agent have been considerably expanded.

An escrow agent or "escrow," as it is commonly called, is an impartial third party who receives and disburses documents, money, and papers from every person involved in a real estate transaction.

The escrow agent holds everything while it is being determined that the seller's title is clear (as his title is searched).

When it is determined that the title is clear, instructions are agreed upon by buyer and seller and disbursements made of the deed and the moneys involved, to the appropriate parties.

WHO ARE THE PARTIES TO THE ESCROW?

BUYER The buyer has made a firm contract to purchase the real property involved, but will not want to part with his money until he is sure of what he is getting: that the seller's deed will convey clear title.

When the buyer has performed in full (paid the purchase price), he is entitled to a deed transferring title, subject only to encumbrances agreed to by both parties.

CAUTION

In the event of death, incompetency, or bankruptcy of the seller in the interim, the buyer may be put to extra expense in order to eventually secure clear title.

SELLER Although the seller has made a firm contract to sell his real property, he will not want to give up his title until he is certain of getting his money. He therefore retains legal title to the property as security.

The seller's legal title can be transferred by deed, passing all the seller's interest in the contract; the grantee, who has notice of the prior contract, takes title subject to the contract.

CAUTION

Upon his death, the right of the seller to the unpaid part of the purchase price passes to his heirs as personal property.

LENDER The lender has committed himself to lending the money to the buyer to complete the purchase price, but, like the buyer, the lender will not want to commit funds until he has been assured that the title to the property in question is free and clear.

Thus, to solve these problems, an impartial third party (an escrow agent) will hold the money, deed, and other documents until clear title has been confirmed. Thereafter, it is his responsibility to see that proper disbursements have been made.

WHO MAY ACT AS ESCROW?   The law makes it necessary for escrow agencies to be licensed by the Corporations Commissioner of California.

The law applies only to those organizations actively engaged in conducting escrow agencies and title companies.

EXEMPT FROM SPECIAL LICENSING ARE:

Banks
Trust companies
Savings and loan associations
Insurance companies
Licensed attorneys

NOTE

Also exempt is any broker or agent licensed by the real estate commissioner while performing acts in the course of or incidental to the real estate business.

CAN A REAL ESTATE BROKER ACT AS AN ESCROW OFFICER?   Yes, but only when he represents either the buyer, the seller, or both. He may not hold escrows for another broker or for anyone acting without the services of a broker.

CAUTION

Escrow funds held by the broker must be placed in a special trust account, subject to a periodic inspection by the commissioner, and, at the broker's own expense, subject to an independent audit annually.

CAUTION

The broker cannot advertise that he conducts an escrow department unless he specifies in the advertisement that such services are only in connection with his real estate brokerage business.

In Northern California the majority of the escrow transactions are handled by the title insurance companies.

In Southern California escrow companies handle the majority of the escrow transactions.

ESCROW LICENSE APPLICANTS

Anyone applying for license under the Escrow Act must meet the following qualifications:

Be financially solvent.

Furnish a surety bond for $5000.

Arrange for the bonding of responsible employees.

Set up a trust fund for all moneys deposited into the escrow.

Keep accurate records, auditable at any time by the commissioner.

At his own expense, submit an independent audit annually.

ESCROW COMPANIES MUST BE INCORPORATED

According to the laws governing escrows:

1 An individual cannot be licensed as an escrow holder or agent.

2 The license must be held by a duly organized corporation for the express purpose of conducting an escrow business.

3 No escrow licensee may disseminate misleading or deceptive statements referring to the supervision of such licensee by the state of California.

4 A licensee is prohibited from describing either orally or in writing any transaction that is not included under the definition of escrow in the California financial code.

5 Licensed escrow agents are prohibited by law from paying referral fees to anyone except a regular employee of the escrow company.

6 Escrow licensees are prohibited by law from soliciting or accepting escrow instructions, or amended or supplemental instruction, containing any blank to be filled in after instructions are signed.

7 Escrow licensees may not permit any person to make any addition to, deletion from, or alteration of an escrow instruction unless it is signed or initialed by all signees on the original instructions.

8 The escrow holder is at first the agent of both parties. When conditions are performed, he usually becomes the agent of each:

The grantor to deliver the deed.

The grantee to pay over the purchase price.

Regardless of the area of California in which escrow is being held, remember these points when dealing with an escrow officer:

The agent must be a neutral third party to the transaction.

The agent can act only according to the terms of the written and signed escrow instructions.

The agent can only close the escrow when all parties have mutually agreed upon all items.

The agent cannot give legal advice.

WHAT ARE THE FUNCTIONS OF A TITLE INSURANCE COMPANY?

Title insurance companies in California have four major functions:

1 To search for and gather public records relating to the title of real property.

2 To examine and interpret title records.

3 To handle the escrow transaction from beginning to close.

4 To insure the principal against losses resulting from defects in the title.

NOTE

> A fee is charged for these services. The amount of the fee depends upon the selling price of the property, and the loan amount on the property or both.

The amount is negotiable between the parties to the transaction. Usually either one or the other, the buyer or the seller, pays the fee, or it may be shared in any way agreeable to both parties.

WHAT ARE THE TWO CHIEF METHODS OF TITLE SEARCH?

COURTHOUSE SEARCH The title searcher goes through the public records in the county courthouse seeking information concerning condition of the title to that piece of property he is examining.

Documents of these records are reproduced and sent to an examiner for interpretation.

TITLE PLANT SEARCH The title insurance company maintains its own "title plant." This may be likened to a miniature courthouse where all records are copied as they are received by the county recorder (title insurance companies maintain a staff for this purpose) and filed for use at some future date.

Very often information regarding property is kept on microfilm or stored in a computer. This allows easy access and requires far less space for storage than do written records. When it becomes necessary to make a title search, it is an easy matter to review a microfilm or to recall information from a computer bank. This results in a saving of time for both the client and the title insurer.

One large title insurance company in California reports the following: (1) Records compiled for more than a century in some instances cover land transactions in California and Nevada. (2) Maps show railroads, highways, and other installations; more than 1,000,000 maps are available.

WHAT IS A CHAIN OF TITLE?

A chain of title is an unbroken relationship in property ownership from the original owner up through the present owners.

Highly skilled title examiners search the records and make the necessary interpretations. At this time a "chain of title" is compiled, tracing it to the present owner.

ESCROW PROCEDURE

The next important function of the title insurance company is to prepare to open the escrow. The procedure involved will be discussed in the next unit.

UNIT SUMMARY

This lesson points out that the escrow procedure is a vital step in any real estate transaction, where an impartial third party represents both the buyer and seller.

It explains the arrangements, to which the buyer and seller agree, concerning the sale through escrow. These agreements become part of the escrow instructions.

In this unit you also learned that escrow companies must be licensed and that important restrictions accompany this licensing.

You also learned that in Northern California, title companies perform the work of the escrow, while in Southern California, the escrow function is usually handled by an independent escrow company.

1 Under what circumstances is a license required of persons engaged in the escrow business?

_____

_____

2 May individuals be licensed as escrow agents in California?

_____

_____

3 The escrow agent may: (a) give legal advice on the manner of taking title; (b) pay referral fees to real estate licensees; (c) deposit all moneys in a commercial bank; (d) do none of these.

4 A licensed real estate broker handling his own escrows must: (a) deposit all moneys received in a bank trust account; (b) maintain books, records, and accounts subject to periodic inspection by the real estate commissioner; (c) deliver at the time of execution escrow instructions and a copy to all persons executing them; (d) do all of these.

5 Escrow agencies must be licensed by (a) the Secretary of State; (b) insurance commissioner; (c) real estate commissioner; and (d) corporations commissioner.

6 Joe and Susan purchase a new home and an escrow is opened. Susan's parents demand that the escrow agent give them the details of the transaction in case the children need advice. The escrow agent should: (a) comply, since they are Susan's parents; (b) give them the information only if the seller agrees to it; (c) not give them the information since escrows are confidential; (d) obtain permission from the corporations commissioner.

7 An escrow company is: (a) bonded agency formed to arbitrate disputes between buyers and sellers in real estate transactions; (b) a neutral agency for the collection and disbursement of documents and monies; (c) a syndicate of real estate brokers; (d) both a and b.

8 A real estate broker may be an escrow holder for:
  a Any real estate transaction.
  b Any of his own real estate transactions.
  c Any real estate transaction involving the sale of a business opportunity.
  d None of these.

9 All private escrow holders are obligated to:
  a Furnish a surety bond in the amount of $5000.
  b Deposit funds in a separate trust account.
  c Submit annual audits to the corporation commissioner.
  d Do all of the above.

1 Only for people actively engaged in conducting an escrow agency including title companies.

2 No. The license must be held by a duly organized corporation.

3 (d) All are expressly forbidden by law in the Escrow Act.

4 (d) Regulations of the Real Estate Commission Article 19, Section 2950 govern these activities.

5 (d) The *Real Estate Reference Book,* 1975, page 119, stipulates that only the corporations commissioner can license an escrow corporation.

6 (c) Escrow information is highly confidential.

7 (b)

8 (b)

9 (d)

19

This unit is concerned with some of the reasons why an escrow is essential and the steps in opening an escrow, including the responsibilities of all parties involved.

The instructions given to the parties to the escrow, the buyer, and seller are presented and the obligations of each are explained.

The general escrow rules, including closing statements and closing costs, are explored so that as a buyer or seller you may understand the steps needed in opening and closing an escrow.

Read this study guide (pages 162–177).
View the TV program, number 19.

At the conclusion of this unit, you will be able to:

1 Explain the importance of an escrow and list five advantages of an escrow.

2 List the steps necessary in an escrow transaction.

3 Explain the procedure involved in opening an escrow.

4 Complete an escrow statement form and be able to explain the entries therein.

5 Compute the closing costs involved in an escrow procedure.

buyer's instructions   recordation
seller's instructions   beneficiary
prorations   settlement sheet
closing costs   trust fund

WHY IS AN ESCROW NECESSARY?

If you decide to buy a TV set, you go to an appliance store, select the set you want, and pay for it with cash or charge it to your account.

Do you ever give a second thought as to whether or not the store has a right to sell the product to you or whether or not you need written evidence of your right to own the appliance?

No—it becomes a simple sales transaction.

Not so with a real estate transaction—the procedure is not quite so simplified.

The seller could sign over a simple deed of conveyance and deliver to the buyer in exchange for the purchase price. However, neither the buyer nor the seller would agree to such an arrangement. Why not?

BECAUSE:

Title to the proper may be encumbered. The buyer needs someone to make a title search to clear the title.

An accurate description of the property is necessary for legal purposes.

The buyer needs an experienced person to prepare the instrument of conveyance for his signature.

The buyer needs assurance that his instructions have been carried out and the deed delivered only when all terms of the contract have been met.

WHAT ARE THE ADVANTAGES OF AN ESCROW?

What, then, are the distinct advantages of using a neutral third party in the transaction?

ADVANTAGES:

An escrow provides a custodian of papers, instructions, funds, and documents until the transaction is closed.

It makes possible the handling of accounting details in a professional manner.

It assures the validity of a binding contract between participating parties.

It is of value to the buyer, assuring him that his monies will not be used until the title is cleared.

It is of value to the seller, assuring him that the deed will not be delivered until the monies have been paid and all other terms and conditions have been met.

HOW IS AN ESCROW OPENED?

The steps in opening an escrow may vary, depending on the location in the northern or southern part of the state. There is a general order to follow in any case, however.

The broker will usually open the escrow after obtaining a completed deposit receipt signed by all concerned parties.

The real estate broker prepares the escrow instructions or requests the escrow agent to do so.

Escrow instructions are signed by all parties to the contract.

The escrow agent orders a title search from a title company, which sends its report to escrow.

The real estate broker will either prepare a deed or have escrow prepare one.

Buyer's and seller's instructions, along with the deed and the buyer's deposit, are sent to escrow.

NOTE

Communities will usually vary in their escrow procedure. However, a title or escrow company uses forms for instructions, while a bank or other authorized agency may issue instructions by letter.

Buyers will, if required, go to the lending institution to sign a note and a deed of trust prepared by the lender.

HOW IS AN ESCROW CLOSED?

When instructions have been completed and monies have been deposited and arranged for, the escrow arrangements are complete.

The basic steps in closing an escrow are as follows.

1 A statement showing the condition of indebtedness and the unpaid balance of the loan is requested from the beneficiary, the lender.

2 When the escrow agent receives all the funds, documents, and instructions necessary to close the escrow, he then makes any necessary adjustments and prorations on a settlement sheet.

3 All instruments pertinent to the transaction are then sent to the title insurance company for recording.

CAUTION

> At this point, *time* becomes an important factor.

4 The title search is run as late as the close of business on the date set for close of escrow and, if no changes have taken place, the deed and other instruments are recorded on the following morning at 8:00 A.M. Thus a title policy can be issued with the assurance that there are no intervening matters of record against the real property involved since the last search.

5 On the day the deed is recorded, the escrow agent may disburse funds to the parties as their interests appear.

6 The escrow agent presents closing statements to the parties who should receive them.

7 The title insurance company tries to issue a policy of title insurance on the day of recordation.

8 Shortly thereafter the recorded deed is sent to the escrow agent for forwarding to the *buyer*.

In Northern California, essentially the same steps are taken; however, the title company issues the policy of title insurance, arranges for the recording, and performs all other escrow functions as well.

(The title insurance policy will be explained later in the unit.)

In Southern California, independent escrow companies perform these duties.

WHAT COMPRISES ESCROW INSTRUCTIONS?

CAUTION

> The escrow must act according to the instructions from the various parties defining the authority of the escrow.

As the buyer and seller meet together at escrow, instructions are agreed on and entered on basic forms or worksheets.

One such worksheet (Figure 1) is presented at the conclusion of this unit for your information along with a brief explanation of the entries to be made. Each entry has been numbered for better clarification. Items 1–14 of the following explanation relate to Figure 1, page 171.

EXPLANATION OF INSTRUCTION SHEET

1 Type of transaction
Sale—Loan—Exchange for $_____

2 Total consideration
Total amount of transaction deposit plus any later payments

3 Time limit
Agreeable closing time for escrow

4 First party
Seller's name and address

5 Second party
Buyer's name and address

6 Type of title insurance policy
CLTA—standard or extended coverage

7 An exact description
''Legal'' description, not street address

8 Vest in (title vesting)
Names of the ''new'' owners insured in title policy

9 Subject to
A ⎫
B ⎪ Includes all matters that buyer approves
C ⎬ as liens and encumbrances against property
D ⎭

10 Adjustments
Adjustments are made on the premise that seller remains the owner until title has passed. He continues to bear expenses, taxes, interest, and the like. Instructions provide that rents, interest, taxes, and insurance be prorated between buyer and seller.

11 Charges
Includes title policy premium, escrow fee, and other costs. These charges are divided as per agreement.

12 Transfer tax
State tax to be paid at time of recording

13 Commission
For the protection of the broker, as a seller, you authorize the escrow to pay a commission to the real estate broker directly.

This item will list the name of the real estate broker to whom the commission will be paid.

14 Other payments

To be paid at close of escrow

Seller will authorize payments of other encumbrances for which he is obligated at the close of escrow.

ITEMS INCIDENTAL TO THE ESCROW TRANSACTION AND PART OF ESCROW INSTRUCTION

These include:

1 Trust fund.

2 Balance of existing loan.

3 Reconveyance fee.

4 Title insurance.

5 Prorations.

6 Closing costs.

TRUST FUND

For the protection of the lender, when a real estate loan is made, monthly payments for taxes and fire insurance may be required; this is called an ''impound account.'' An estimate is made by the *lender* of needed funds for taxes and insurance, which vary from year to year. A deposit may be required equal to one or more months' taxes. These funds constitute a ''trust fund.''

When the sale of the property is made and you pay off the loan, the seller is entitled to the unused portion of the ''trust fund.''

BALANCE OF EXISTING LOAN

If an existing loan is to be paid or assumed by the buyer, the escrow will obtain a ''beneficiary statement'' that shows the exact balance due from the one holding the ''deed of trust'' so that the proper amount may be paid, or so that the buyer can receive the proper amount of credit if the loan is to be assumed by the buyer.

RECONVEYANCE FEE

If the seller has a loan that is not being assumed by the buyer, the loan must be paid off in order to clear the title.

The seller instructs the escrow to pay off the loan, for which he receives a ''deed of reconveyance.'' A reconveyance fee is charged the seller for this service.

CAUTION

The sum due the lender is entered in the seller's escrow instructions as an estimate; the final figure will not be known until the final computations are made by the lender at the time of closing.

WHAT IS TITLE INSURANCE?

A title insurance policy is a contract of indemnity that insures the ownership of real property, subject to any encumbrances and other items that may cloud the title.

The buyer is assured that a thorough search has been made of all public records affecting the property being purchased.

This insurance covers county data and also applies to:

Federal records.

State records.

Lien-levying agencies, such as tax and assessment districts and homeowners' associations.

WHAT ARE OFF-RECORD RISKS? A title policy protects against "off-record" defects that are not disclosed in the search of public records.

EXAMPLES

Forged deeds.

Incompetency of parties
(minorities, insanity, deaths).

Status of parties
(community property rights, etc.).

BASIC GROUPS OF POLICIES **STANDARD POLICY**

An owner's policy insures the owner for amount of purchase price.
A lender's policy insures the lender for the amount of the loan.
A joint protection policy insures both the owner and the lender under one policy.

INCLUDED IN THE STANDARD POLICY The policy assures that title is free and clear of all encumbrances of public record.

EXCLUDED FROM STANDARD POLICY The policy excludes:

Physical inspection of property.

Zoning assessments not yet liens.

Sewer charges.

Mining claims.

Water rights.

Land patents.

A loss caused by the owner or by defects known to him.

WHAT IS EXTENDED COVERAGE INSURANCE? It is primarily for the benefit of lenders. A physical inspection of property is required.

It is frequently used by out-of-state lenders who can't inspect properties on which they are making loans.

It is more expensive.

WHAT DOES TITLE INSURANCE DO FOR YOU? It assures you of a thorough examination of all public records.

It insures you, the buyer, of acquiring an undisputed title, clear of defects and subject only to encumbrances revealed in the title examination.

It means the buyer has a marketable title.

At the conclusion of this unit is a sample title insurance policy (Figure 2).

WHAT ARE PRORATIONS AND CLOSING COSTS?

The amount that the buyer must pay beyond the purchase price, such as loan charges, recording charges, prorations on taxes, insurance, interest and other financial items that require adjustments.

TAXES   Taxes usually require proration. If, for example, the seller had paid only the first installment of his taxes in a given year, this would cover the months during which he had the property, resulting in a credit to the seller. If the period for which the taxes had been paid was not fully used up, all credit for taxes due would be given to the buyer, on a prorated basis.

INTEREST   If the buyer assumes a fire insurance policy that has not yet expired, the seller is entitled to a prorated refund of the unused premium.

RENTS   Rents will be prorated in those cases involving income producing properties.

When the title has cleared, the escrow becomes the agent of the *seller* and the *buyer*—to the seller as to money and to the buyer as to the deed.

QUESTION

Is an escrow cancelled by the death or incapacity of a party during the escrow procedure?

No. The competent party may compel completion of the transaction against the incompetent's personal representative.

THE ESCROW IS COMPLETE WHEN:

Escrow sends the deed and deeds of trust to the recorder's office for recordation. This offers protection to the *buyer* as to his title and the *lender* as to his lien.

Escrow sends the closing statement to the *seller* and the *buyer* showing disbursement of funds.

Escrow issues its title policy insuring the buyer of clear title, sending the original copy to the *lender* and a copy to the *buyer*.

UNIT SUMMARY

In this unit, you learned that the escrow procedure is necessary in order to protect the rights and privileges of buyers and sellers and to spell out the obligations of each in a real property transaction.

The step-by-step procedure in opening and closing an escrow was explained.

By use of a sample instruction sheet the parts of the form were listed, and each item was explained in terms of its position in the written instructions.

Title insurance, as a protection to the buyer, was explained and the difference between a standard policy and extended coverage insurance were noted.

REVIEWING YOUR UNDERSTANDING

MULTIPLE CHOICE

(   ) **1** A complete and accurate history of the ownership of a property is known as (a) an abstract, (b) a title flow, (c) a chain of title, (d) a title policy.

(   ) **2** A binding contract and conditional delivery of transfer documents are the elements of:
  a a binding escrow
  b a valid escrow
  c a perfect escrow
  d a complete escrow

(   ) **3** An escrow agent is most likely subject to disciplinary action if he:
  a refuses to pay a commission to the broker referring the escrow
  b holds funds after close of escrow
  c refuses to handle an escrow
  d accepts escrow instructions with blanks to be filled in by him after instructions have been signed

(   ) **4** Title insurance does not protect a buyer against:
  a zoning restrictions
  b unrecorded easements
  c forgery in the chain of title
  d lack of capacity of any grantor in the chain of title

(   ) **5** A title insurance company is least likely to inspect property for:
  a a standard policy
  b an ATA policy
  c an extended coverage policy
  d none of these

TRUE OR FALSE

(   ) **1** An escrow agent must be a neutral third party and cannot give legal advice.

(   ) **2** It is common practice for a real estate broker to open the escrow.

(   ) **3** Escrow instructions are legally required and must be followed to the letter.

(   ) **4** The seller's instructions include authorization to the escrow to pay commissions directly to the real estate broker.

(   ) **5** "Closing costs" include those costs over and above the purchase price, such as loan charges, recording charges, and other prorations that a buyer must pay when buying real estate.

SUGGESTED LEARNING ACTIVITIES

Visit an escrow or title company to observe the procedure involved in an escrow.

REVIEWING YOUR UNDERSTANDING—ANSWERS

MULTIPLE CHOICE

1 (c)	**3** (d)	**5** (a)
2 (b)	**4** (a)	

TRUE OR FALSE

1 True

2 True

3 True

4 True

5 True

(1) SALE - LOAN - EXCHANGE_____

CASH THROUGH ESCROW   NOW $_____
                       LATER $_____

MTG - TRUST DEED _____ $_____

MTG - TRUST DEED _____ $_____

CASH OUTSIDE OF ESCROW $_____

(2) TOTAL CONSIDERATION $_____

ON **(7)** _____

VEST IN **(8)** _____

(3) TIME LIMIT _____

FIRST PARTY **(4)** _____
ADDRESS _____

SECOND PARTY **(5)** _____
ADDRESS _____

(6) ISSUE: (CLTA) JT PRO; OWNER'S; LOAN; ATA; LEASEHOLD;_____ FOR $_____

SUBJECT TO____ **(9a)** GENERAL AND SPECIAL TAX 19_____ 19_____; _____ BONDS AND ASSESSMENT

(9b) COVENANTS, CONDITIONS, RESTRICTIONS, AND EASEMENTS OF RECORD _____

(9c) MORTGAGE - TRUST DEED (OF RECORD)_____ FORM EXECUTED BY _____

TO SECURE A NOTE FOR $_____ PAYABLE IN INSTALLMENTS TO _____

AT_____ WITH INTEREST FROM_____ ON UNPAID PRINCIPAL AT_____% PER ANNUM (PAYABLE_____

PRINCIPAL (AND INTEREST) PAYABLE IN INSTALLMENTS OF $_____ OR MORE ON THE_____ DAY OF EACH_____ MONTH

BEGINNING_____ MATURITY DATE_____ PREPAYMENT PRIVILEGE_____

PRESENT UNPAID BALANCE $ _____

(9d) MORTGAGE - TRUST DEED (OF RECORD)_____ FORM, EXECUTED BY_____

TO SECURE A NOTE FOR $_____ PAYABLE IN INSTALLMENTS TO _____

AT_____ WITH INTEREST FROM_____ ON UNPAID PRINCIPAL AT_____% PER ANNUM (PAYABLE_____

PRINCIPAL (AND INTEREST) PAYABLE IN INSTALLMENTS OF $_____ OR MORE ON THE_____ DAY OF EACH_____ MONTH

BEGINNING_____ MATURITY DATE_____ PREPAYMENT PRIVILEGE_____

PRESENT UNPAID BALANCE $ _____

(9)

ADJUSTMENTS

TAXES AS OF **(10a)** _____

    BASIS _____

INSURANCE AS OF **(10b)** _____

INTEREST AS OF **(10c)** _____

    BASIS **(10d)** _____

RENTS AS OF_____

    BASIS _____

WATER STOCK & SEC'Y STATEMENT _____

_____

WE DRAW_____

(10)

PAYMENTS

CHARGES PAID BY **(11)** _____

TRANSFER TAX $_____ **(12)** TAX SERVICE _____

COMM. $ **(13)** _____ TO _____

ADDRESS _____ BROKER No._____

TAXES_____ TAX SALES_____ ASSESSMENTS_____

PAY THE FOLLOWING AT CLOSE OF ESCROW **(14)** _____

_____

ESCROW OPENED AND CHARGES GUARANTEED BY }_____

REMARKS_____

FIGURE 1

FIGURE 2
Policy of title insurance

TO 1012 FC (5.72)
California Land Title Association
Standard Coverage Policy Form
Copyright 1963

POLICY OF TITLE INSURANCE

ISSUED BY

Title Insurance and Trust Company

Title Insurance and Trust Company, a California corporation, herein called the Company, for a valuable consideration paid for this policy, the number, the effective date, and amount of which are shown in Schedule A, hereby insures the parties named as Insured in Schedule A, the heirs, devisees, personal representatives of such Insured, or if a corporation, its successors by dissolution, merger or consolidation, against loss or damage not exceeding the amount stated in Schedule A, together with costs, attorneys' fees and expenses which the Company may become obligated to pay as provided in the Conditions and Stipulations hereof, which the Insured shall sustain by reason of:

1. Any defect in or lien or encumbrance on the title to the estate or interest covered hereby in the land described or referred to in Schedule C, existing at the date hereof, not shown or referred to in Schedule B or excluded from coverage in Schedule B or in the Conditions and Stipulations; or

2. Unmarketability of such title; or

3. Any defect in the execution of any mortgage shown in Schedule B securing an indebtedness, the owner of which is named as an Insured in Schedule A, but only insofar as such defect affects the lien or charge of said mortgage upon the estate or interest referred to in this policy; or

4. Priority over said mortgage, at the date hereof, of any lien or encumbrance not shown or referred to in Schedule B, or excluded from coverage in the Conditions and Stipulations, said mortgage being shown in Schedule B in the order of its priority;

all subject, however, to the provisions of Schedules A, B and C and to the Conditions and Stipulations hereto annexed.

In Witness Whereof, Title Insurance and Trust Company has caused its corporate name and seal to be hereunto affixed by its duly authorized officers on the date shown in Schedule A.

Title Insurance and Trust Company

by John Baker Butler
PRESIDENT

Attest Charles F. Stahl
SECRETARY

FIGURE 2 (Continued) **CONDITIONS AND STIPULATIONS**

1. DEFINITION OF TERMS

The following terms when used in this policy mean:

(a) "land": the land described, specifically or by reference, in Schedule C and improvements affixed thereto which by law constitute real property;

(b) "public records": those records which impart constructive notice of matters relating to said land;

(c) "knowledge": actual knowledge, not constructive knowledge or notice which may be imputed to the Insured by reason of any public records;

(d) "date": the effective date;

(e) "mortgage": mortgage, deed of trust, trust deed, or other security instrument; and

(f) "insured": the party or parties named as Insured, and if the owner of the indebtedness secured by a mortgage shown in Schedule B is named as an Insured in Schedule A, the Insured shall include (1) each successor in interest in ownership of such indebtedness, (2) any such owner who acquires the estate or interest referred to in this policy by foreclosure, trustee's sale, or other legal manner in satisfaction of said indebtedness, and (3) any federal agency or instrumentality which is an insurer or guarantor under an insurance contract or guaranty insuring or guaranteeing said indebtedness, or any part thereof, whether named as an insured herein or not, subject otherwise to the provisions hereof.

2. BENEFITS AFTER ACQUISITION OF TITLE

If an insured owner of the indebtedness secured by a mortgage described in Schedule B acquires said estate or interest, or any part thereof, by foreclosure, trustee's sale, or other legal manner in satisfaction of said indebtedness, or any part thereof, or if a federal agency or instrumentality acquires said estate or interest, or any part thereof, as a consequence of an insurance contract or guaranty insuring or guaranteeing the indebtedness secured by a mortgage covered by this policy, or any part thereof, this policy shall continue in force in favor of such Insured, agency or instrumentality, subject to all of the conditions and stipulations hereof.

3. EXCLUSIONS FROM THE COVERAGE OF THIS POLICY

This policy does not insure against loss or damage by reasons of the following:

(a) Any law, ordinance or governmental regulation (including but not limited to building and zoning ordinances) restricting or regulating or prohibiting the occupancy, use or enjoyment of the land, or regulating the character, dimensions, or location of any improvement now or hereafter erected on said land, or prohibiting a separation in ownership or a reduction in the dimensions or area of any lot or parcel of land.

(b) Governmental rights of police power or eminent domain unless notice of the exercise of such rights appears in the public records at the date hereof.

(c) Title to any property beyond the lines of the land expressly described in Schedule C, or title to streets, roads, avenues, lanes, ways or waterways on which such land abuts, or the right to maintain therein vaults, tunnels, ramps or any other structure or improvement; or any rights or easements therein unless this policy specifically provides that such property rights or easements are insured, except that if the land abuts upon one or more physically open streets or highways this policy insures the ordinary rights of abutting owners for access to one of such streets or highways, unless otherwise excepted or excluded herein.

(d) Defects, liens, encumbrances, adverse claims against the title as insured or other matters (1) created, suffered, assumed or agreed to by the Insured claiming loss or damage; or (2) known to the Insured Claimant either at the date of this policy or at the date such Insured Claimant acquired an estate or interest insured by this policy and not shown by the public records, unless disclosure thereof in writing by the Insured shall have been made to the Company prior to the date of this policy; or (3) resulting in no loss to the Insured Claimant; or (4) attaching or created subsequent to the date hereof.

(e) Loss or damage which would not have been sustained if the Insured were a purchaser or encumbrancer for value without knowledge.

4. DEFENSE AND PROSECUTION OF ACTIONS—NOTICE OF CLAIM TO BE GIVEN BY THE INSURED

(a) The Company, at its own cost and without undue delay shall provide (1) for the defense of the insured in all litigation consisting of actions or proceedings commenced against the Insured, or defenses, restraining orders, or injunctions interposed against a foreclosure or sale of the mortgage and indebtedness covered by this policy or a sale of the estate or interest in said land; or

FIGURE 2 (Continued)

(2) for such action as may be appropriate to establish the title of the estate or interest or the lien of the mortgage as insured, which litigation or action in any of such events is founded upon an alleged defect, lien or encumbrance insured against by this policy, and may pursue any litigation to final determination in the court of last resort.

(b) In case any such action or proceeding shall be begun, or defense interposed, or in case knowledge shall come to the Insured of any claim of title or interest which is adverse to the title of the estate or interest or lien of the mortgage as insured, or which might cause loss or damage for which the Company shall or may be liable by virtue of this policy, or if the Insured shall in good faith contract to sell the indebtedness secured by a mortgage covered by this policy, or, if an Insured in good faith leases or contracts to sell, lease or mortgage the same, or if the successful bidder at a foreclosure sale under a mortgage covered by this policy refuses to purchase and in any such event the title to said estate or interest is rejected as unmarketable, the Insured shall notify the Company thereof in writing. If such notice shall not be given to the Company within ten days of the receipt of process or pleadings or if the Insured shall not, in writing, promptly notify the Company of any defect, lien or encumbrance insured against which shall come to the knowledge of the Insured, or if the Insured shall not, in writing promptly notify the Company of any such rejection by reason unclaimed unmarketability of the Company in regard to the subject matter of such action, proceeding or matter shall cease and terminate; provided, however, that failure to notify shall in no case prejudice the claim of any Insured unless the Company shall be actually prejudiced by such failure and then only to the extent of such prejudice.

(c) The Company shall have the right at its own cost to institute and prosecute any action or proceeding or do any other act which in its opinion may be necessary or desirable to establish the title of the estate or interest or the lien of the mortgage as insured; and the Company may take any appropriate action under the terms of this policy whether or not it shall be liable thereunder and shall not thereby concede liability or waive any provision of this policy.

(d) In all cases where this policy permits or requires the Company to prosecute or provide for the defense of any action or proceeding, the Insured shall secure to it, the right to so prosecute or provide defense in such action or proceeding, and all appeals therein, and permit it to use, at its option, the name of the Insured for such purpose.

Whenever requested by the Company the Insured shall give the Company all reasonable aid in any such action or proceeding, in effecting settlement, securing evidence, obtaining witnesses, or prosecuting or defending such action or proceeding, and the Company shall reimburse the Insured for any expense so incurred.

5. NOTICE OF LOSS—LIMITATION OF ACTION

In addition to the notices required under paragraph 4(b), a statement in writing of any loss or damage for which it is claimed the Company is liable under this policy shall be furnished to the Company within sixty days after such loss or damage shall have been determined and no right to action shall accrue to the Insured under this policy until thirty days after such statement shall have been furnished, and no recovery shall be had by the Insured under this policy unless action shall be commenced thereon within five years after expiration of said thirty day period. Failure to furnish such statement of loss or damage, or to commence such action within the time hereinbefore specified, shall be a conclusive bar against maintenance by the Insured of any action under this policy.

6. OPTION TO PAY, SETTLE OR COMPROMISE CLAIMS

The Company shall have the option to pay or settle or compromise for or in the name of the Insured any claim insured against or to pay the full amount of this policy, or, in case loss is claimed under this policy by the owner of the indebtedness secured by a mortgage covered by this policy, the Company shall have the option to purchase said indebtedness; such purchase, payment or tender of payment of the full amount of this policy, together with all costs, attorneys' fees and expenses which the Company is obligated hereunder to pay, shall terminate all liability of the Company hereunder. In the event, after notice of claim has been given to the Company by the Insured, the Company offers to purchase said indebtedness, the owner of such indebtedness shall transfer and assign said indebtedness and the mortgage securing the same to the Company upon payment of the purchase price.

7. PAYMENT OF LOSS

(a) The liability of the Company under this policy shall in no case exceed, in all, the actual loss of the Insured and costs and attorneys' fees which the Company may be obligated hereunder to pay.

FIGURE 2 (Continued)

(b) The Company will pay, in addition to any loss insured against by this policy, all costs imposed upon the Insured in litigation carried on by the Company for the Insured, and all costs and attorneys' fees in litigation carried on by the Insured with the written authorization of the Company.

(c) No claim for damages shall arise or be maintainable under this policy (1) if the Company, after having received notice of an alleged defect, lien or encumbrance not excepted or excluded herein removes such defect, lien or encumbrance within a reasonable time after receipt of such notice, or (2) for liability voluntarily assumed by the Insured in settling any claim or suit without written consent of the Company, or (3) in the event the title is rejected as unmarketable because of a defect, lien or encumbrance not excepted or excluded in this policy, until there has been a final determination by a court of competent jurisdiction sustaining such rejection.

(d) All payments under this policy, except payments made for costs, attorneys' fees and expenses, shall reduce the amount of the insurance pro tanto and no payment shall be made without producing this policy for endorsement of such payment unless the policy be lost or destroyed, in which case proof of such loss or destruction shall be furnished to the satisfaction of the Company; provided, however, if the owner of an indebtedness secured by a mortgage shown in Schedule B is an Insured herein then such payments shall not reduce pro tanto the amount of the insurance afforded hereunder as to such Insured, except to the extent that such payments reduce the amount of the indebtedness secured by such mortgage. Payment in full by any person or voluntary satisfaction or release by the Insured of a mortgage covered by this policy shall terminate all liability of the Company to the insured owner of the indebtedness secured by such mortgage, except as provided in paragraph 2 hereof.

(e) When liability has been definitely fixed in accordance with the conditions of this policy the loss or damage shall be payable within thirty days thereafter.

8. LIABILITY NONCUMULATIVE

It is expressly understood that the amount of this policy is reduced by any amount the Company may pay under any policy insuring the validity or priority of any mortgage shown or referred to in Schedule B hereof or any mortgage hereafter executed by the Insured which is a charge or lien on the estate or interest described or referred to in Schedule A, and the amount so paid shall be deemed a payment to the Insured

under this policy. The provisions of this paragraph numbered 8 shall not apply to an Insured owner of an indebtedness secured by a mortgage shown in Schedule B unless such Insured acquires title to said estate or interest in satisfaction of said indebtedness or any part thereof.

9. SUBROGATION UPON PAYMENT OR SETTLEMENT

Whenever the Company shall have settled a claim under this policy, all right of subrogation shall vest in the Company unaffected by any act of the Insured, and it shall be subrogated to and be entitled to all rights and remedies which the Insured would have had against any person or property in respect to such claim had this policy not been issued. If the payment does not cover the loss of the Insured, the Company shall be subrogated to such rights and remedies in the proportion which said payment bears to the amount of said loss. If loss should result from any act of the Insured, such act shall not void this policy, but the Company, in that event, shall be required to pay only that part of any losses insured against hereunder which shall exceed the amount, if any, lost to the Company by reason of the impairment of the right of subrogation. The Insured, if requested by the Company, shall transfer to the Company all rights and remedies against any person or property necessary in order to perfect such right of subrogation, and shall permit the Company to use the name of the Insured in any transaction or litigation involving such rights or remedies.

If the Insured is the owner of the indebtedness secured by a mortgage covered by this policy, such Insured may release or substitute the personal liability of any debtor or guarantor, or extend or otherwise modify the terms of payment, or release a portion of the estate or interest from the lien of the mortgage, or release any collateral security for the indebtedness, provided such act does not result in any loss of priority of the lien of the mortgage.

10. POLICY ENTIRE CONTRACT

Any action or actions or rights of action that the Insured may have or may bring against the Company arising out of the status of the lien of the mortgage covered by this policy or the title of the estate or interest insured herein must be based on the provisions of this policy.

No provision or condition of this policy can be waived or changed except by writing endorsed hereon or attached hereto signed by the President, a Vice President, the Secretary, an Assistant Secretary or other validating officer of the Company.

FIGURE 2 *(Continued)*

11. NOTICES, WHERE SENT

All notices required to be given the Company and any statement in writing required to be furnished the Company shall be addressed to it at the office which issued this policy or to its Home Office, 433 South Spring Street, Los Angeles, California 90051.

12. THE PREMIUM SPECIFIED IN SCHEDULE A IS THE ENTIRE CHARGE FOR TITLE SEARCH, TITLE EXAMINATION AND TITLE INSURANCE.

121470022	K	23

ALTA LOAN POLICY—1970 WITH STREET IMPROVEMENT ASSESSMENT COVERAGE OR CALIFORNIA LAND TITLE ASSOCIATION STANDARD COVERAGE POLICY—1963

SCHEDULE A

PREMIUM   : $126.20
AMOUNT   : $25,000.00
EFFECTIVE DATE: FEBRUARY 10, 1971 at 8:00 A.M.
POLICY NUMBER: 4410980

INSURED

JOHN STRONG AND HELEN STRONG:

1. TITLE TO THE ESTATE OR INTEREST COVERED BY THIS POLICY AT THE DATE HEREOF IS VESTED IN:

    JOHN STRONG AND HELEN STRONG, HUSBAND AND WIFE, AS JOINT TENANTS.

2. THE ESTATE OR INTEREST IN THE LAND DESCRIBED OR REFERRED TO IN SCHEDULE C COVERED BY THIS POLICY IS A FEE.

SCHEDULE B

THIS POLICY DOES NOT INSURE AGAINST LOSS OR DAMAGE BY REASON OF THE FOLLOWING:

PART ONE

ALL MATTERS SET FORTH IN PARAGRAPHS NUMBERED 1 TO 5 INCLUSIVE ON THE INSIDE COVER SHEET OF THIS POLICY UNDER THE HEADING SCHEDULE B PART ONE.

PART TWO

1. GENERAL AND SPECIAL COUNTY AND CITY TAXES FOR THE FISCAL YEAR 1970–1971

SECOND INSTALLMENT: $240.00

2. AN EASEMENT AFFECTING THE PORTION OF SAID LAND AND FOR THE PURPOSES STATED HEREIN, AND INCIDENTAL PURPOSES,

IN FAVOR OF   : SOUTHERN CALIFORNIA EDISON COMPANY, A CORPORATION
FOR   : POLE LINES
RECORDED   : JANUARY 12, 1953 IN BOOK 40710 PAGE 117, OFFICIAL RECORDS
AFFECTS   : THE NORTH 6 FEET

FIGURE 2 (Continued)

121470022   K   23

ALTA LOAN POLICY—1970 WITH STREET IMPROVEMENT ASSESSMENT COVERAGE OR CALIFORNIA LAND TITLE ASSOCIATION STANDARD COVERAGE POLICY—1963

3. AN EASEMENT AFFECTING THE PORTION OF SAID LAND AND FOR THE PURPOSES STATED HEREIN, AND INCIDENTAL PURPOSES,

IN FAVOR OF   : ASSOCIATED TELEPHONE COMPANY, LTD., A CORPORATION

FOR   : POLE LINES AND CONDUITS

RECORDED   : JANUARY 20, 1953 IN BOOK 40777 PAGE 256, OFFICIAL RECORDS

AFFECTS   : THE NORTH 6 FEET

4. AN EASEMENT AFFECTING THE PORTION OF SAID LAND AND FOR THE PURPOSES STATED HEREIN, AND INCIDENTAL PURPOSES, DISCLOSED BY A DECLARATION OF RESTRICTIONS

EXECUTED BY : EMPIRE BUILDERS

FOR   : UTILITY INSTALLATION AND MAINTENANCE

RECORDED   : FEBRUARY 25, 1953 IN BOOK 41053 PAGE 360, OFFICIAL RECORDS

AFFECTS   : THE REAR 6 FEET

5. COVENANTS, CONDITIONS AND RESTRICTIONS IN THE DECLARATION OF RESTRICTIONS ABOVE MENTIONED.

WHICH PROVIDE THAT A VIOLATION THEREOF SHALL NOT DEFEAT OR RENDER INVALID THE LIEN OF ANY MORTGAGE OR DEED OF TRUST MADE IN GOOD FAITH AND FOR VALUE.

RESTRICTIONS, IF ANY, BASED ON RACE, COLOR, RELIGION OR NATIONAL ORIGIN ARE DELETED.

SCHEDULE C

THE LAND REFERRED TO IN THIS POLICY IS SITUATED IN THE COUNTY OF LOS ANGELES, STATE OF CALIFORNIA, AND IS DESCRIBED AS FOLLOWS:

LOT 22 OF TRACT NO. 18268, IN THE CITY OF WEST COVINA, IN THE COUNTY OF LOS ANGELES, STATE OF CALIFORNIA, AS PER MAP RECORDED IN BOOK 451 PAGES 24 AND 25 OF MAPS, IN THE OFFICE OF THE COUNTY RECORDER OF SAID COUNTY.

20

This unit will discuss the ownership of real property, including the ways in which a purchasor may take title to that property.

Either an individual or a corporation may take title in the same manner; this constitutes individual ownership. This is explained to help you decide that decision that best fits your desires and needs.

The co-ownership features of title possession are covered, including those ownerships between man and wife; the characteristics of each are pointed out, so that the proper decision regarding taking title can be made.

Read the study guide (pages 180–187).
View TV program, number 20.

At the conclusion of this unit, you will be able to:

1 Distinguish between the following methods of holding title;
a Ownership in severalty.
b Joint tenancy.
c Tenancy in common. Undivided interest.
d Tenancy in partnership.
e Tenancy by the entirety.
2 List some advantages and disadvantages of each method of holding title.
3 Identify the fourfold unity existing in joint tenancy and be able to explain the meaning of each.
4 Define ''separate property'' as it is described in the California Civil Code.
5 Define right of survivorship as it applies to holding title.

ownership in severalty   tenancy in common
joint tenancy   community property
unity of interest   separate property
unity of title   chain of title
unity of time   certificate of title
unity of possession   abstract of title
right of survivorship

All property must have an owner. It must be owned by either the federal, state, or local government, or by some private institution or party. In this unit we are particularly concerned with ownership by private persons.

Title to real property can be held by one person alone or by two or more persons together. To avoid difficulties you might encounter in conjunction with real estate transactions, it is necessary for you to understand the various ways in which property may be owned.

If title is held by one person or corporation, it is termed an estate or ownership in severalty. If title is held by persons jointly, they may take title as tenancy in common, joint tenancy, tenancy in partnership, or as community property.

OWNERSHIP IN SEVERALTY This term applies to that condition wherein an individual (corporation with the same rights and privileges as an individual) owns property without anyone else having an interest in it. As indicated, this may apply to a corporation as well. (In the eyes of the law, a corporation is an individual.)

An individual or corporation (through its board of directors) may acquire, lease, and convey property, and may borrow money using the property as security. The individual or corporation may also enter into contracts or do anything incidental to the transaction of business, including becoming a party to a mortgage or deed of trust.

JOINT TENANCY When two or more persons own real property jointly with equal ownership rights and undivided interest, where no one owns any specific part of the property, it is known as *joint tenancy*.

A fourfold unity is created when the condition exists where each owner has exactly the same rights as any other.

This fourfold unity includes unity of *interest*, unity of *title*, unity of *time*, and unity of *possession*.

Unity of Interest. Means that each tenant has the same interest in the property—in other words their interest is equal. For example, if there are two owners, each owns one-half; if there are three owners, each owns one-third.

Unity of Title. Means that the joint tenants must own in the same manner evidenced by the same conveyance or means of title transfer and have equal rights to the property.

Unity of Time. Means that, on the part of each owner, he possesses his interest and his title at one and the same time.

Unity of Possession. Means that each tenant has an equal right to possession over the whole of the property.

It may be said, then, that joint tenants have one and the same interest, accruing by one and the same conveyance, commencing at one and the same time, and enjoyed by one and the same possession.

In addition to the four unities, the most important characteristic of joint tenancy is the right of survivorship. Survivorship is the right possessed by the surviving tenant or tenants to succeed automatically to the interest of a tenant who dies.

The right of survivorship is often known as the "grand incident of the joint tenancy."

EXAMPLE

When Mr. Miller and Mr. Sykes hold titles in joint tenancy and Mr. Miller dies, the title to the entire property passes to Mr. Sykes.

Because of this situation and the contingencies involved, many states have laws requiring that the words "joint tenancy" be definitely written in the deed. California does not require any specific language. However, the courts are aware of possible problems as to the status of the property and have established the rule that the true intention of husband and wife shall prevail over the record title.

EXAMPLE

If you are purchasing real property jointly with your wife and both of you wish to have the ownership go to one on the death of the other, you might consider taking title in *joint tenancy*.

Each joint tenant has the right to the use of the whole property. None can exclude the others or claim any specific portion for himself. If he receives rent from premises, he must divide the profits with others in accordance with interest owned. This also implies an equal sharing of tax payments, loan payments, and maintenance expenses.

CREATION OF JOINT TENANCY   A joint tenancy can be created by deed or by will.

The most common method is creation by deed. In any event, it must be declared to be a joint tenancy. Simple wording might be "To A and B as joint tenants, with right of survivorship."

It is possible for an owner in severalty to add the name of someone else to the records as joint tenant with himself. He would prepare a deed granting to himself and others as joint tenants. Other transfers may be made between tenants, including husband and wife.

TERMINATION OF JOINT TENANCY   If any of the essential unities cease to exist or are destroyed, joint tenancy will no longer exist.

A joint tenant may convey his interest to others, thus resulting in the termination of joint tenancy as far as his interest is concerned. If at any time the owners wish to terminate the joint tenancy arrangement and all are agreeable, joint tenancy would no longer exist and each tenant would then have and own an equal interest in severalty.

SURVIVORSHIP   A joint tenant cannot will his property, since his interest passes to surviving tenant or tenants upon his death.

POINT OF INTEREST

The surviving joint tenant takes the estate free from any creditor's claims or debts against the estate of the person who died. This may include tax liens or any judgment liens.

ADVANTAGES IN JOINT TENANCY The principle advantage is that of survivorship, which eliminates probate proceedings in the event of death and allows the surviving tenants a right to interest in the title free and clear from claims or debts.

Because of the simplicity of passing title to the surviving tenant, the usual delay of upward of 6 months as well as additional costs are avoided.

DISADVANTAGES OF JOINT TENANCY The disadvantages center around the area of taxation, specifically the obligation of income, gift, inheritance, and estate taxes on both federal and state levels. Joint tenancy can be a pitfall for the ignorant or unwary.

TENANCY IN COMMON

Tenancy in common exists when two or more persons are owners of an undivided interest in a single estate.

This type of ownership is created whenever an instrument conveying an interest in real property to two or more persons does not specify that the interest is acquired by them in joint tenancy, in partnership, or as community property.

EXAMPLE

The interest of any cotenant may be any fraction of the entire property. Thus, a parent could grant to his two sons and a daughter property with varied interests. To son A he may grant two-tenths, to son B four-tenths, and the remainder to his daughter. They would all hold their interest as tenants in common.

If you held ownership as a tenant in common, your share of the property cannot be identified, since your share is in the whole of the property. You own an undivided interest with others. In the event of your death or the death of any of the tenants, the right of survivorship does not apply. The remaining tenants do not acquire the property. The interests of any deceased tenant in common goes to the designated heirs.

All tenants have equal rights of possession. Any one is free to sell, convey, or transfer his interest as he sees fit; the new owner then becomes a tenant in common.

Tenancy in common differs from joint tenancy in regard to the four unities. It does not require three of the unities, unity of title, unity of interest, and unity of time. However, it does require unity of possession. This means that each tenant has a right to possession and, unless by mutual agreement of all tenants, none of them can exclude the others or claim any specific portion for himself.

EXAMPLE

If you are living in a home and hold ownership as a tenant in common, you are not responsible to pay rent to any of the cotenants; but if you rent to a third party, the proceeds must be divided among the tenants in proportion to the shares owned in the property.

When property is deeded to a husband and wife and no reference to title is made, it is presumed to be community property.

EXAMPLE

If a parent deeds property to child A and B, without specifying the extent of the interests of each, each will be presumed to have received an undivided one-half interest in the property. Interests do not have to be equal in tenancy in common; one tenant may own one-third and the other may own two-thirds.

TENANCY IN PARTNERSHIP

Real estate may be owned in partnership. The California Corporations Code defines a partnership as an association of two or more persons to carry on as co-owners a business for profit.

Under the Uniform Partnership Act in California:

1 A partner has an equal right with his other partners to possession of specific partnership property for partnership purposes only, and generally has no other rights of possession except by special agreement between the partners.

2 A partner's rights in specific partnership property are not assignable except in connection with the assignment of rights of all partners in the same property.

3 A partner's rights in specific partnership property are not subject to attachment or execution of a judgment based on a claim exclusively against him as an individual, but must be based on a claim against the partnership itself.

4 Upon the death of a partner, his rights in partnership real property rest in the surviving partner or partners. The heirs of the decedent are entitled to the value of his interest in the partnership at the time of his expiration.

TENANCY BY THE ENTIRETY

Most states have superseded the common law expressed in joint tenancy by statute that provides for joint tenancy rights of survivorship through *tenancy by the entirety*. This method is limited to husbands and wives only; neither spouse can transfer any interest during his or her joint life without the consent of the other.

Tenancy by entirety is not recognized in community property states, including California.

COMMUNITY PROPERTY

California is one of a number of states that has community property laws. These originated in old Spanish and Mexican rules about marital property. In a nutshell, these laws give both spouses equal interest in all property they accumulate by their *combined* efforts during their marriage. Under the California community property laws, the wife has equal rights to the husband in all cases; however, in some states the wife has little if any rights to property jointly accumulated by combined efforts.

WHAT ABOUT PROPERTY OWNED BEFORE MARRIAGE?   This is considered to be *separate property,* and each spouse can dispose of his interest or retain it as he wishes.

WHAT ABOUT PROPERTY CONVEYED BY WILL?   If either the husband or the wife receives property under a will or is given property, it is owned separately and may be dealt with as the spouse wishes.

REMEMBER

Property earned or acquired by husband and wife together is considered community property.

In the event that the value of *separate property* increases or there are any earnings from separate property, they belong to the spouse owning that interest.

EXAMPLE

If Mary Jones was willed an apartment house prior to her marriage to Jerry Jones, the rents received therefrom belong to Mrs. Jones as separate property.

Separate property is defined in the California Civil Code as follows:

1 All property owned by either husband or wife before marriage.

2 All property acquired by either spouse during marriage by gift or inheritance.

3 All rents and profits from separate property; proceeds from the sale of separate property; property acquired with the rents and profits of separate property.

4 The earnings and profits of the wife from her own business as a sole trader.

5 Earnings and accumulations of each party after rendition of a court decree of separate maintenance.

6 Money damages awarded to either spouse in a civil action for personal injuries.

PRESUMPTIONS MADE

1 All property acquired by husband and wife after marriage is presumed to be community property.

2 Property conveyed to a married man in his name alone is presumed to be *community property*, and the burden of proof is on the husband to show that the property is his separate property.

3 Property conveyed to a married woman in her name alone is presumed to be her separate property.

MANAGEMENT OF PROPERTY   The California Civil Code states that the husband and wife during the marriage have equal interests but under the management and control of the husband.

The husband may not give it away without his wife's written consent. He may dispose of it for a valuable consideration, but only with the wife's consent in writing.

Neither spouse may sell community real property without the consent of the other.

In managing the community real property, the husband cannot sell or mortgage community real property or lease it for more than a year without the written consent of the wife. The wife must join in executing any instrument by which community real property or any interest therein is leased for a longer period than 1 year, or is sold, conveyed, or encumbered.

OWNERSHIP IN GENERAL   Not only does all property have to be owned, but ownership of real property must be evidenced by a document in writing. This document is usually a deed or other instrument.

The land involved in any transaction must be described on the deed or conveyance so that there can be no mistake or misunderstanding about it.

The deed, too, must be recorded so that the title can be protected. There must also be a "chain of title" manifest; in other words, there must be an unbroken line of ownership of the land from the beginning.

The ownership of any property is governed by the laws of the state where the property is located, not the laws of the state where the owner lives.

In Unit 24 a more detailed discussion of deeds is given.

Before concluding this unit, there are several important definitions regarding titles that will assist in your understanding of the unit title, "How Should You Take Title?"

CERTIFICATE OF TITLE This is an opinion on the condition of the title after examination of the records. It differs from the guarantee of title in that those making guarantees must deposit a guarantee fund with the state treasurer. In the event of any negligence, the injured party may be reimbursed from this fund. The guarantee does not cover anything not of record, such as forged instruments, violations of restrictions, or defective documents.

POLICY OF TITLE INSURANCE This is what the name implies. The standard coverage policy insures against matters disclosed by public records, lack of capacity or authority of parties, forgery in the chain of title, and defective delivery of the deed. Further discussion of this subject is included in Unit 18.

ABSTRACT OF TITLE This is a file of documents that affects the title to property. It usually contains statements as to the condition of taxes, records of court action, and the like.

UNIT SUMMARY

In this unit we have discussed the difference in holding title in severalty and those methods that represent ownership by more than one person.

Terms such as ownership in severalty, joint tenancy, tenancy in common, tenancy in partnership, tenancy by the entirety, and community property were defined, and the method by which each could be acquired was explained.

The meaning of each of the four unities required for joint tenancy was described and the importance of each was reviewed. These unities are unity of interest, unity of title, unity of time, and unity of possession. The right of survivorship and its importance in joint tenancy was pointed out.

The place of tenancy in common as an ownership form was discussed. The relationship between the two methods of holding title—joint tenancy and tenancy in common—was compared with the responsibilities, rights, and privileges of those possessing property as community property.

In conclusion, related items such as chain of title, certificate of title, and abstract of title were added to show the relationship of title ownership to title protection.

REVIEWING YOUR UNDERSTANDING

MULTIPLE CHOICE

( ) 1 Severalty ownership of real property means: (a) ownership by several persons; (b) that there are several ways to own real estate; (c) sole ownership by a single person; (d) severance resulting from condemnation proceedings.

( ) 2 If a mother and son wish to purchase a home and take title in such a manner that they would each hold half the title, it should be taken as: (a) tenants in common; (b) joint tenants; (c) partnership; (d) any of above.

( ) 3 Not having his wife's consent, a husband may sign a voidable contract for the purpose of: (a) exchanging community real property; (b) managing community real property; (c) selling community real property; (d) leasing community real property for 2 years.

( ) 4 A real property contract for the sale of community property signed by a husband alone is: (a) enforceable; (b) valid; (c) void; (d) illegal.

( ) 5 Property held in joint tenancy, upon the death of one of the tenants, passes to the: (a) landlord; (b) state; (c) county assessor; (d) surviving joint tenant.

( ) 6 Community property is property owned by: (a) churches; (b) husband and wife; (c) the municipality; (d) the community.

( ) 7 The basis of community property law is : (a) Spanish law; (b) Anglo-Saxon common law; (c) federal tax laws; (d) state tax laws.

( ) 8 A married woman can will: (a) the separate property of her husband; (b) none of the community property; (c) half of the community property; (d) all property held as joint tenants.

( ) 9 A wife has no legal redress if the husband does which of the following with community property without her consent: (a) buys real property; (b) signs and leases for more than a year as lessor of real property; (c) sells personal property for less than value; (d) exchanges real property.

( ) 10 If property held by John and Mary Smith as joint tenants is sold, the new owner of the property must take title: (a) as husband and wife in joint tenancy; (b) as tenants in common; (c) as husband and wife in severalty; (d) in anyone's name and in any manner they see fit.

SUGGESTED LEARNING ACTIVITIES

Determine the manner in which you hold title to your property. If you do not own real property, ask someone who does—your parents, other family members, neighbors, or friends; then review the advantages and disadvantages of that form of ownership.

REVIEWING YOUR UNDERSTANDING—ANSWERS

MULTIPLE CHOICE

1 (c)	5 (d)	9 (a)
2 (b)	6 (b)	10 (d)
3 (b)	7 (a)	
4 (c)	8 (c)	

In this unit we will discuss two basic areas: capital improvements and preventive maintenance.

Suggestions will be given in properly planning improvements that you might contemplate, including those that are actually needed and those that are primarily for improved appearance and beautification of the inside and outside of your house.

The areas in which improvements might be made are explored in depth, and the pros and cons of employing professional help are discussed.

Suggestions for additions and improvements in various living areas, such as the kitchen, bathroom, laundry room, living room, and outside areas, are presented.

Suggestions for preventive maintenance cover adjuncts to living, such as insulation, moisture control, heating and air conditioning, pipes and plumbing, wiring and lighting, and painting and "fix-up."

Read this study guide (pages 190–197).
View TV program, number 21.

ASSIGNMENT

PERFORMANCE OBJECTIVES

At the conclusion of this unit, you will be able to:

1 Draw up a plan for the improvement and beautification of your home.

2 Decide on those areas that, through new construction and "add-ons," might increase the capital value of your home.

3 Make a list of those possible factors that might add to the value of your investment if taken care of periodically.

4 Inspect, repair, maintain, or employ assistance in repairing items, such as insulation, moisture control, heating and air conditioning, pipes and plumbing, and wiring and lighting.

TERMS YOU SHOULD KNOW

cosmetic changes
National Home Improvement Council
moisture control

Perhaps you've decided to "fix-up" or improve your home in order to protect your investment. It has been estimated that approximately 42 percent of all American families were involved in home improvements last year. These improvements ranged from simple living room redecoration to an ambitious face-lifting of the entire exterior.

CAPITAL IMPROVEMENTS Important considerations are involved before any type of renovation is attempted. You should not act on impulse. Each step should be carefully planned ahead of time. These plans may include choice of color, materials, style, and the overall personality of the house. One of the basic problems that must be faced is the financing of the projected improvements.

PLANNING

Study magazines that include suggestions for home improvement.

Read real estate sections of newspapers and periodicals.

Take advantage of house tours to see how others have used "add-on's" and other improvements in their homes.

Visit model showrooms and form the habit of procuring appropriate pamphlets in housewares and building supply stores and departments.

Keep an up-to-date file of all usable and helpful ideas and techniques.

Even though you may not have artistic tendencies, you should begin to make rough sketches of how you might want to change certain rooms, create more space for storage, or add on to present area.

Many renovations or changes may have to have prior official approval from building, electrical, and plumbing inspectors. You should therefore be acquainted with all building inspection codes, regulations, and permits.

Zoning laws need to be checked; some apply to exterior architectural styles and codes, and they may determine the minimum distance each building must be from the property line.

NEEDED AND COSMETIC CHANGES The needed changes are usually reflected after you have purchased an old home to fix up or remodel. Homes that need some remodeling and basic changes are attracting many buyers today.

In a previous unit you were given detailed instructions about what to look for in buying an old home. Regardless of the care with which the house is examined, there may be certain changes and innovations that may increase the market value of your home, for example:

New roofing.

Bathroom fixtures.

Change in flooring.

Replace piping.

The "cosmetic changes" refer to the appearance and the beautification of your home, inside and outside. These changes may include new paint, wallpaper, carpeting, and fixtures.

DOING IT YOURSELF Since the amount paid for labor is the biggest share of remodeling costs, you may decide to "do it yourself." There are several important points to consider when you start your plans.

1 Will you have sufficient time to give to the work?

2 Are you skilled enough to do a professional-looking job?

3 If you are married, will your marriage stand up under the stress?

If you decide to "do it yourself," you may be able to save money by shopping around for materials and supplies at junkyards, auction sales, estate sales, small lumberyards, or garden supply houses.

SELECTING A CONTRACTOR It is a sad but true commentary that in the construction business there are many fly-by-night contractors who may be unreliable and incompetent.

CAUTION

> It has been estimated that upwards of three of every four contractors go out of business after a relatively short time.

The question, then, is: "How can you go about locating the proper contractor for the job?"

Make inquiries at a building supply firm, who may be able to direct you to a reliable contractor among their customers.

Check with your immediate friends and relatives who may have had a successful experience with a specific contractor.

Your banker may be able to direct you to a competent contractor.

A movement that started in Kansas City, Missouri in 1973 resulted in the formation of an association of quality contractors whose main function was to raise the professional standards in the business. This group is now nationwide and is associated with the National Home Improvement Council, with branches in 33 cities.

Check with your local Better Business Bureau; they often have information about contractors. At least they can warn you against dealing with certain companies that have been found to be disreputable.

It may be a good idea to get bids from several contractors. If the bid is unrealistically low, be cautious. The contractor may need cash to write off an outstanding bill, and he may submit a low bid just to get the job.

If the bid is unusually high, it may indicate that he is so busy that he is not too interested in the job.

A competent contractor who, from a structural standpoint knows what can and cannot be done and whose work will add obvious value to your home, is well worth what he might charge you for his services.

WHAT MIGHT YOUR HOME IMPROVEMENTS INCLUDE?

Home improvements, to increase the value of your home, most likely will include one or more of the following.

Kitchens, bathrooms, and laundries.

Fireplaces.

Swimming pool.

Expansion of unused space.

Outdoor improvements.

KITCHENS, BATHROOMS, AND LAUNDRIES In improving the market value of your home, the kitchen is one of the most important rooms to consider. A kitchen can be improved without too much renovation.

The bathroom is another room to consider. Adding an additional bathroom back to back with an existing bathroom will not mean a major construction job.

The addition of a laundry room or renovation of the present laundry room area will add to the value of the home at a minimal cost.

It is significant that these three areas—kitchens, bathrooms, and laundries—have significant renovation areas in common.

Plumbing is a common area for each of these rooms. Usability, durability, and appearance can be considerably improved by a renovation of the plumbing system. This might include completely new pipes or an addition to the old system.

Ventilation is another area common to the three aforementioned rooms. If you don't have the necessary ventilation, moisture will damage walls, ceilings, and floors. Wall finishings for the three areas must be moisture resistant and easy to clean.

Lighting is also a commonality in these three rooms. Strong overhead lighting is important in each area. Fluorescents might be considered for added candlepower and decorative purposes.

Since these areas are so important and ready changes may be made, additional suggestions for each area are discussed below.

Kitchens If you had your "druthers," the feature that would probably interest you most in considering the kitchen would undoubtedly be *convenience*. If the kitchen isn't convenient, remodeling may be desirable.

Other essential characteristics of a kitchen are cheerfulness, attractiveness, and good lighting.

Take a close look at the cabinets and storage space. These can undoubtedly be improved with a little redecorating and "do-it-yourself" carpentry work.

If your kitchen doesn't have some form of exhaust release, this is a small change that may result in large returns.

Existing flooring can often be improved with little effort and little cost. Vinyl chips to cover unseemly floors are easily and inexpensively installed. Carpeting is fast becoming a popular way to improve a kitchen.

Kitchen walls should be able to be cleaned quickly and easily. Surfaces prepared with vinyl coating, either with vinyl wallpaper or vinyl paint, will make the surface resistant to water stains and household chemicals. Improvements of this type will make it easy to get rid of grease and grime and will add considerably to the value of your investment.

Bathrooms Perhaps your home can use an extra bathroom. If this becomes an actuality, try to make additional installations as close as possible to existing plumbing lines.

The installation of mirrors in a bathroom can give the appearance of spaciousness. If plate glass proves too expensive, mirror tiles may do the job.

Often the addition of fluorescent lighting or vanity lights can do wonders. Try it.

For use on bathroom walls and floors, ceramic tile will outlast most any other materials and will give the room a richer look. Tub and shower kits of ceramic tile are easily installed and will add to the market value.

Laundries With very little effort, the laundry room can be changed to a multipurpose room. A combination laundry and sewing room arrangement may be the most efficient and least expensive way to go.

FIREPLACES To many people, a fireplace is a necessary component of a home. A traditional fireplace may be too expensive, but a prebuilt fireplace costs approximately half that of a built-in fireplace. Many styles are available, since there are about 21 major manufacturers of prebuilts and prefabs.

The amount invested in a fireplace can be tripled when your home is placed on the market.

SWIMMING POOL Not all homes will profit by the installation of a swimming pool. In spite of the fact that 5 million American families own private swimming pools of one kind or another, in some cases a pool is prohibitive due to size or shape of lot.

If pool installation is feasible from a space and cost standpoint, it may be a plus value in the marketability of your home.

EXPANSION OF UNUSED SPACE Regardless of the size of a home, there hardly ever seems to be sufficient storage space. If you want your home to seem roomier, add more closets and storage space. Having a place to put things helps to avoid a cluttered house.

Ready-made shelves come in various wood textures, wood compositions, and metal. They're easy to install with simple hand tools.

If you are a "do it your-selfer," take care in selecting your woods, nails, and screws.

Turning a garage into a living space can increase the value of a single-family dwelling. You may have to install subflooring over the slab floor of the garage, which involves a considerable financial investment.

OUTDOOR IMPROVEMENTS The statement has been made that "a beautiful lawn can add $1000 to the resale of a house."

First impressions are important, so the front yard, driveway and entrance way should be a welcome invitation to visitors. The manner in which the yard is beautified tells much about the character of the occupants of the house.

Foundation shrubbery is extremely important, and will add many dollars to resale value. Wooden decks, patios, and flower beds also add to the beauty and intrinsic value.

PREVENTIVE MAINTENANCE

It's "what you do with what you've got" that pays off in the end. If you take care of your house, it will pay off to you in increased value when you wish to place it on the market. This accentuates the importance of preventive maintenance.

INSULATION   By checking your insulation periodically, you will be able to save considerably on your fuel and other utility bills. One of the first places where insulation should be checked and installed if present insulation is less than satisfactory is the attic. Check the thickness of the existing material and add to it where it is warranted.

There are other areas that should be insulated or, at best, the present insulation should be checked periodically. These areas include insulation for the floors and foundation. Access is ordinarily gained through the crawl hole beneath the house.

Weather stripping and caulking placed around outside doors and windows will prevent heat loss and eliminate chilling drafts.

A test made by the National Bureau of Standards proved that in a properly insulated house, with the outdoor temperature at 21° Farenheit and the furnace heat turned off during the night, the indoor temperature dropped only 6 degrees.

MOISTURE CONTROL   One of the first things a potential house hunter will check for is telltale signs of moisture damage or water seepage. Mildew is a sign of excess moisture. It can be washed from the walls and mildew-resistant paint applied.

Ventilation in the basement area should be a regular procedure. This can be done by opening windows. If there are no windows, a ventilating fan will help.

Properly placed down-spouts will drain excess water from the roof area. Drainage tiles placed at the foot of the down-spout will help carry the water away from the house.

If a periodic check is made of the roof area and bad shingles are replaced and potential leaks are stopped, reroofing may be delayed for some time.

HEATING AND AIR CONDITIONING   "Climate control" is another item that rates high on the want list for a potential home buyer. If it's necessary to update your heating and air conditioning system, it would be well worth the cost.

A thermostat is a worthwhile investment that will correspondingly increase the house value. By the same token, an automatic timer that turns off the air conditioner during the night when the temperature drops and turns it on again in the morning is a means of economizing.

PIPES AND PLUMBING   If there is any water damage in the house it can usually be traced to worn-out and leaking pipes and fixtures. If needed repairs and replacements are made you'll notice a decided difference in your water bill. Leaky faucets should be replaced immediately.

Check the age of your present plumbing. If it is 20 years old or more it should be repaired or replaced.

WIRING AND LIGHTING   Check to see if you have a strong enough electric line to carry your current appliances and electrical outlets. You may need to have a heavier line installed. If so, it should be changed.

MAKING THE OLD SEEM LIKE NEW   Tasteful decorations can do a lot to rejuvenate a house. The vast choice of patterns and colors makes it difficult to decide what is best. In mixing patterns you take risks. It is better to stick to a distinctive pattern in each room.

As indicated earlier, it is a good idea to keep a file on ideas that you have picked up over an extended period of time. If you prefer, you may receive the free decorating services that are offered by department stores or furniture or drapery stores to advertise and promote their products.

REMEMBER
Color can change the size, shape, and personality of a room.

If you plan on redecorating to any degree, why not start in the foyer or entrance to your house? After all, it is the first place visitors see, and first impressions go a long way.

If you decide to redo your living room, try to add ideas that create the illusion of spaciousness. This can be done by proper use of carpeting, furniture, drapes, mirrors, and the like.

Furniture can add to or detract from the value of your home when it is viewed by a prospective buyer. Repainting and reupholstering "sagging" furniture gives a new dimension to your investment.

Painting and fixing up your home, along with capital improvement and preventive maintenance, offers you a double bonus. The changes you make not only increase the value of your home, but you can be the receipient of the benefits of these improvements while living within its walls.

UNIT SUMMARY

This unit stressed the importance of planning any projected capital improvements. Improvements were divded into two major areas: improvements that were needed and cosmetic improvements.

Whether the improvements become part of a "do-it-yourself" plan or professional assistance is used, the most likely areas for improvement would be kitchens, bathrooms, laundry rooms, and areas outside of the house.

Another improvement area stressed in the unit that is related to all rooms was the areas where unused space might be used for closets and storage space.

In addition to the capital improvements that might increase the market value of your property, the unit stressed preventive maintenance in areas such as insulation, moisture control, heating and air conditioning, pipes and plumbing, and wiring and lighting.

MULTIPLE CHOICE

(   )   1   Cosmetic changes include all but one of the following (a) new paint; (b) copper pipes; (c) shrubbery; (d) shade trees.

(   )   2   In planning improvements you should: (a) keep a file on ideas; (b) read home improvement magazines; (c) be aware of zoning laws; (d) do all of the foregoing.

(   )   3   It has been estimated that what percent of contractors go out of business in a relatively short time? (a) 10 percent; (b) 75 percent; (c) 50 percent; (d) 25 percent.

(   )   4   Which one of the rooms in the house is usually improved before the others? (a) basement; (b) bedroom; (c) kitchen; (d) living room.

(   )   5   What improvements will be noticed first by "house lookers?" (a) the closets; (b) bathroom fixtures; (c) wall-to-wall carpeting; (d) outside landscaping.

(   )   6   Preventive maintenance includes all but one of the following: (a) moisture control; (b) built-in shelves; (c) insulation; (d) pipes and plumbing.

(   )   7   How old should plumbing be before you should consider replacing it? (a) 5 years; (b) 10 years; (c) 20 years; (d) 30 years.

(   )   8   If you plan on redecorating your house, you should start in which area? (a) basement; (b) attic; (c) back porch; (d) none of these.

Prepare a written report on an article obtained from a home improvement magazine concerning the improvement of one room in a house.

MULTIPLE CHOICE

1 (b)	5 (d)
2 (d)	6 (b)
3 (b)	7 (c)
4 (c)	8 (d)

22

In this unit we discuss other methods of acquiring title in addition to those described in Unit 20. A distinction is made between voluntary and involuntary title transfer.

Voluntary title transfer includes discussion of topics such as: transfer by will, transfer actions by nature or man, transfer by various types of occupancy and transfer by private and public grants.

The topics covered under involuntary transfer are those in which courts of law are called on to establish legal title.

Read this study guide (pages 200–207).
View TV program, number 22.

At the conclusion of this unit, you will be able to:

1 Determine the difference between the voluntary and involuntary transfer of property.

2 Describe three major types of wills that can be used to transfer title.

3 Trace the step-by-step procedure for the various types of voluntary transfer of title: that is, by will, succession accession, occupancy, and transfer.

4 Trace the step-by-step procedure followed in involuntary title transfer: that is, those instituted by operation of the law and through the courts.

holographic will	abandonment
witnessed will	prescription
nuncupative will	bankruptcy
intestate succession	forfeiture
accession	eminent domain
accretion	condemnation proceedings
avulsion	escheat
adverse possession	estoppel

In addition to the methods of taking title discussed in Unit 20, there are additional methods by which this action may be taken. These methods are divided into two areas: voluntary and involuntary transfer.

VOLUNTARY TRANSFER

TRANSFER BY WILL   Through various means an individual may accumulate real and personal property during his lifetime. On his death, title to the property may go to his beneficiaries by means of a will.

A will is a legal declaration by which a person disposes of his or her property, effective only at his death.

A male person who makes a will is called a *testator;* a female person making a will is known as a *testatrix.*

The term, *to bequeath,* is used in connection with the leaving of *personal property.* The property is the *bequest* or *legacy.* The person receiving the property is the *legatee.*

When *real property* is left by will, it is said to be devised. The one receiving the property is the *devisee.*

In the event the *testator* is leaving both real and personal property, the will usually reads "bequeath and devise."

There are three types of wills. They are:

1 A witnessed will.

2 A holographic will.

3 A nuncupative will.

A WITNESSED WILL   A witnessed will is a formal written document signed by the individual who is making it, wherein he declares in the presence of at least two witnesses that it is his will. The witnesses in turn sign the will. It is recommended that this document be prepared by an attorney.

A HOLOGRAPHIC WILL   A holographic will is a document dated and signed in the handwriting of the individual making the will. No formal documentation by an attorney is necessary.

A NUNCUPATIVE WILL   The nuncupative will is rarely used and when it is, it can only be used to dispose of personal property. It need not be in writing but is only employed in contemplation of death.

THE PROCEDURE OF A WILL

When a person dies and leaves a will, bequeathing certain property to his or her beneficiaries, there is little difficulty encountered in transfer of the property. On death the property is not immediately marketable or insurable until it is cleared by the person designated to handle the will, the executor or executrix.

The transaction must go through probate court to determine and pay off any creditors' claims and to establish the identity of the beneficiaries named in the will.

When a deceased person leaves a will, he is said to have died, *testate*. When he fails to leave a will he is said to have died, *intestate*. Heirs then must go through probate proceedings to prove their right to the property. In such cases, the court appoints an administrator or administratrix to handle the estate.

Where no will is present, the separate property of either spouse is distributed through the courts. If one child remains, the child will receive one-half and the surviving spouse the other one-half. If there is more than one child, the surviving spouse receives one-third and the remaining two-thirds are divided between the surviving children on an equal basis.

TRANSFER BY INTESTATE SUCCESSION

When a person dies without leaving a will, the law provides for the disposition of his property. The decedent's share of the estate automatically passes to the surviving spouse by *intestate succession*.

Depending on things such as the relationship of the next of kin and the character of the property, this situation is governed by a large number of special rules and regulations.

Property held as community property goes to the surviving spouse.

TRANSFER BY ACCESSION

This term refers to the right of an owner of property to an increase in the property he owns, regardless of whether it was caused by nature or man. This type of addition to ownership includes:

Accretion.

Avulsion.

Addition of fixtures.

ACCRETION This term applies to a gradual increase in the amount of land owned through the deposit of sand and dirt on the bank of a river or lake boundary.

These deposits are known as *alluvium deposits*. The loss to the landowner on the eroded side is permanent, and the gain by the landowner on the side where the soil is deposited is also permanent.

AVULSION This term applies to the violent tearing away of soil from a river bank and the redepositing of it elsewhere. (This is usually due to a violent storm or flood.) This soil immediately becomes part of the land on which it is deposited. However, unlike accretion, this land is not a permanent acquisition. It can be reclaimed by the original owner if he does so within one year of the date of occurrence.

ADDITION OF FIXTURES Acquisition of title by addition of fixtures occurs when an individual affixes his property to the land of another without an agreement permitting him to remove it. The thing so affixed belongs to the owner of the land unless he requires the former tenant to remove it.

When it has been determined whether a given item is or is not a fixture, this question remains: Who gets it? Between the seller and buyer of the land, if there is no agreement to the contrary, things affixed to the land at the time of the contract of sale, go to the buyer by grant of the land.

TRANSFER BY OCCUPANCY

Title to real property and certain other rights may be acquired through occupancy by several methods. Three methods are:

Adverse possession.

Abandonment.

Prescription.

ADVERSE POSSESSION This term applies to the actual physical possession of property for a period of time by a person who is not the actual owner, and the person's acquiring title to that property after the following *five* requirements are met.

1 It must be hostile to the true owner's title—rather than involve a permissive use.

2 Possession must be continuous and uninterrupted for a period of five years.

3 The possession must be by actual occupation, and be open and notorious. (This means that the claim of possession must not be kept a secret. He does not actually have to reside on the property but must show his intentions of holding and possessing the land, through some type of improvement to the land.)

4 The possession must be under the claim of right or color of title. (This means that the possessor's actions must give the impression that he has the absolute right to the possession of the property.)

ABANDONMENT Abandonment as it applies to real property is a situation wherein a lessee abandons a lease; that is, moves out. The landlord thus reacquires possession and full control of the premises.

The lessor also has the right to sue the lessee for the difference between the total payments made to date of abandonment and the original amount for which the lessee contracted.

PRESCRIPTION The occasion may arise when a claimant has fulfilled all but one of the five requirements for adverse possession. For example, he has not been paying the taxes and assessments on the property; they have been paid by the true owner. The claimant may require an easement by prescription rather than title to the property.

TRANSFER

Title to property is conveyed from one person to another in one of four ways. The four ways are:

Private grant.

Public grant.

Gift.

By operation of law or through court action.

PRIVATE GRANT   The private grant results in an owner's voluntarily conveying his ownership rights to another. Today this is the most common method used to transfer title to real property.

PUBLIC GRANT   In our country's early history, the government made many land grants through laws enacted by Congress. These grants were made to settlers to encourage the land's development and improvement. Land was also granted for educational institutions, national parks, railroads, cities and towns, and to private citizens.

GIFT   A property owner may voluntarily transfer his property to another party without giving or receiving any consideration or remuneration. In the case of real property, the transaction would normally be evidenced by a gift deed.

INVOLUNTARY TRANSFER   There are a variety of situations in which courts of law are called on to establish legal title. The most common of these involuntary transfers are:

Execution sale.

Bankruptcy.

Forfeiture.

Marriage.

Eminent domain.

Escheat.

Estoppel.

EXECUTION SALE   When a judgment goes against an owner of property, the court directs the sheriff or marshal to satisfy the judgment out of the property of the debtor. Real property belonging to the debtor, and not exempt from execution, is seized by the sheriff or marshal and sold at public auction.

BANKRUPTCY   When an individual cannot meet his credit obligations, he may either voluntarily "take out" bankruptcy or may be adjudged bankrupt by the courts. In either event, the court under federal statute takes possession of his property and distributes the proceeds proportionately to his creditors.

Real property may have to be sold to pay the claims against the bankrupt.

FORFEITURE In selling real property, the owner may impose a "condition subsequent" in his deed. If the condition so included is breached (if it is not adhered to), the grantor or his successor can terminate the estate and reacquire title. In this situation, property is said to be acquired by forfeiture with no new consideration paid.

MARRIAGE According to California law, although the wedding ceremony itself has no direct effect on the transfer of the title to property, anything earned or acquired, including real property, by husband and wife or either during marriage is considered to be community property. Each spouse has a present, existing, and equal interest in property acquired in this manner.

ESTOPPEL Title to real property can be transferred by the court under the following circumstances: the true owner of property allows a friend or acquaintance to appear to everyone as the true owner of his property, and an innocent third party buys the land from the apparent owner. The true owner is barred or estopped from claiming any further ownership.

If a person had a lesser estate in real property than he claims, or if he had a defective title in the land he conveys, and he later acquires full title, the person to whom he had conveyed the original title will be entitled to receive the full title by estoppel.

ESCHEAT Based on the premise that all property must be owned, when a person dies and leaves no apparent heirs, ownership reverts back to the state who was the original owner. This action is called the principle of escheat.

It is not, however, an automatic action, as it is presumed that heirs capable of taking title exist somewhere. Legal proceedings are instituted to determine if the doctrine of escheat applies.

The probate courts will do all in their power to locate possible heirs. After escheat proceedings are instituted, the title is held in trust by the state for five years. If at the end of that time no heirs have come forth, the title will transfer to the state with all rights of ownership.

EMINENT DOMAIN This is the term applied to action taken by bodies such as the federal government, states, cities, counties, improvement districts, public utilities, education institutions, and similar public and semipublic bodies. Eminent domain is the power to obtain private property, through condemnation proceedings, for public use.

When privately owned land is needed for public uses such as streets, irrigation, railroads, electric power, public housing, or off-street parking, condemnation action can be instituted and the land can be procured by paying the property owner "just compensation for the property."

Most courts have ruled that "market value" or "fair market value" is the proper basis for determining just compensation.

UNIT SUMMARY

In this unit you have learned that property rights can be transferred in a variety of ways, both voluntarily and involuntarily.

Ways of transferring property voluntarily include: will, intestate succession, accession (including actions such as accretion, avulsion, and addition of fixtures), transfer by occupancy (including actions such as adverse possession), abandonment, prescription, transfer (including methods such as private grant, public grant, and gift), and operation of law or court action.

Involuntary action, which is imposed by the courts, includes incidents of title transfer such as sheriff's or marshal's sale, bankruptcy, forfeiture, marriage, estoppel, escheat, and eminent domain.

REVIEWING YOUR UNDERSTANDING

MULTIPLE-CHOICE

( )   1   A will which is written, dated and signed in the handwriting of the testator is:
  a A monographic will.
  b A nuncupative will.
  c A holographic will.
  d None of the foregoing.

( )   2   The term "voluntary transfer" refers to all but one of the following:
  a Accretion.
  b Estoppel.
  c Accession.
  d Abandonment.

( )   3   When land is needed for public use, title can be acquired by:
  a Public domain.
  b Abandonment.
  c Eminent domain.
  d Right of escheat.

( )   4   When new land is formed along the shore of a body of water, from natural causes, slowly and deliberately, the action is termed:
  a Avulsion.
  b Accretion.
  c Prescription.
  d None of the foregoing.

( )   5   When a person dies without leaving a will, he is said to have died:
  a Without recourse.
  b Testate.
  c Nuncupatively.
  d Intestate.

TRUE AND FALSE

( )   6   All property must have an owner.

( )   7   Title by adverse possession can be acquired against a city or county.

( )   8   A bequest is a gift of money by will.

( )   9   If an intestate who has never been married leaves no heirs, his estate goes to the state through escheat proceedings.

SUGGESTED LEARNING ACTIVITIES

REVIEWING YOUR UNDERSTANDING—

ANSWERS

(   ) **10** An administrator is a person appointed by will to administer the estate of a decedent.

Review your own will to see if the disposition of your property is clearly stated. (If you have no will check that of a relative or close friend.)

1	c	**6**	True
2	b	**7**	False
3	c	**8**	True
4	b	**9**	True
5	d	**10**	False

23

OVERVIEW

In this unit we discuss the reasons why you may decide to sell the real property in your possession.

The reasons include the desire to move into a larger home, a reduced need for space as your family grows up, job transfer, an increase in family size, health conditions, and a change in income.

How to prepare your home for selling and how to get the best price for your property are also described.

The unit concludes with the arguments for and against selling your own home as opposed to employing a professional real estate agent for this purpose.

ASSIGNMENT

Read this study guide (pages 210–216).
View TV program, number 23.

PERFORMANCE OBJECTIVES

At the conclusion of this unit you will be able to:

1 Determine the compelling reasons for selling your home.

2 List the steps necessary to prepare your home for selling.

3 Test the advantages and disadvantages of employing a real estate broker as opposed to selling your own property.

TERMS YOU SHOULD KNOW

realtor
amenities

Regardless of your plans at the time that you purchase your home, you may eventually find it necessary to sell. Nearly one out of five American families move to a new location each year.

Incidentally, if there is a possibility that you are going to move, before you purchase, it is advisable to consider carefully the amount you must pay down. You will be "money ahead" if you do.

REASONS FOR SELLING   Some of the specific reasons for selling might be the following.

Job change, thus necessitating a move, particularly if the transfer involves a job beyond commuting distance from your present location. Nearness to place of employment may not dictate your move, but it will at least influence it.

Advancement or improvement in your job status, thus enabling you to live in better surroundings with more of the amenities, that is, improvements and additions, to improve your standard of living.

Addition to your family, which could require a larger home with another bedroom, larger yard facilities, closer proximity to schools, and the like.

Your family may be grown and the last child may be leaving. You may no longer need as large a house as you have been living in.

Weather and atmospheric changes that are not good for your health, or for members of the family. You may be forced to leave the area, necessitating the sale of your property.

NOTE
A home is something that you buy, use—and when it no longer fits your needs—sell, or retain as an investment.

PREPARING YOUR HOME TO SELL   Your property will sell faster and at a better price if you follow these helpful suggestions:

Prepare house carefully for inspection by prospective buyers. Have it looking its best at all times.

OUTSIDE APPEARANCE   First impressions are important: they have a lasting effect on the would-be buyer. A first impression is often based on the outside appearance of the house. You cannot rely on the buyer's falling in love with the interior of the house. He may never stop to look further unless he finds the exterior pleasing. So, keep your yard neat and clean—have the shrubs trimmed and the lawn cut.

Make a prospect want to come inside.

"Dress up" your windows; they are the eyes of the house.

Ask yourself these questions:

Is the exterior in need of paint?

Are there any loose hinges, shutters or screens?

Does the shrubbery need trimming?

Is the garage free of old tools, equipment, or odds and ends, that are not being used?

A prospective buyer will not be in a receptive mood after he has "tangled" with an errant skate or with an icy spot on the sidewalk. (Besides, he could sue if he were injured.)

Make all minor repairs, such as fixing broken window panes, loose door-knobs, sticking doors, leaky plumbing, and broken light switches. Little things like these make a house difficult to show, and often kill a sale.

INTERIOR COMES NEXT   A clean, well-kept interior indicates that the house has been properly maintained. The buyer many times will be so impressed with its tidiness that he may overlook some minor problems.

Throughout the house, clean shiny windows brighten the interior.

Fill cracks in the walls, they may denote a structural weakness.

If there are water spots on the ceilings in any of the rooms, even though the roof has been repaired, they are damaging to the image of the house and should be repainted.

CAUTION

Buyers are wary and will look for damp spots, an indication of poor construction, ventilation, and plumbing.

Ask yourself this question: What did I look for when I bought? The answer is probably: A neat home in reasonably good condition.

WHEN ACTUALLY SHOWING YOUR HOME   Be prepared at all times to show your home. The prospect you turn away might be the ultimate buyer.

If the prospect asks questions about the house and neighborhood, answer them directly and honestly. Questions about the transaction should be referred to your real estate agent, if you have employed one.

If a real estate broker or salesman has been employed, leave the showing of the house to him. Interrupting his sales presentation may lose a sale.

If you have a dog, keep him out of the house and under control. Many buyers are afraid of dogs.

Shut off or turn down the radio and TV. They can be distracting.

Nothing adds to cheerful atmosphere more effectively than light. Use your lights carefully and artistically for the best effect. For example, if the house is shown in the evening, make sure there is proper illumination both inside and out-side of the house.

A moderate amount of heat adds a feeling of coziness in cold weather while fresh air is equally desirable on hot days.

Never apologize for the appearance of the house. It only emphasizes the faults.

Display full value of your storage space, free from a crowded condition.

If you have an attractive fireplace, have a cozy fire burning, weather permit-ting—at least, shine the fireplace brass and accoutrements in the fireplace.

Add little homey touches—a vase of flowers, a plant, small pillows, and the like. Aim for a restful, happy look.

REMINDER

Sell a home, not a house.

ADDITIONAL TIPS IN SHOWING YOUR HOME   Prepare a detailed fact sheet to give prospects. This should include:

1 Basic financial information, that is, mortgage, monthly payments, interest, and the like.

2 Assessed valuation and tax rate.

3 Extras—draperies, carpets, and appliances.

4 Average cost of electricity, fuel, and water.

5 Location of nearby schools, churches, shopping centers, parks, and recreation areas.

Prepare a floor plan that includes the number and size of rooms and closets. Specify when house is open for showing.

When showing the home, have the prospect *do* things, *feel* things, and *measure* things.

WHO SHOULD SELL YOUR HOME?

Some people attempt to sell their homes without professional help. This decision usually ends in frustration and dissatisfaction.

Why Use a Licensed Real Estate Salesman or Broker?   Do you know what your home is really worth?

An agent has a great deal more knowledge about fair prices than you do, and he or she has access to marketing surveys and records of sales transactions. You may set your price too low and lose money, or you may set it too high and lose prospects.

Aren't You a Little Afraid To Show Your Home to Any Stranger?   It can be dangerous. When you hang out a sign reading, "For Sale by Owner." you leave your door wide open to all kinds of people. A licensed salesman or broker will screen all applicants and eliminate all undesirable characters, as well as professional house hunters. This is added protection for your home, and makes certain that your home is only opened to interested buyers.

Do You Want To Be Tied to Your Home Day and Night?   Your salesman or broker will allow you to come and go as you please, while he shows your home by appointment only. Phone calls at all hours necessitating your answering difficult questions will be eliminated.

Can You Guarantee That Your Own Advertising Will Suffice?   If you're not an expert in this field, leave it to an expert—you won't be able to compete with professional ad writers. Your salesman or broker will be able to design advertising to get the reader's attention, arouse interest, and stimulate action. He will answer the question what type of person is most likely to be attracted to this home?

He will aim his ad toward attracting the proper prospects.

He will be honest—use careful and not misleading words.

He will make himself clearly understood.

He will make his ads interesting and to the point.

He will be enthusiastic, not funny or cute.

He will provide factual, honest information in simple concise language.

Are You an Enthusiastic Well-Informed Salesperson?   If you are fortunate enough to get qualified prospects, will you be able to bargain with them successfully? Without a professional background it will be extremely difficult for you to discuss intelligently prices, terms, financing, and other pertinent subjects.

Can You Close That Sale?   Are you aware of the best possible financing?

Favorable financing is vitally important to the transaction of any real property transaction. Are you able to secure for your prospect the best possible loan, or should you leave that to the "loan experts?" Your salesman or broker can screen buyers for loans, saving you valuable time.

Are you able to handle complicated real estate forms and documents successfully and safely?

Your salesman or broker knows what is required. He knows what must be included in a sales agreement, escrow, or deed. You can be assured that he will protect your interests.

In spite of the pitfalls discussed above, some people still attempt to sell their own home without professional help. They attempt to justify their decision with these reasons:

We're not in a hurry to sell.

Houses in our area are in demand.

Mortgage money is generally available.

Others in the neighborhood have sold their own home.

We want to save the commission that we would have to pay for professional service.

If you're one of these—think twice before making one of the biggest decisions of your life.

WHERE CAN YOU FIND A REAL ESTATE AGENT?   There are 800,000 real estate licensees in the United States—many experienced and some inexperienced. Selecting the proper one is not easy, but these suggestions will be helpful.

Ask neighbors and friends who have bought or sold for their recommendations. If they were pleased with their treatment, the recommendation will be helpful.

Ask your local bank for a recommendation.

Look for an agency that has a well-located and well-maintained office. One that uses dignified advertising.

The terms Realtors and Realtists are not synonyms for just any real estate agent. They are individuals engaged in the real estate business who are members of national associations. As members they are required to subscribe to a strict code of ethics established by their associations.

You should be able to discuss frankly with your real estate agent any problems that may arise relative to the marketing of your property.

The selling of property, especially a home, involves some inconvenience to the occupant. All real estate salesmen and brokers are aware of this and will try to be as considerate as possible. With your cooperation, they will work energetically to find a buyer. The possibility of a sale is greatly enhanced when the transaction is placed in the hands of a professional.

UNIT SUMMARY

In this unit we have discussed the reasons why it may become necessary for you to sell your home. These reasons include job changes, advancement or improvement in job status, increase in family size, decrease in family size, and health conditions.

In preparing your home for sale, you should be aware of the importance of outside as well as inside appearances.

Suggestions were given for the showing of your home, including discussion of the items that enhance the beauty and value of the property.

The question as to whether you should employ a real estate salesman or broker was given careful consideration. It was suggested that, because of the complicated nature of a real estate transaction, professional help is needed. Your agent will know what your home is really worth and how best to advertise it to make the sale. He takes the risk and the inconvenience, releasing you from details that you are not in a position to handle, such as financing, preparing for escrow, and completing necessary documents and reports.

REVIEWING YOUR UNDERSTANDING

1 List five reasons why you might be required to sell your home.
   a
   b
   c
   d
   e

2 List four steps to follow when showing your home.
   a
   b
   c
   d

3 List five pitfalls that might be avoided by employing a licensed real estate salesman or broker to sell your home.
   a
   b
   c
   d
   e

4 Give three suggestions for locating a qualified real estate agent.
   a
   b
   c

SUGGESTED LEARNING ACTIVITIES

Visit your local real estate board office and ask to see, and then read and reflect on the contents of the "Realtor's Code of Ethics" or "Creed."

REVIEWING YOUR UNDERSTANDING—ANSWERS

1 a Your job location may change.
  b There may be an advancement or job improvement.
  c There may be an addition to your family.
  d There may be a decrease in family size.
  e You may have to move for health purposes.

2 a Keep house well and tastefully lighted.
  b Show how storage space may be utilized.
  c Add little homey touches.
  d Prepare a detailed fact sheet on basic information on your home.

3 a Determining best price.
  b Opening house to all comers.
  c Tying up all your time.
  d Preparing advertising that sells.
  e Recommending favorable financing.

4 a Ask your neighbors or friends.
  b Ask your local banker.
  c Look for the sign "Realtor," or "Realtist."

24

In this unit it will be assumed that you are putting your home on the market for sale. In so doing, certain preliminary steps must be taken. In our discussion, analysis of the market is stressed, along with the use of a financial report. These steps assist in determining the selling price and the net proceeds to be expected from the sale.

The best methods of contracting with a broker for the sale of your home are explained and forms are provided to clarify this explanation.

The final steps in the sales transaction are then discussed. They are qualifying the buyer, accepting his offer or presenting a counteroffer and getting the buyer to agree, closing the transaction, obtaining the termite inspection report, and taking the transaction to escrow.

Read this study guide (pages 218–228).
View TV program, number 24.

At the conclusion of this unit, you will be able to:

1 Determine the preliminary steps that must be taken before your home can be offered for sale, including the determination of price, and the net proceeds expected from the sale.

2 Decide on the best and most productive system to be used in listing your property for sale.

3 Follow in sequence the steps used by your broker in consummating the sales transaction, including qualifying the buyer, presenting the offer, and accepting or making a counteroffer.

4 Explain the meaning of a "termite report."

competitive market analysis	net listing
estimated seller's net	exclusive listing
listing	MLS
open listing	termite report

SO YOU WANT TO SELL YOUR HOME If the time is right and you have given careful consideration to selling your home, the next step is determining how to go about it.

You naturally want to get the best possible price with the best financing and the most reliable buyer.

You need to seek professional advice. Call a reliable broker and ask for a competitive market analysis.

COMPETITIVE MARKET ANALYSIS The market value of a home can be determined by using the competitive market analysis form (see Figure 1), developed by the California Association of Realtors. The form is divided into two parts.

The top half lists those homes in the area that are presently for sale, those sold during the past 12 months, and those expiring during the last 12 months. The information on each home includes the number of bedrooms and baths, whether there is a den, square footage, type of financing, list price, days on the market, and the terms.

On those homes sold in the preceding 12 months the date sold is given along with the sales price.

F.H.A. and V.A. appraisals on other real properties are listed.

The lower half of the form gives an overall appraisal of the property being sold which includes buyer appeals, marketing position, selling costs, and net proceeds, if any. Figure 1 is a sample copy of the Comparative Market Analysis form.

When this form has been completed you should know what buyers are paying for comparable homes; what buyers have paid in the last 12 months; and what buyers would not pay in the preceding 12 months.

If the form is filled out completely and accurately with current information, the competitive market value of your home will have been tentatively established.

FINANCING ANALYSIS There are four principal factors that are instrumental in affecting the sale of your home. They are location, condition, price, and financing.

Obviously you can do nothing about the location of your property. But you can improve the condition of your home and your price can be competitive. However, the fourth factor, that of financing, is actually the most flexible of the four.

The most effective tool for explaining the avenues open in financing and their effect on your net receipts from the sale of your home is another form provided by the California Realtors Association. It is entitled, Estimated Seller's Net (see Figure 2).

When this form is completed, using the maximum charges that can be expected from the sale of the dwelling, you will have a realistic figure as to the net proceeds that you might expect to receive at the close of escrow.

LISTING PROPERTY Now you are ready to list your property, to procure the best possible buyer.

WHAT IS A LISTING? The Department of Real Estate defines a listing as "a contract by which a principal employs an agent to do certain things for the prin-

PROPERTY ADDRESS _____ DATE _____

FOR SALE NOW	BED-RMS.	BATHS	DEN	SQ. FT.	1ST LOAN	LIST PRICE	DAYS ON MARKET	TERMS			

SOLD PAST 12 MOS.	BED-RMS.	BATHS	DEN	SQ. FT.	1ST LOAN	LIST PRICE	DAYS ON MARKET	DATE SOLD	SALE PRICE	TERMS

EXPIRED PAST 12 MOS.	BED-RMS.	BATHS	DEN	SQ. FT.	1ST LOAN	LIST PRICE	DAYS ON MARKET	TERMS		

F.H.A—V.A. APPRAISALS

ADDRESS	APPRAISAL	ADDRESS	APPRAISAL

BUYER APPEAL   MARKETING POSITION
(GRADE EACH ITEM 0 TO 20% ON THE BASIS OF DESIRABILITY OR URGENCY)

1. FINE LOCATION _____%   1. WHY ARE THEY SELLING _____%
2. EXCITING EXTRAS _____%   2. HOW SOON MUST THEY SELL_____%
3. EXTRA SPECIAL FINANCING _____%   3. WILL THEY HELP FINANCE ....YES___NO___%
4. EXCEPTIONAL APPEAL_____%   4. WILL THEY LIST AT COMPETITIVE MARKET
                                                      VALUE ....YES___NO___%
5. UNDER MARKET PRICE _____YES___NO___%   5. WILL THEY PAY FOR APPRAISAL ....YES___NO___%

          RATING TOTAL_____%   RATING TOTAL_____%

ASSETS _____
DRAWBACKS _____
AREA MARKET CONDITIONS _____

RECOMMENDED TERMS _____

TOP COMPETITIVE MARKET VALUE ....

PROBABLE FINAL SALES PRICE ....

FIGURE 1 Sample listing form

SELLER'S NAME _____ DATE _____

PROPERTY ADDRESS _____

BROKER _____

SALES REPRESENTATIVE _____ SELLING PRICE $_____

ENCUMBRANCES:

First Trust Deed ....Source: Seller ☐ Lender ☐ Document ☐ ....$

Second Trust Deed ......Source: Seller ☐ Lender ☐ Document ☐ ....

Other Encumbrances ....Source: Seller ☐ Lender ☐ Document ☐ ....

TOTAL ENCUMBRANCES .... $

GROSS EQUITY $

ESTIMATED SELLING COSTS

Policy of Title Insurance ....$

State & County Tax Stamps ....

Estimated Escrow Fees ....

Termite Inspection and Report ....

(Possible repairs not included) ....

Prepayment penality, if any:

GI............None ....

FHA.........1% of original amount of loan if less than 10 yrs. old ....

No charge if refinanced FHA

Conventional..Varies, but safe to figure 6 months' interest ....

on unpaid balance

Reconveyance fee (only if existing loan is being paid off) ....

Lender's Demand or Beneficiary Statement ....

Proration of interest on existing loan ....

(Interest is always 1 month in arrears. Allow 1 month's interest maximum)

FHA or VA loan discount fee of new loan ....

Brokerage ....

Discount Second T.D. (if applicable) ....

Other ....

Other ....

APPROXIMATE TOTAL COSTS $ $

$

APPROXIMATE SELLER'S PROCEEDS

(Gross Equity Less Total Costs)

POSSIBLE CREDITS OR DEBITS

Proration of property tax

Return of balance in Impound Account

This estimate has been prepared to assist the seller in computing his costs. Whenever possible we have used the MAXIMUM charges that can be expected. Lenders and escrow companies will vary in their charges; therefore, these figures cannot be guaranteed by the broker or his representatives.

I have read the above figures and acknowledge receipt of a copy of this form.

Presented by: _____

_____

Address: _____

Seller

_____

Phone No.: _____

Seller

THE APPROXIMATE SELLER'S PROCEEDS CALCULATED ABOVE WILL VARY ACCORDING TO ANY DIFFERENCES IN UNPAID LOAN BALANCES, IMPOUND ACCOUNT, IF ANY, AND ANY EXPENSES FOR REQUIRED CORRECTIVE WORK. ALL INFORMATION IS FROM SOURCES BELIEVED RELIABLE BUT NOT GUARANTEED.

ESN-11

FIGURE 2 Sample listing form

cipal.'' It is often called an authorization to sell, and the most commonly used listing forms are captioned ''Authorization to Sell.'' An agent holding a listing is always bound by the law of agency and is charged with obligations to his principal that do not exist between two principals.

In your case, the listing becomes a contract whereby you hire the services of a licensed real estate broker to sell your home.

One of your major decisions will be: What type of listing should I use? Your choice lies in one of four categories: open, net, exclusive, and multiple.

Open Listing   This listing takes the form of a written memorandum in which you authorize one or more brokers to act as agent in the sale of your property.

Open listings are actually the simplest form of written authorization to sell. Usually no time limit is specified for the employment, and you may withdraw the property from the market. If your property is sold, it automatically cancels all outstanding listings and it is not necessary to notify each agent.

Where open listings are used, the commission is earned by the first broker to find a buyer who meets the terms of the listing, or whose offer is accepted by you, the seller. If by chance you sell your own property, you do not have to pay a commission to any of the brokers holding ''open listings.''

The drawback to an open listing is that the broker generally will spend less money, time, and energy on this type of listing because, often, he does not make the sale and his efforts are in vain.

Net Listing   Because of the nature of this type of listing it is generally confined to sales of nonresidential property. In a net listing the compensation is not definitely determined, but you set a sales price and say to the listing broker, ''You may retain all money received in excess of the predetermined net price.''

EXAMPLE

You decide to sell your home so that you can realize $50,000. The listing broker finds a buyer willing to pay $58,000. If the broker is able to close the transaction, his compensation is $8000.

This arrangement is seldom used as it tempts the broker to put his interests ahead of yours. Special regulation is necessary to avoid charges of misrepresentation and fraud. Under the Real Estate Law, failure of an agent to disclose the amount of his compensation in connection with a net listing is cause for revocation or suspension of his license. This disclosure must be done prior to, or at the time that you bind yourself to the transaction. The net listing may be either exclusive or nonexclusive.

Exclusive Listing   The exclusive listing may be of two types, that of an exclusive agency, or an exclusive right to sell.

Exclusive agency listing is a contract containing the words ''exclusive agency.'' You agree that the agent you select shall be the only one with whom the house will be listed for a specified period of time. Under this type of listing the commission for a sale is payable to the broker named in the contract. If the broker or any other broker finds the buyer and effects the sale, the broker holding the exclusive listing is entitled to a commission. You do not, however, rule out the possibility of finding a buyer yourself. In the event that you do make the sale, the agent is not entitled to a commission because under the law you are not an agent.

Under the exclusive right to sell listing, the listing agent is entitled to the commission on the sale of the property, if sold within the time limit by him, by any other broker, or by the owner. Since the listing broker gets the commission no matter who makes the sale, the listing office will put all its effort into the merchandising of your property. Because of this arrangement, misunderstandings regarding commissions are greatly alleviated, if not eliminated entirely.

Multiple Listing   This is a variation of the exclusive right to sell listing. With a multiple listing, you give the exclusive right to sell to an agent of your choice for a specified period. An exclusive right to sell listing form (see Figure 3) is completed and filed with a central bureau. This bureau is made up of cooperating brokers who find it to their mutual advantage to group together, creating a broader market for the advertising of your listing.

Through this multiple listing service known as the MLS, the listing is printed, sometimes with a picture of your home, and is distributed to all agents who are members of the multiple listing service. This means that, although you have listed your property with only a single agent, it is placed in the hands of a great many agents.

The buyer of your home likes to do business with a Realtor, or a Realtist. These professional designations are worn by only those brokers who are members of national associations. As such, they are subject to their rules and regulations, observe ethical standards of conduct, and are entitled to their association's benefits.

Multiple listing is a public service conducted by a group of brokers, who are usually members of a real estate board. Multiple listing is nationwide, a proven service in hundreds of cities for more than 30 years. In our community we have many offices cooperating to give you action. This extra service costs you no more than the standard sales commission.

FIGURE 3   **14. EXCLUSIVE AUTHORIZATION AND RIGHT TO SELL**

CALIFORNIA REAL ESTATE ASSOCIATION STANDARD FORM

1. Right to Sell. I hereby employ and grant _____, hereinafter called "Agent", the exclusive and irrevocable right to sell or exchange the real property situated in _____, County of _____, California described as follows:

_____

_____

_____

2. Term. Agent's right to sell shall commence on _____, 19_____ and expire at midnight on _____, 19_____

3. Terms of Sale.

(a) The price for the property shall be the sum of $_____, to be paid as follows:

_____

(b) The following items of personal property are to be included in the above-stated price:

FIGURE 3 *(Continued)*

(c) Agent is hereby authorized to accept on my behalf a deposit upon the purchase price in an amount to be not less than $_____.

(d) Evidence of title to the property shall be in the form of a California Land Title Association Standard Coverage Policy of Title Insurance in the amount of the selling price to be paid for by _____

(e) I warrant that I am the owner of the property or have the authority to execute this agreement. I hereby agree to permit a FOR SALE sign to be placed on my property by Agent named herein.

4. Compensation to Agent. I hereby agree to compensate Agent as follows:

(a) _____% of the selling price if the property is sold during the term hereof, or any extension thereof, by Agent, on the terms herein set forth or any other price and terms I may accept, or through any other person, or by me, or _____% of the price shown in 3.-(a), if said property is withdrawn from sale, transferred, conveyed, leased without the consent of Agent, or made unmarketable by my voluntary act during the term hereof or any extension thereof.

(b) The compensation provided for in subparagraph (a) above if property is sold, conveyed or otherwise transferred within 90 days after the termination of this authority or any extension thereof to anyone with whom Agent has had negotiations prior to final termination, provided I have received notice in writing, including the names of the prospective purchasers, before or upon termination of this agreement or any extension thereof. However, I shall not be obligated to pay the compensation provided for in subparagraph (a) if a valid listing agreement is entered into during the term of said 90 days protection period with another licensed real estate broker and a sale, lease or exchange of the property is made during the term of said 90 days protection period.

5. If action be instituted on this agreement to collect compensation or commissions, I agree to pay such sum as the Court may fix as reasonable attorney's fees.

6. I authorize the Agent named herein to cooperate with sub-agents.

7. This property is offered without respect to race, creed, color, or national origin.

8. In the event of an exchange, permission is hereby given Agent to represent all parties and collect compensation or commissions from them, provided there is full disclosure to all principals of such agency. Agent is authorized to divide with other agents such compensation or commissions in any manner acceptable to them.

9. I agree to hold Agent harmless from any liability or damages arising from any incorrect information supplied by me or any information I fail to supply.

10. Other provisions:

_____

11. I acknowledge that I have read and understand this Agreement, and that I have received a copy hereof.

Dated _____, 19____ _____, California

_____	_____
Owner	Owner
_____	_____
Address	City · State · Phone

12. In consideration of the execution of the foregoing, the undersigned Agent agrees to be diligent in endeavoring to obtain a purchaser.

	Agent		Address · City
By	_____		_____
			Phone Date

FORM A-11

Selling Your Property Through MLS   This process is followed in offering your home for sale through MLS.

Your property is analyzed and with available market information, price is decided on.

Your broker prepares an appropriate listing form with all pertinent data.

A printed description of your property is prepared in quantity.

Copies of this information are sent to the multiple listing service.

Buyers learn of the availability of your house through offices of brokers participating in MLS.

In selling your property in this way, you are represented by only one broker, but you enjoy the services of many, for the cost of one.

Reasons for Using MLS   The California Association of Realtors suggests six reasons why you should consider MLS.

1 Proven results at no extra cost.

2 Offers an organized market for your property.

3 Property is exposed to more potential buyers.

4 You receive the benefit of the professional knowledge of many realtors.

5 Realtors from coast to coast have had successful practical results for both buyers and owners of real estate through MLS.

6 Through the great distribution you save the three T's—time, tires, and tempers.

When you use the multiple listing service, you must agree to abide by certain regulations. By mutual agreement you may decide to have the listing be in effect for at least 30, 60, or 90 days—even up to six months in some parts of the country. Such a period is sometimes necessary for the service to have the listings printed and distributed and to permit time for agents to line up prospects.

If you wish to withdraw from the multiple listing before the expiration date, you usually must obtain the written consent of the listing agent. Before you sign a multiple listing agreement, you should be sure that there are no unreasonable terms in any withdrawal provisions. You might obtain a letter from the listing broker stating the conditions under which the listing may be withdrawn. If the conditions seem unreasonable, check with your attorney before you give the listing.

QUALIFYING THE BUYER   Your broker will be interested in selling your home as quickly and efficiently as he possibly can. Time is money to him, so he will endeavor to eliminate undesirable prospects through a careful system of qualifying prospective buyers.

As a potential prospect appears, your agent will gather information concerning his intentions, his needs, and his financial capability. When a worthy prospect is found, the broker will "present your offer."

PRESENTING THE OFFER   When your home has been prepared for showing, the prospective buyer has been shown the home, and the deposit receipt has been prepared as explained in Unit 16, the offer is made.

You need not accept the first offer presented to you. It is your prerogative to listen to the offer presented and to negotiate with your broker until a satisfactory agreement is reached.

An important point to consider will be the qualifications of the buyer. If your broker is on his toes he will be able to answer intelligently any questions you may have concerning the character and financial condition of the proposed buyer.

In your negotiations there may be points on which you cannot agree. You would then make a counteroffer which is relayed to the prospective buyer by your agent.

If the counteroffer is accepted by the buyer, the transaction is ready to go to a neutral third party known as escrow.

TERMITE REPORT   Most lenders require a structural pest control inspection (often incorrectly referred to as a "termite inspection") before making a loan. This inspection is required on all V.A. and F.H.A. loans in areas where infestation or infections are found. The charge for this inspection varies from $15 to $25, plus mileage charges for property that is located some distance from cities. This fee may be paid by the buyer, since he is requesting the loan. However, in some areas of southern California, the seller customarily pays for this inspection.

The expression "termite inspection" or "termite clearance," so commonly used in many real estate transactions, is possibly misleading to the parties concerned, including the agent.

All structural pest control operators use a form prescribed by the State of California Structural Pest Control Board. It is entitled Standard Structural Pest Control Inspection Report, and has a subheading entitled Wood Destroying Pests or Organisms. The report deals with all forms of pests and infestations. A structural pest control inspector cannot limit his inspection to one type of infestation or infection. The report, however, may be made on only part of a building, providing that the report is designated as a limited one. The inspector reports any and all evidence of infestation, infections, and adverse conditions found in the building inspected.

When a real estate licensee requests an inspection from a pest control firm, he should ask for a structural pest control inspection report. The question of whether all or some of the recommendations made in the report are to be completed or not is a matter decided by someone other than the pest control operator.

UNIT SUMMARY

In this unit we have pointed out the advantages of having a competitive market analysis in determining the selling price for your property. The Estimated Seller's Net form is explained as a tool in determining the net proceeds that can be expected from the sale of a home.

The advantages and disadvantages of the various types of listings, such as open listings, net listings, exclusive listings, and multiple listing, were explored. The Exclusive Authorization and Right to Sell form was explained in detail.

This unit stated that when the above-mentioned preliminaries are completed and the deposit receipt is filled out, offers may be forthcoming from prospective buyers. An offer may then be accepted or a counteroffer may be made.

The unit concludes with an explanation of the procedure involved in taking the transaction to escrow, including the ''termite inspection'' report.

REVIEWING YOUR UNDERSTANDING

MULTIPLE-CHOICE

(   )   1   A broker earns his commission:
    a At close of escrow.
    b At the time he lists property.
    c When he finds a buyer ready, willing, and able to purchase on terms agreed to by owner.
    d none of above.

(   )   2   A competitive market analysis:
    a Determines proceeds you may expect.
    b Lists only homes for sale.
    c Lists only listings that have expired.
    d None of the above.

(   )   3   A financial analysis report refers to:
    a Estimated selling costs.
    b Gross equity in property.
    c Deposit receipt.
    d Both (a) and (b).

(   )   4   An open listing authorizes that:
    a One or more brokers may act as agent.
    b You may sell your own property.
    c The commission amount is open.
    d Both (a) and (b).

(   )   5   A net listing is usually used with:
    a Single family dwellings.
    b Commercial property.
    c Mobile homes.
    d Multiple unit dwellings.

(   )   6   In an exclusive right to sell listing:
    a Broker making the sale receives the full commission.
    b If you make the sale the exclusive agent receives part of the commission.
    c The broker holding the exclusive receives a commission even if the sale is made by another broker.
    d All of the above.

(   )   7   In listing your property through MLS:
    a One of many brokers may make the sale.
    b Commission can be paid to the listing broker as well as the one who makes the sale.
    c All members of MLS are Realtors or Realtor Associates.
    d All of the above.

( ) **8** When the buyer presents an offer:
    a It must be accepted by the seller.
    b It is dangerous to attempt to negotiate changes.
    c The seller may issue a counteroffer.
    d All of the above.

( ) **9** One of the following statements is true concerning termite inspections:
    a The term termite inspection is listed on the required form.
    b All loans require a termite inspection.
    c F.H.A. and V.A. loans in California require such a report.
    d Both (a) and (b).

( ) **10** The commission received for listing is not fixed in:
    a An exclusive listing.
    b A net listing.
    c An open listing.
    d All of the above.

SUGGESTED LEARNING ACTIVITIES

Visit a multiple listing office to observe first hand the operations of MLS.

REVIEWING YOUR UNDERSTANDING—ANSWERS

1 c		**6** c	
2 d		**7** d	
3 d		**8** c	
4 b		**9** c	
5 b		**10** b	

25

A basic understanding of income taxes is becoming more important each year as taxes continue to increase. We will learn how income taxes affect you and real estate. Understanding that the income tax is complex, we will deal with this unit in simplified terms to enable you to understand the basic tax principles and laws involved.

Read this study guide (page 230–236).
View TV program, number 25.

At the conclusion of this unit, you will be able to:

1 List three types of basis and the characteristics of each.
2 Give the requirements for long-term capital gain treatment.
3 Identify two requirements of an installment sale.
4 Be able to solve problems concerning depreciation.
5 List at least three tax advantages of home ownership.
6 List at least three requirements regarding eligibility for tax assistance to the aged.

basis, adjusted cost basis   exchange
capital gain   economic life
installment sale   indicated gain

BASIS It is important that the homeowner or investor understand the relationship between basis and the ultimate sale price of the property. Basis is the beginning point for computing the amount of gain or loss on the sale.

Although property is acquired in many different ways, we will discuss the three main methods of acquiring ownership; basis by purchase, basis by gift, and basis by inheritance.

Basis by purchase is the price paid for the property.

Basis by gift is the donor's (giver of the gift) adjusted basis plus the gift tax paid but not to exceed the fair market value at the time of the gift.

Basis by inheritance is the fair market value at time of death or 1 year later if elected.

ADJUSTED COST BASIS While basis is the beginning point for the calculation of gain or loss on the sale, a number of adjustments to basis occur throughout the period of ownership. The adjusted cost basis (ACB) reflects the final calculations that represent these changes.

Basis is increased by certain closing costs such as title insurance paid, appraisal or legal fees, capital improvements made, and sale costs on disposition. Basis is reduced by accumulated depreciation taken.

The ACB, then, reflects the original basis plus and minus any of these changes. The ACB is subtracted from the sales price to determine the extent of any gain or loss. Below is an example.

$ 40,000	original basis	
+	500	applicable closing costs on purchase
+ 2,000	capital improvements (new roof, not a roof repair)	
+ 4,000	sales costs on disposition	
$ 46,500		
− 10,500	accumulated depreciation	
$ 36,000	adjusted cost basis	
$ 60,000	sales price	
−36,000	adjusted cost basis	
$ 24,000	indicated gain	

The basis of property wherein title is held as community property is fair market value as of time of death or one year later. The above example would be represented as follows if one of the spouses died, regardless of the development of the ACB prior to death.

$ 60,000	sales price immediately after death
−60,000	basis
0	indicated gain

As of this writing, it appears that joint tenancy property will be accorded the same tax treatment to the surviving spouse as community property under the new law. Check with your own tax counsel, however, on this point.

CAPITAL GAINS OR ORDINARY Generally, most real estate is considered a capital asset. As such, real estate is afforded the advantage of capital treatment upon sale under certain conditions. If property is held for longer than 6 months, the gain is treated as a long-term capital gain. Only one-half of the net long-term capital gain is included in the taxpayer's income. The taxpayer may elect to use the alternate method of a flat 25 percent of the gain up to $50,000 and 35 percent on the excess above $50,000.

$ 60,000 sales price
$-36,000$ adjusted cost basis
_____
$ 24,000 indicated gain

$24,000 indicated gain × 50 percent = $12,000 added to the taxpayer's income from gainful employment.

If the holding period is 6 months or less, the entire indicated gain is added to the taxpayer's income as ordinary income.

INSTALLMENT SALES Under Internal Revenue Code Section 453 a taxpayer may elect to use the installment sale, which spreads the tax on gain over a number of years. This avoids paying tax on the entire gain in the year in which the property is sold. Two requirements must be observed to qualify for the installment sale.

1 The down payment plus principal payment on the mortgage must not exceed 30 percent of the sales price in the year of the sale.

2 The taxpayer must claim the installment sale election on his tax return for the year in which the property is sold.

EXCHANGES Under Internal Revenue Code Section 1031, gain or loss is not recognized under a properly structured real estate exchange. The property must be held for use in trade or business, for increase in value, or for the production of income. This section does not apply to personal residences.

The property must be exchanged for other "like" property, which is real estate meeting the above requirements. Any "unlike" property is termed "boot" and is taxable unless offset.

Through a tax-deferred exchange, the gain is deferred until the new property is sold. Exchanges are extremely complex, and we will not go into greater detail in this text.

DEPRECIATION Taxpayers who own investment properties are entitled to deductions for depreciation. An owner of a personal residence is not entitled to depreciation under the tax laws.

Land is not depreciable, since it is not subject to physical deterioration. If an investor paid $100,000 for a property and $25,000 was allocated to the land, $85,000 was allocated to the improvements, and $5000 was deducted for salvage value, he would be able to depreciate the only $80,000. Salvage value is the reasonably anticipated fair market value of the property at the end of its useful life and must be taken into account with all but the declining balance method. Personal property may also be depreciated if applicable.

The economic life of the improvement must be established. This is the period of time over which the improvement's economic existence can be justified. Under Revenue Procedure 62-21, suggested economic lives are given. Forty years is the suggested life for a new apartment building. Consequently, an apartment building that is 15 years old would have a remaining economic life of 25 years, and the depreciation schedule would be set up on that basis unless a shorter or longer life could be justified.

The taxpayer must select the method of depreciation that is consistent with current laws. There are several methods available, but the most commonly used are straight line depreciation and declining balance depreciation.

STRAIGHT LINE DEPRECIATION Straight line depreciation is characterized by equal annual deductions that are computed by dividing the improvement value less salvage value by the economic life.

$100,000 purchase price
−15,000 land
− 5,000 salvage value

$ 80,000 total allowable for depreciation

$80,000 × 4 percent = $3,200 per year depreciation

$$\frac{\$80,000}{40\text{-year life}} = \$2,000 \text{ per year depreciation}$$

OR

$$\frac{100 \text{ percent total depreciation}}{40\text{-year life}} = 2\frac{1}{2} \text{ percent per year}$$

$80,000 × 0.025 = $2,000 per year depreciation

If the economic life was 25 years:

$$\frac{100 \text{ percent total depreciation}}{25\text{-year life}} = 4 \text{ percent per year}$$

DECLINING BALANCE DEPRECIATION Declining balance depreciation takes the form of 125 percent, 150 percent, or 200 percent of straight line depreciation. The following shows which properties are eligible for the declining balance method.

	NEW	USED
Apartments	200 percent declining balance if first user of new building	125 percent if economic life of at least 20 years
		Straight line if less than 20 years
Commercial	150 percent declining balance if first user of new building	Straight line

Owners do not have to use the declining balance method. They may use straight line depreciation even on a new building if they prefer. Salvage value is not considered for declining balance.

HOW DECLINING BALANCE IS COMPUTED   Depreciation will decline annually under this method. To compute the first year's depreciation, multiply the straight line rate by 125 percent, 150 percent, or 200 percent.

$100,000   improvement value, 40-year life, 2.5 percent declining balance
  × 0.025 (100 percent ÷ 40 years = 2   percent)
_____

$ 2,500   straight line depreciation
      × 2   (200 percent)
_____

$ 5,000   first year depreciation 200 percent declining balance

To compute the second year depreciation, you must deduct the amount of depreciation taken the first year from the original amount and repeat the percentage calculations.

$100,000   original improvement value
  −5,000   first year depreciation

$ 95,000   balance
× 0.025

   2,375   straight line
     × 2
_____

$ 4,750   second year depreciation 200 percent declining balance

As a short cut, it should be apparent that you can double the straight line depreciation rate to $0.025 \times 2 = 0.05$ and eliminate one step.

DEPRECIATION RATES

Useful Life, Years	Straight Line, %	125% Declining Balance, %	150% Declining Balance, %	200% Declining Balance, %
50	2.00	2.50	3.00	4.00
40	2.50	3.13	3.75	5.00
25	4.00	5.00	6.00	8.00
20	5.00	6.25	7.50	10.00

PERSONAL RESIDENCES   You are entitled to deductions for property taxes and interest payments on your mortgage. You cannot take deductions for repairs, nor may you depreciate your home. Capital improvements may be added to your basis to reduce the indicated gain on sale. You are entitled to capital gain treatment, but you cannot deduct losses.

Under Internal Revenue Code Section 1034, no gain is recognized if you exchange your home for another personal residence (not a second or vacation home). The cost of the newly acquired residence must equal or exceed the adjusted sales price of the former residence. The adjusted sale price is the gross sale price less fixing-up expenses, which are incurred within 90 days before the sale and paid within 30 days after the sale.

You may also sell your personal residence and defer any gain if you purchase another personal residence within 18 months before or after the sale of the former residence, provided that the cost of the newly acquired residence exceeds the adjusted sale price of the former residence. If the new home is under construction within 1 year before or after the sale of the former residence and it is completed and used as your personal residence within 2 years of the former sale, the gain is deferred, provided that the cost equals or exceeds the adjusted sale price of the former residence.

TAX ASSISTANCE FOR THE AGED

Internal Revenue Code Section 121 affords tax relief for those who are 65 or older when their personal residence is sold. You are allowed an exclusion of the first $20,000 of the adjusted sale price, provided you have owned and used the property as your personal residence for 5 out of the last 8 years preceding the sale. Either the husband or wife may be 65 or older, provided you are legally married at the time the property is held as either community property or joint tenancy. This exemption is available only once during your lifetime.

UNIT SUMMARY

We discussed three different types of basis and the characteristics of each. We learned the technical aspects of capital gains, installment sales, exchanges, depreciation, and tax assistance for the aged. Obviously, you should consult your personal tax advisor when the occasion arises. However, you now have the basic tools to do some tax preplanning, which you will find invaluable in later years.

REVIEWING YOUR UNDERSTANDING

TRUE OR FALSE

( ) **1** The adjusted cost basis by gift is developed by starting with the fair market value of the gift.

( ) **2** To be eligible for a long-term capital gain, the holding period must be over 6 months.

( ) **3** One requirement of the installment sale is the 30 percent rule.

( ) **4** If the economic life of a property was 33 years, the percent factor to be applied would be 3 percent.

( ) **5** Salvage value must be considered in all methods of depreciation.

FILL-INS

1 The _____ of an investment property is the period of time over which it can justify its economic existence.

REVIEWING YOUR UNDERSTANDING—ANSWERS

2 Spreading the tax on the gain over a number of years is an election to use the _____ _____.

3 Under a properly structured section 1031 transaction, the tax is _____.

TRUE OR FALSE
1 False
2 True
3 True
4 True
5 False

FILL-INS
1 economic life
2 installment sale
3 deferred

26

SHOULD YOU CONSIDER A SMALL INVESTMENT PROPERTY?

Perhaps you should consider a small investment property. Here, we discuss several of the significant factors involved in investment properties, including the four internal factors and two additional factors. We conclude with an analysis of a typical property.

Read this study guide (page 238–247).
View TV program, number 26.

At the conclusion of this unit you will be able to:

1 Identify and describe the characteristics of the four internal factors affecting investments.

2 List and give examples of the effects of two additional factors affecting investments.

3 Give your own example of the significance of leverage.

risk, liquidity   leverage
increment   tax shelter

AN INVESTMENT DEFINED

Most people try to save a portion of their income for future investment. They understand that their money will work harder for them if it is invested prudently. An investment is the allocation of funds for income or for profit.

There are many different types of investments. Each has its advantages and disadvantages. Some individuals invest their money in savings accounts, life insurance, and stocks and bonds. Others invest in real estate. Whichever form their investment takes, investors are primarily concerned with the income to be received and the potential profit to be made when the investment is sold. The income to be received can take the form of interest, dividends, or rents. The profit that is made when the investment is sold is referred to as appreciation.

FOUR FACTORS INFLUENCING INVESTMENTS

There are generally four internal factors that influence all investments. They are risk, liquidity, management, and increment.

Risk is the chance that the investor takes that he may lose all or a part of his initial investment. Risk is relative to the return expected. If an investor desires a high return, he can expect a higher risk. The risk involved with savings accounts, life insurance, and bonds is considered low. However, the return on these investments is also considered low. The risk involved in stocks and real estate will vary, depending on the quality and the market conditions at the time of purchase and sale.

Liquidity is the quality of being able to convert the investment to cash. Savings accounts, life insurance, and stocks and bonds are considered very liquid. Real estate is not as liquid as these other investments. However, real estate priced right will sell in a reasonable period of time. Also, if sufficient equity is present the property may be refinanced, thus releasing cash.

Management is required in all investments. Although the cost of management is negligible on savings accounts and insurance, it is nonetheless present and the net return to the investor is reduced accordingly. Management is usually necessary when stocks and bonds are bought and sold. On smaller real estate investments, the owner may choose to manage the property himself. On larger properties, professional management is usually required.

Increment is the hope of selling the investment at a later date for more than was originally paid for it. Consequently, appreciation is an important factor. Investments such as savings accounts and insurance generally have no increment value. It is true that interest is accumulated. However, the dollar amount of the capital investment remains the same. The same is true of bonds which earn interest. Stocks often have substantial appreciation. Sometimes, however, they drop significantly in value depending on the market. Real estate has statistically tended to increase significantly in value over the years.

ADDITIONAL FACTORS INFLUENCING INVESTMENTS

There are two external factors that influence investments. They are taxes and inflation.

An important consideration to many investors is not how much they earn, but how much they keep after paying income taxes. Investments are taxed differently. Savings account interest and stock dividends are taxed as ordinary income. Income from annuities is also taxed as ordinary income, although only a portion is subject to tax since it is a partial return of capital. Real estate income in the form of rents can be offset by operating expenses and deductions for depreciation and interest payments on a mortgage. This increases spendable income which, in most cases, is wholly or at least partially sheltered from income taxes.

Another tax consideration is the method of taxation that is applied to the profit from a sale. Stocks held more than six months are afforded capital gains treatment as is real estate. However, real estate enjoys a particular advantage not afforded to other investments. Under Internal Revenue Code Section 1031, real estate may be exchanged for other real property on a tax-deferred basis if certain requirements are met.

Inflation takes its toll on fixed income investments such as savings accounts, preferred stocks, annuities, and bonds. The investor receives a stipulated interest rate regardless of the effect of inflation. People on fixed incomes have learned this hard lesson in the past several years. Common stock has normally kept pace with inflation. Real estate has been one of the best hedges against inflation.

INDIVIDUAL DECISIONS

As we have learned, real estate is an attractive investment. However, each person's motivation and circumstances must be considered. A retired investor would probably want a high return of cash spendable income to supplement his income. He therefore would want a low risk investment. A younger person paying high taxes might not want additional income but would prefer tax shelter and appreciation. He would prefer leverage that maximizes loans and minimizes his down payment.

We now consider two examples that illustrate this point. Both involve the same apartment building with a sales price of $85,000. In the first example (see Figures 1 to 3) the buyer has a first deed of trust of $60,000 only. In the second example (see Figures 4 to 6) we add a second deed of trust of $10,000 to illustrate the effects of leverage for an investor with different motivations.

COMPARISON OF THE TWO EXAMPLES

	Example 1	Example 2	Difference
Cash flow	$1,291	$ 91	−$1,200
Equity buildup	648	948	+300
Tax savings	688	1,126	+438
Appreciation	2,550	2,550	0
Total net return	$5,177 (19.1%)	$4,715 (27.7%)	−462

As you can see from the above comparison, the buyer in Example 2 has a total net return of only $462 less the first year than the buyer in Example 1. This is true even though his initial investment was $10,000 less. His percentage return is higher as his money is working harder for him. Of course, his risk is greater, since he has less cash flow to cover a major unforeseen expenditure. He also has to be concerned with paying off the second deed of trust when it comes due. Typically, this is done through refinancing the first deed of trust, assuming the property has increased in value and the balance of both loans has been reduced by principal payments.

It should be emphasized that cash flow and tax shelter are tangible money

FIGURE 1

ESTIMATED ANNUAL INCOME
AND EXPENSE STATEMENT

Property <u>123 Elm St.</u>

INCOME:

_____(un) furnished_____bedroom units @ $_____per month = $_____

_____(un) furnished_____bedroom units @ $_____per month = _____

_____(un) furnished_____bedroom units @ $_____per month = _____

_____(un) furnished_____bedroom units @ $_____per month = _____

_____(un) furnished_____bedroom units @ $_____per month = _____

Miscellaneous_____per month _____

_____per month _____

Total Monthly Income ....$ <u>1,905</u>

Scheduled Gross Income ....$ <u>13,140</u>

   Less: Reserve for Vacancies <u>2</u> % ....$ <u>263</u>

Gross Operating Income ....$ <u>12,877</u>

LESS OPERATING EXPENSES:

Taxes	$ 2,268	or	%
Insurance	$ 200	or	%
Gas and Electricity	$ 745	or	%
Water	$ 135	or	%
Sewer and Refuse	$ 225	or	%
Reserves & Maintenance	$ 920	or	%
Management ⎫	$ 920	or	%
Resident Mgr. ⎭	$	or	%
Bus. License	$ 25	or	%
Miscellaneous	$ 100	or	%
	$	or	%
	$ 5,538	or	% × $

                                            $ <u>5,538</u>

ESTIMATED NET OPERATING INCOME ....$ <u>7,339</u>

LOAN SERVICE: Sales Price $85,000

  1st T.D. $<u>60,000</u>, <u>25</u> years, <u>9</u> % interest.

  Monthly <u>$504</u>. Yearly Payments interest $<u>5,400</u>

  and principal $<u>648</u> ....$ 6,048

  2nd T.D. $_____, _____years, _____% interest.

  Monthly_____. Yearly Payments interest $_____

  and principal $_____ ....$

  Other. $_____, _____years, _____% interest.

  Monthly_____. Yearly Payments interest $_____

  and principal $_____ ....$

                           Total Payments $ <u>6,048</u>

ANNUAL GROSS SPENDABLE INCOME: $ <u>1,291</u>

Date_____

FIGURE 2

ANALYSIS OF TAX SHELTER

Property __123 Elm St.__

NOTE: The depreciation schedules listed below are estimates to demonstrate the depreciation benefits available from this investment. We suggest you consult your tax counselor regarding your individual needs.

ESTIMATED BASIS FOR DEPRECIATION:

Land (Non-depreciable)	20 %	.... $	17,000
Building	75 %	....	63,750
Equipment ... ⎫	.... %	....	
Rugs & Drapes ⎬	5 %	....	4,250
Furniture ..... ⎪	.... %	....	
Other .... ⎭	.... %	....	

....

$ __85,000__

ESTIMATED DEPRECIATION—First Year
$63,750 ÷ 25 yrs. = $2,550/yr. depreciation

Building: _25_ years estimated life, Method _straight line_ $ __2,550__
balance

Appliances & Equipment: ____ years estimated life, Method _____
balance

$4,250 ÷ 5 yrs. = $850/yr. depreciation

Rugs & Drapes: _5_ years estimated life, Method _straight line_   850
balance

Furniture: ____ years estimated life, Method _____
balance

Other: ____ years estimated life, Method _____
balance

$ __3,400__

ESTIMATED INTEREST—First Year

First Deed of Trust	$ __5,400__	
Second " " "	_____	
Third " " "	_____	
_____ " " "	_____	
	$ __5,400__	$ __5,400__

TOTAL DEPRECIATION AND INTEREST—FIRST YEAR	$ __8,800__
ESTIMATED NET OPERATING INCOME	$ __6,048__
FIRST YEAR REAL ESTATE TAXABLE LOSS	$ __⟨2,752⟩__

Note: Loss may be applied to income from other sources.

THIS STATEMENT WITH THE INFORMATION IT CONTAINS IS GIVEN WITH THE UNDERSTANDING THAT ALL NEGOTIATIONS RELATING TO THE PURCHASE, RENTING OR LEASING OF THE PROPERTY DESCRIBED ABOVE SHALL BE CONDUCTED THROUGH THIS OFFICE. THE ABOVE INFORMATION, WHILE NOT GUARANTEED, HAS BEEN SECURED FROM SOURCES WE BELIEVE TO BE RELIABLE.

Date _____

FIGURE 3

**ANALYSIS OF RETURN
ON INVESTMENT**

Property ___123 Elm St.___

INVESTMENT (including costs of $__2,000__)* $__27,000__

I. *CASH FLOW*
Estimated Annual Gross Spendable Income | $1,291 |
or Cash Return on Investment of . . . . | 4.8 % |

II. *EQUITY BUILDUP*
Annual loan payments of $__6,048__less Interest
of $__5,400__amounts to Equity Buildup of | $ 648 |
which is equal to a return of . . . . | 2.4 % |

III. *TAX SAVINGS*
1st year tax loss of $__2,752__in the __25__% tax
bracket results in estimated tax savings of | $ 688 |
or return on investment of . . . . | 2.5 % |

IV. *APPRECIATION*
Property values in this vicinity have appreciated at
the rate of approximately __3__% per year recently.
This would result in an increase in value of | $2,550 |
or an additional return on investment of . . . . | 9.4 % |

V. *TOTAL NET RETURN ON INVESTMENT*
I plus II plus III plus IV . . . . | $5,177 | | 19.1 % |

* Closing Costs: Estimated costs of transaction. Some of these costs may be depreciation
items, added to the basis of property for tax purposes.

THIS STATEMENT WITH THE INFORMATION IT CONTAINS IS GIVEN WITH THE UNDERSTANDING THAT ALL
NEGOTIATIONS RELATING TO THE PURCHASE, RENTING OR LEASING OF THE PROPERTY DESCRIBED ABOVE
SHALL BE CONDUCTED THROUGH THIS OFFICE. THE ABOVE INFORMATION, WHILE NOT GUARANTEED, HAS
BEEN SECURED FROM SOURCES WE BELIEVE TO BE RELIABLE.

Date_____

FIGURE 4

**ESTIMATED ANNUAL INCOME
AND EXPENSE STATEMENT**

Property 123 Elm St.

INCOME:

_____(un) furnished_____bedroom units @ $_____per month = $_____

_____(un) furnished_____bedroom units @ $_____per month = _____

_____(un) furnished_____bedroom units @ $_____per month = _____

_____(un) furnished_____bedroom units @ $_____per month = _____

_____(un) furnished_____bedroom units @ $_____per month = _____

Miscellaneous_____per month _____

_____per month _____

Total Monthly Income .... $ 1,095

Scheduled Gross Income .... $ 13,140

    Less: Reserve for Vacancies 2 % .... $ 263

Gross Operating Income .... $ 12,877

LESS OPERATING EXPENSES:

Taxes	$ 2,268 or	%
Insurance	$ 200 or	%
Gas and Electricity	$ 745 or	%
Water	$ 135 or	%
Sewer and Refuse	$ 225 or	%
Reserves & Maintenance	$ 920 or	%
Management ⎤ Resident Mgr. ⎦	$ 920 or	%
	$ or	%
Bus. License	$ 25 or	%
Miscellaneous	$ 100 or	%
	$ or	%

$ 5,538 or ____% × $ $ 5,538

ESTIMATED NET OPERATING INCOME .... $ 7,339

LOAN SERVICE: Sales Price $85,000

1st T.D. $ 60,000 , 25 years, 9 % interest.

Monthly $504 . Yearly Payments interest $ 5,400

and principal $ 648 .... $ 6,048

2nd T.D. $ 10,000 , 8 years, 9 % interest.

Monthly $100 . Yearly Payments interest $ 900

and principal $ 300 .... $ 1,200

Other. $_____years, _____% interest.

Monthly_____. Yearly Payments interest $_____

and principal $_____ .... $_____

Total Payments $ 7,248

ANNUAL GROSS SPENDABLE INCOME: $ 91

THIS STATEMENT WITH THE INFORMATION IT CONTAINS IS GIVEN WITH THE UNDERSTANDING THAT ALL NEGOTIATIONS RELATING TO THE PURCHASE, RENTING OR LEASING OF THE PROPERTY DESCRIBED ABOVE SHALL BE CONDUCTED THROUGH THIS OFFICE. THE ABOVE INFORMATION, WHILE NOT GUARANTEED, HAS BEEN SECURED FROM SOURCES WE BELIEVE TO BE RELIABLE.

Date_____

FIGURE 5 **ANALYSIS OF TAX SHELTER**

Property __123 Elm St.__

NOTE: The depreciation schedules listed below are estimates to demonstrate the depreciation benefits available from this investment. We suggest you consult your tax counselor regarding your individual needs.

ESTIMATED BASIS FOR DEPRECIATION:

Land (Non-depreciable)	_20_ %	$	_17,000_
Building	_75_ %		_63,750_
Equipment ... ⎫	_____ %		_____
Rugs & Drapes ⎬	_5_ %		_4,250_
Furniture ..... ⎪	_____ %		_____
Other .... ⎭	_____ %		_____

.... _____

$ _____

ESTIMATED DEPRECIATION—First Year

$100\% \div 25 \text{ yrs.} = 4\% \text{ yr.} \times .25 = 1.0 + 4.0 = 5\% \times \$63{,}750 = \$3{,}188$

Building: _25_ years estimated life, Method _125% D.B._ $ _3,188_
    (balance)

Appliances & Equipment: _____ years estimated life, Method____   _____
    (balance)

$100\% \div 5 \text{ yrs.} = 20\% \text{ yr.} \times .25 = 5 + 20 = 25\% \times \$4{,}250 = \$1{,}063$

Rugs & Drapes: _5_ years estimated life, Method _125% D.B._   _1,063_
    (balance)

Furniture: _____ years estimated life, Method _____   _____
    (balance)

Other: _____ years estimated life, Method _____   _____
    (balance)

$ _4,251_

ESTIMATED INTEREST—First Year

First Deed of Trust	$ _5,400_
Second '' '' ''	_900_
Third '' '' ''	_____
_____ '' '' ''	_____
	$ _6,300_

$ _6,300_

TOTAL DEPRECIATION AND INTEREST—FIRST YEAR $ _10,551_

ESTIMATED NET OPERATING INCOME $ _6,048_

FIRST YEAR REAL ESTATE TAXABLE LOSS $ ⟨4,503⟩

Note: Loss may be applied to income from other sources.

Date_____

FIGURE 6

ANALYSIS OF RETURN ON INVESTMENT

Property __123 Elm St.__

INVESTMENT (including costs of $__2,000__)* $ __17,000__

I. *CASH FLOW*
Estimated Annual Gross Spendable Income | $ 91 |
or Cash Return on Investment of .... | .5 % |

II. *EQUITY BUILDUP*
Annual loan payments of $__7,248__ less Interest
of $__6,300__ amounts to Equity Buildup of | $ 948 |
which is equal to a return of .... | 5.6 % |

III. *TAX SAVINGS*
1st year tax loss of $__4,503__ in the __25__ % tax
bracket results in estimated tax savings of | $1,126 |
or return on investment of .... | 6.6 % |

IV. *APPRECIATION*
Property values in this vicinity have appreciated at
the rate of approximately __3__ % per year recently.
This would result in an increase in value of | $2,550 |
or an additional return on investment of .... | 15.0 % |

V. *TOTAL NET RETURN ON INVESTMENT*
I plus II plus III plus IV............................ | $4,715 | | 27.7 % |

* Closing Costs: Estimated costs of transaction. Some of these costs may be depreciation items, added to the basis of property for tax purposes.

THIS STATEMENT WITH THE INFORMATION IT CONTAINS IS GIVEN WITH THE UNDERSTANDING THAT ALL NEGOTIATIONS RELATING TO THE PURCHASE, RENTING OR LEASING OF ALL THE PROPERTY DESCRIBED ABOVE SHALL BE CONDUCTED THROUGH THIS OFFICE. THE ABOVE INFORMATION, WHILE NOT GUARANTEED, HAS BEEN SECURED FROM SOURCES WE BELIEVE TO BE RELIABLE.

Date_____

amounts realized each year. Possible appreciation and equity build (loan reduction) are not realized until sale. Accelerated depreciation (depreciation in excess of straight line) is recaptured as ordinary income on sale. It can be deferred through a properly observed tax deferred exchange, however.

UNIT SUMMARY

REVIEWING YOUR UNDERSTANDING

In this unit we have shown that a real estate investment has certain advantages over other types of investments. You have learned that there are many factors to take into consideration concerning investments. Like any investment, real estate has certain risks. However, historically, real estate has proved to be one of the best investments.

TRUE OR FALSE

( ) **1** The most liquid investment is real estate.

( ) **2** Only real estate is afforded the advantage of the tax deferred exchange.

( ) **3** Stocks and real estate traditionally do better than most other investments in inflationary times.

( ) **4** Retired individuals normally prefer leverage in a real estate transaction.

( ) **5** Management of most investments relative to real estate is less expensive and less burdensome to the investor.

FILL-INS

1 That investment factor that describes appreciation is called _____.

2 The investment that has the most tax advantages is _____.

3 Interest earned on savings accounts is taxed at_____ _____.

REVIEWING YOUR UNDERSTANDING—ANSWERS

TRUE OR FALSE

1 False

2 True

3 True

4 False

5 True

FILL-INS

1 increment

2 real estate

3 ordinary income rates

27

In this unit you will learn what a lease is and what it should contain.

There are two principal forms of leases. These will be explained and a sample standard lease form will be carefully analyzed.

There are certain statutory restrictions on the power to lease property. Each type of property, with its time limit, will be discussed. Four different types of leaseholds determined by their time duration will be compared. You will learn that leases can be of definite duration and an indefinite duration.

The rights, privileges, and obligations as a landlord or as a tenant are explained in detail.

Renewals, extensions, and terminations of leases will be explained in terms of the legal ramifications of leases.

Property management is explored, and the duties and qualifications of a property manager are reviewed.

Read this study guide (pages 250–260).
View TV program, number 27.

At the conclusion of this unit, you will be able to:

1 Define and describe a lease and list the information that must be included.

2 Distinguish between tenancy for years, periodic tenancy, tenancy at sufferance, and tenancy at will.

3 Distinguish between the rights of the lessor and lessee as parties to a lease agreement.

4 Explain the major legal ramifications related to the creation and termination of a lease.

5 Describe a professional property manager and list his specific duties and responsibilities.

lease
straight lease
percentage lease
tenancy for years
periodic tenancy
tenancy at will

tenancy at sufferance
lien
abandonment
constructive eviction
assignment
sublease

You may desire to derive income from your property by allowing others to use and/or occupy it for a fixed rental fee; that is you may desire to *lease* the property.

WHAT IS A LEASE?

A lease is an agreement between the owner of real property and another party who wishes to rent that property for an agreed period of time for a certain amount of money. The lessor is the one who holds title (or the owner or landlord) and the lessee is the person (or tenant) who wishes to occupy and/or use the property.

The lease itself is the relationship between the lessor and the lessee and not just a piece of paper; however, the paper that contains the rights and responsibilities of each party is termed a lease or leasehold.

CONTENTS OF A LEASE

No exact wording is required to create a leasehold, as long as the intention to rent the property appears. However, there must be a contract or agreement between the lessor and the lessee that includes the names of the parties and a description of the premises; the street address will suffice, but a legal description will cover all contingencies. It should specify what is included, such as parking space.

In order to avoid undesirable use of the premises it should specify for what purpose it "shall be used."

The lease can be for as long as both parties agree. However, a stipulation of time within which the contract remains valid must be given. For any lease of 1 year, the law stipulates that it must be in writing. For 1 year or less the agreement may be oral, but the law presumes a month-to-month tenancy and the burden of proof is on the renter to prove otherwise.

CAUTION

Put *all* leases in writing in order to avoid future problems.

Conditions of occupancy must be set forth in the agreement. This includes questions such as: Who pays the taxes? Can the lease be assigned or sublet? What are the public liability provisions? What is the position of both parties to the contract in case of damage by fire, earthquake, and the like? Is the landlord allowed inspection privileges? Who is expected to make necessary repairs?

FORMS OF LEASES

In a *percentage lease* for business purposes, the lessee pays a percentage of his gross sales as rent. A percentage lease usually requires a minimum rent as well.

The type of business will determine the percent paid for the lease. A fixed scale does not exist, but suggested percentages are available. As a rule, when the sale involves low-cost items with a small markup, the percentage paid is lower. Percentages vary from as low as 1 percent to as high as 12 percent. Four to 8 percent is the average.

A *straight lease* is usually applied to residential property and is the most common form of lease. An agreed upon rental is exchange for use, possession, and quiet enjoyment of premises. A standard form is usually used. Figure 1 is a basic form offered by the California Association of Realtors.

FIGURE 1

𝕷𝖊𝖆𝖘𝖊

CALIFORNIA REAL ESTATE ASSOCIATION STANDARD FORM

This Indenture, made the ....day of................, A.D. 19....

between ....

....

....

...., hereinafter called the lessor,

and ....

....

...., hereinafter called the lessee.

WITNESSETH, that the lessor does by these presents, lease and demise unto the lessee all of the property situated in the ....,

County of ...., State of California, described as follows, to wit:

for the term of ....

beginning ....19...., and ending ....19....

for the total rent or sum of ....

....Dollars,

in lawful money of the United States of America, payable as follows, to wit:

All of said rent shall be paid at the office of..,

the agent of the lessor, ...Street,..........................,

California, or at such other place as may be designated by the lessor.

IN ADDITION THERETO IT IS HEREBY AGREED AS FOLLOWS, TO WIT:

First: That the lessee shall pay the lessor said rent in the manner hereinbefore specified, and shall not let or underlet the whole or any part of said premises, nor sell or assign this lease, either voluntarily or by operation of law, nor allow said property to be occupied by anyone contrary to the terms hereof, without the written consent of the lessor;

Second: That should said rent be not paid when due or should the lessee default in any of the covenants or conditions contained herein, the lessor, or his representative or agent, may re-enter said premises and remove all persons therefrom;

Third: That the lessee shall occupy said demised premises and shall keep the same in good condition, including such improvements as may be made thereon hereafter, the usual wear and tear and damage by the elements excepted, and shall not make any alterations thereon without the written consent of the lessor and shall not commit or suffer to be committed any waste upon said premises;

Fourth: That said premises shall not be used by the lessee, nor anyone else, during the term hereof or any extension thereof, for the sale of any intoxicating liquors, nor for any illegal or immoral purpose, and that possession of said premises by the lessee or his successors or assigns shall not be construed as conveying any title thereto or ownership thereof;

Fifth: That all Governmental laws and ordinances shall be complied with by the lessee;

Sixth: That the lessee waives all rights under Section 1942 of the Civil Code of California and releases the lessor from any and all damages which may be sustained by the lessee or any other party during the time he may be in possession of said premises;

Seventh: That should the occupancy of said premises, by the lessee, cause the present fire and liability insurance rates applicable thereto to be increased, the lessee shall pay the difference upon the amount of fire and liability insurance now being carried by the lessor and said difference shall be in addition to the amount of rental specified herein and shall be paid to the lessor upon demand;

Figure 1 (*Continued*)

Eighth: That should the lessor be compelled to commence or sustain an action at law to collect said rent or parts thereof or to dispossess the lessee or to recover possession of said premises, the lessee shall pay all costs in connection therewith including a reasonable fee for the attorney of the lessor;

Ninth: That the waiver, by the lessor, of any covenant or condition herein contained shall not vitiate the same or any other covenant or condition contained herein and that the terms and conditions contained herein shall apply to and bind the heirs, successors and assigns of the respective parties hereto;

Tenth: That should the lessee occupy said premises after the expiration date of this lease, with the consent of the lessor, expressed or implied, such possession shall be construed to be a tenancy from month to month and said lessee shall pay said lessor for said premises the sum of $_____per month for such period as said lessee may remain in possession thereof;

Eleventh: That said premises shall not be used by the lessee during the term of this lease for other than _____purposes except with the written consent of the lessor;

Twelfth: That at the expiration of said term or the sooner determination thereof, the lessee shall peacefully quit and surrender possession of said premises in as good condition as reasonable use and wear thereof will permit;

Thirteenth: That all words used herein in the singular number shall include the plural and the present tense shall include the future and the masculine gender shall include the feminine and neuter.

IN WITNESS WHEREOF, the lessor and the lessee have executed this indenture as of the day and year first above written.

_____

_____

_____

_____

For these forms address California Real Estate Association,
520 So. Grand Ave., Los Angeles 90017
(Copyright, 1928, by California Real Estate Association)

FORM #L-14

LEASE

TO

Dated

CONTENTS OF STANDARD LEASE FORM

1 Date that lease was made, including the termination date.
2 Names of lessor and lessee.
3 Location and description of property.
4 Terms of the lease.
5 Stipulation of rent to be paid.
6 Where rent is to be paid.
7 Special conditions and provisions.
8 Signatures of lessor and lessee.

Forms may differ slightly but all contain the basic legal requirements. No particular language is required so long as the intention to rent the property is clear.

Items 1 and 5 above require additional explanation.

The law stipulates a time limit for leases based on the types of real property involved.

Property within a city or town—99 years.

Municipal property—55 years.

Agricultural or horticultural property—51 years.

Property with mineral lands—35 years.

Tidelands property—66 years.

Property belonging to a minor or incompetent person cannot be leased by guardians or custodians for longer than—10 years.

As in all types of contracts, there must be a consideration in a lease. The consideration is rent for the use of the property. The form specifies when the rent is to be paid or if it is to be paid in advance. (Incidentally, the law states that it is due at the end of the term, unless otherwise agreed. In practice it is usually paid in advance.)

There are actually four types of leaseholds, as determined by their duration: tenancy for years; periodic tenancy; tenancy at will; and tenancy at sufferance.

TENANCY FOR YEARS

This is the most commonly used leasehold, and it specifically states a mutually agreeable time period. The term need not be stated in years but may be for 24 hours, or in months or weeks. Under this agreement the tenant has the right to exclusive possession for a fixed time period, as beginning and termination dates are definitely established.

PERIODIC TENANCY

In this type of agreement, ownership rights are established over an indeterminable period of time. It is commonly called month-to-month tenancy, but can, of course, be day-to-day or week-to-week tenancy. It is deemed to be renewable at the end of each rental period. There is a definite beginning date, but the termination date is not definite. It is usually terminated by a 30-day notice.

TENANCY AT WILL The term of this lease is indefinite and is seldom used. It is created by mutual agreement and can be terminated by either party at any time. Most states, including California, require that some form of notice be given.

TENANCY AT SUFFERANCE When a tenant has completed a tenancy for years and continues to remain on the property, he has a tenancy at sufferance. If the lessor continues to receive rental payments, the lessee may remain, but his rights are limited to those rights that are allowed by the lessor.

There is no implied warranty that the premises are suitable; it is the responsibility of the lessee to inspect the premises and to certify that they are acceptable.

If the lessor refuses payments, all rights and interests of the tenant terminate and he, the lessee, may be treated as a trespasser and ejected by the lessor.

Your rights, privileges, and obligations either as a lessor or a lessee are set forth in the contract as specified by law.

RIGHTS OF LESSOR/LANDLORD The landlord/lessor has no right of entry except as specified in the lease. In case of emergency or other dire need entry is permitted.

There is no implied warranty that the premises are suitable; it is the responsibility of the lessee to inspect the premises and to certify that they are acceptable.

The landlord has a lien on a delinquent tenant's property. This means that he may take possession of certain property of the tenant until rent is paid if this is so stipulated in the law of the state.

Multiple-unit dwellings must post a notice on the premises, showing the name and address of the owner, and/or the owner's agent on whom service calls may be made.

RIGHTS OF LESSEE/TENANT There is an implied agreement that the lessee will deliver premises to the lessor on completion of lease—and to pay rents as agreed.

There is no implied agreement that the lessor pay the lessee for any improvements that the lessee may make. The enjoyment of the use of the improvement is termed to be payment enough.

The lessor must maintain the exterior of the premises and usually has no liability to maintain the interior, in the absence of an agreement to the contrary.

If the premises become unfit and demands for repair are refused, the tenant may leave, terminating the lease, or he may make repairs. If an owner refuses to make necessary repairs after being notified by the tenant, the tenant may spend 1 month's rent for repairs.

If the lessor does not conform to the terms of the lease and the place is deemed untenable and the tenant is forced to leave, he is said to have been "constructively evicted." Under "constructive eviction," the lessee is not liable for the remainder of the rent under the lease.

RIGHT OF QUIET POSSESSION The right of quiet possession is an essential right of the tenant. The law implies a covenant by the lessor for "quiet enjoyment and possession" of leased premises to lessees. Constructive eviction mentioned in the previous paragraph can occur through the landlord's attempts to lease property to others or through making extensive and unwarranted alterations to the leased premises.

Other remedies are available to the tenant if the landlord fails to maintain or repair property.

1 He may make his own repairs (maximum of 1 month's rent can be deducted).
2 He may abandon the premises.

ABANDONMENT OF PREMISES

If the premises are abandoned or the lessee leaves the property, he is still obligated to comply with the terms of the lease, and the lessor may sue for the rent as it becomes due. If he in turn rerents the property, he can only recover the difference between the amount owed and the amount recovered from the new lessee.

The lease is not automatically cancelled by the death of either party. The lease usually binds the heirs and successors of the lessee.

If, during the lease of commercial property, the lessee goes out of business, vacates the premises, and discontinues the rent, it is termed abandonment and the lessor may choose one of several remedies.

1 He can allow the premises to remain idle and sue for the rent as it is due.

2 He may rerent the property and hold the lessee responsible for the difference between the delinquent rent and the proceeds of reletting.

3 He may sue for damages as provided within the limits of the law.

Obligations of a dual nature are created in a lease relationship: those growing out of a landlord and tenant relationship (discussed earlier in this unit), and those growing out of the expressed stipulations of the lease.

PREPAID RENT

The lessee is usually required to pay the first and last month's rent in advance and/or make a security deposit that will cover possible rent delinquencies or damage to property.

INSURANCE, TAXES, AND THE LIKE

The lessee may have to maintain fire insurance or liability insurance. He may also have to pay property taxes or increases. An "inflation clause" may be written into the agreement whereby lessee agrees to a rent increase if some index figure increases or taxes increase.

RIGHTS OF ENTRY BY LESSOR

Lessee is entitled to quiet possession. This means that he is entitled to exclusive possession without interference by the lessor. However, the lessor may enter in case of emergencies.

ASSIGNMENT AND SUBLEASE

If it is not forbidden in the agreement, the tenant may make an assignment of his lease or create a sublease. An assignment is a transfer of the entire leasehold which, in a sublease, the lessee sublets the premises but still remains responsible to the lessor for payments of the rent under the lease.

EXAMPLE

At the end of a 3-year lease, if the tenant wishes to assign to a third party his rights for the remainder of the contract he may do so, or he may choose to sublet for only 2 years and reoccupy the premises the third year.

REPAIRS Unless the premises are a dwelling house, the lessee bears the burden of the ordinary repairs needed to keep the premises in good condition, allowing for normal expected wear and tear.

LEGAL RAMIFICATIONS TO CONSIDER If the tenant does not comply with the terms of the lease and fails to remedy the default, he is guilty of "unlawful detainer" and may be sued for three times the amount of back rent and ordered to leave the premises—this is an eviction notice. This notice is served by a landlord or his agent on a defaulting tenant.

"Unlawful detainer action" is initiated as follows.

1 Complaint is served on the tenant and he is given 3-days notice to "pay rent or quit."

2 If he doesn't pay the delinquent rents within 3 days, he must vacate.

3 Notice must be personally served or, in the case of commercial property, the notice may be posted on the premises.

Property can be sublet unless the lease specifies otherwise. The original lessee is then liable to the lessor for the rent payments.

If a lease is renewed a new contract should be written. If the lease is extended the terms of the original agreement remains in force unless specifically removed. Since all contracts require a consideration to pass between the parties, rent paid is the consideration paid by the lessee, in exchange for the granting of the premises by the lessor.

TERMINATION OF LEASE A lease agreement may be terminated by one or both parties for various reasons.

1 When the agreed term has expired.

2 Constructive eviction when tenant terminates lease because he did not receive reasonable privacy and enjoyment to which he was entitled.

3 When owner refuses to make necessary repairs after being notified by tenant.

4 Eviction for failure to pay rent.

5 In case of destruction of property there is usually a termination.

6 A breach or violation of conditions of lease.

7 By mutual agreement commonly called "surrender." One cannot force the other to terminate without reason.

PROPERTY MANAGEMENT The management of that property is of interest to anyone who invests in real property as a source of income.

If you do not have the time or the ability to personally manage your property, you need professional help. Properties that need managing might be office buildings, store buildings, apartment houses, single-family residences, rental units, public housing, lofts, factories, garages, hotels, shopping centers, single purpose buildings such as theaters, restaurants, churches, hospitals, mortuaries, service stations, and public buildings.

In the simplest form, an owner desires to rent space that will bring sufficient return to pay all expenses and yield a return on the investment, while the tenant wishes to rent facilities within his income.

Many owners of real property have found that using a professional property manager results in savings and is not an expense because of the money saved through efficient management procedures.

SELECTING A PROPERTY MANAGER OR RESIDENT MANAGER

A professional property manager is an independent contractor paid by the owner through fees and/or commission on rents.

A resident manager is an employee of the owner and performs work specified by him.

Either one should be a person of experience and of good moral character. His experience should have rendered him capable of dealing with businessmen, husbands and wives, doctors and lawyers, engineers, financiers, and so forth. With this experience he should be a well-rounded, socially conscious, alert, and aggressive individual—in short, a skillful businessman.

Because the professional activity of property management has increased tremendously lately, a method of training and preparation for this group has arisen. Today the Institute of Real Estate Managers, under the designation IREM, operates to raise the professional standards of property managers and, through them, you can be assured of proper professional help in this area.

In keeping with IREM standards, the professional property manager today must:

Be a specialist in merchandising.

Be a leasing expert.

Have maintenance know-how.

Understand accounting.

Be a tax expert.

Be an expert in psychology.

Be interested in research.

Know every facet of insurance as it pertains to buildings.

Be a credit and finance expert.

SPECIFIC DUTIES OF A PROPERTY MANAGER

Among his duties, a property manager must:

Create and supervise maintenance schedules and repairs.

Establish the rental schedule.

Supervise all purchasing.

Develop a tenant-relations policy.

Develop employee policies and supervise their operations.

Maintain proper records and make regular reports to the owner.

Qualify and investigate the tenant's credit.

Prepare and execute liens.

Hire and instruct satisfactory personnel to staff the building(s).

Audit and pay bills.

Advertise vacancies through selected media and broker lists.

Plan alterations and modernizing programs.

Inspect vacant space periodically.

Keep abreast of the times and conditions.

Pay insurance premiums and taxes.

RESIDENT MANAGEMENT If you have property to rent and you are not living on or near the premises it's a good idea to hire a resident manager. Of course, this depends on your available time and the number of rental units on the premises.

A resident manager should possess the following qualifications: a pleasant personality that attracts tenants; the temperament and ability to meet the responsibilities required; a good appearance; honesty and integrity; willingness to perform housekeeping work; and availability for showing vacancies, collecting rents, and performing other necessary duties.

UNIT SUMMARY

In this unit we have defined and described a lease and, using a sample lease form, we identified the parts of the lease that are required.

We discussed "percentage lease" and the "straight lease" and learned how each is used.

We learned that the law requires a time limit for leasing various types of property and that there are four types of leases, determined by their duration: tenancy for years; periodic tenancy; tenancy at will; and tenancy at sufferance.

We discussed the rights, privileges, and obligations of the parties to a lease and learned that those of the lessor differed from those of the lessee.

We learned that a lease can be terminated by either party upon proper notice and that the actions of both are governed by law.

The conditions under which a professional property manager should be engaged and suggestions as to what type of person should be hired were explored.

REVIEWING YOUR UNDERSTANDING

MULTIPLE CHOICE

(   ) **1** A tenant under a written lease may break the lease if: (a) the property is uninhabitable; (b) the property is destroyed; (c) lessor breaks any of the lease provisions; (d) any of the above.

(   ) **2** Farm land in California may be leased for a period not to exceed (a) 10 years; (b) 15 years; (c) 99 years; (d) 51 years.

(   ) **3** Urban property can be subleased: (a) for up to 99 years; (b) for less than the term of the original lease; (c) for the full term of the original lease; (d) all of the above.

(   ) **4** The first action in an eviction procedure for nonpayment of rent would be: (a) the actual eviction notice; (b) 30-day notice; (c) 3-day notice; (d) unlawful detainer.

(   )   **5**   You rent a mountain cabin from October 1 to January 1. This is: (a) an estate for years; (b) a periodic tenancy; (c) a tenancy at will; (d) a tenancy at sufferance.

(   )   **6**   A lessee may terminate a lease if: (a) the lessor interferes with the lessee's peaceful possession; (b) the property is destroyed; (c) the lessor breaks the provisions of the lease; (d) all of the above.

TRUE OR FALSE

(   )   **1**   A tenancy from month to month is a form of periodic tenancy.

(   )   **2**   In California, renting a home for an unspecified term is not presumed to be for 1 month.

(   )   **3**   A lease is a relationship between the lessor and the tenant.

(   )   **4**   If a tenant is constructively evicted, he may not terminate his tenancy and sue for damages.

Read and study the *Real Estate Reference Book,* Chapter 25.

SUGGESTED LEARNING ACTIVITIES
REVIEWING YOUR UNDERSTANDING—ANSWERS

MULTIPLE CHOICE

1 (d)	**4** (c)
2 (d)	**5** (a)
3 (d)	**6** (d)

TRUE OR FALSE

1 True	**3** True
2 False	**4** False.

28

Brushing up on your knowledge of mathematics is a vital step in helping you to cope with the problems of daily living.

In preceding units, you have only been exposed to the application of some mathematical formulas and the need for some practical application of theory and philosophy.

This unit is a "thumbnail" review of five basic areas of mathematics: numbers, fractions, decimals, interest, and percent.

With the information given you will not be able to solve all mathematical problems, but it will help you to face some of the most common problems encountered in dealing in real estate.

Read this study guide (pages 262–271).
View TV program, number 28.

At the conclusion of this unit, you will be able to:

1 Add, subtract, multiply, and divide fractions and decimals as they apply to your real estate transactions.

2 Using the interest formulas, compute ordinary interest by using the regular computation methods and the special "6%-60 day method."

3 Using the percentage, base and rate formulas, compute problems involved in finding unknown quantities and in changing a percent to its equivalent decimal or fraction, or to change a decimal or fraction to its equivalent percent.

WHOLE NUMBERS   This type of number is made up of *digits* from 0 to 9. The value of the number depends on its position.

EXAMPLE

7265

7 is in the thousand position = 7000
2 is in the hundred position = 200
6 is in the ten position   =   60
5 is in the unit position   =   5
                                 ————
                                 7265

The number reads seven thousand two hundred sixty five.
Symbols are used to make any number meaningful.

$200 —dollars

200%—percent

200   —acres, feet, rods, miles, units, and so forth

FRACTIONS   A *fraction* is part of a whole.

EXAMPLE

$\frac{2}{3}, \frac{3}{4}, \frac{1}{8}$

In these examples the numbers above the line, 2, 3, and 1, are called the *numerator;* those below the line are the *denominator.*

¾ of an acre means an acre divided into 3 or 4 parts.

Proper fractions are those in which the denominator is larger than the numerator.

EXAMPLE

$\frac{1}{2}, \frac{7}{8}, \frac{13}{15}$

Mixed numbers are a combination of a whole number and a proper fraction.

EXAMPLE

$1\frac{2}{3}, 6\frac{5}{8}, 12\frac{3}{8}$

Improper fractions are those in which the numerator is larger than the denominator.

EXAMPLE

$\frac{8}{7}, \frac{12}{8}, \frac{23}{15}$

COMPUTATION RULES WITH FRACTIONS

Rule 1

In adding and subtracting fractions you must find a common denominator.

EXAMPLE

$$\begin{array}{l} 1/2 = 2/4 \\ + \, 3/4 = 3/4 \\ \hline = 5/4 \text{ or } 1\frac{1}{4} \end{array} \qquad \begin{array}{l} 6\frac{2}{3} = 6\frac{8}{12} \\ + \, 3\frac{1}{4} = 3\frac{3}{12} \\ \hline = 9\frac{11}{12} \end{array}$$

Rule 2

In multiplying fractions, multiply the numerator by the numerator and the denominator by the denominator.

EXAMPLE

$\frac{2}{3} \times \frac{3}{8} = \frac{6}{24}$ or $\frac{1}{4}$

$8 \times \frac{1}{4} = \frac{8}{4}$ or 2

Rule 3

In multiplying mixed numbers convert to an improper fraction and multiply.

EXAMPLE

$3\frac{1}{5} \times 4\frac{2}{3} = \frac{16}{5} \times \frac{14}{3} = \frac{224}{15}$ or $14\frac{14}{15}$

Rule 4

In dividing fractions, invert the divisor, the number below the line, and multiply.

EXAMPLE

$\frac{7}{8} \div \frac{2}{4} = \frac{7}{8} \times \frac{4}{2} = \frac{28}{16}$ or $1\frac{12}{16}$ or $1\frac{3}{4}$.

$15 \div \frac{5}{8} = \frac{15}{1} \times \frac{8}{5} = 24$

DECIMALS   A *decimal* is the *period* that sets apart the whole number from a fractional part of a number.

The value of a decimal number depends on the position of the number relative to the decimal.

EXAMPLE

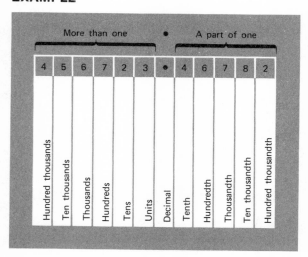

Rule 5

In adding or subtracting numbers with decimals, keep the decimal in the exact position. Zeros in a number must be given a position just as the digits are given a position.

EXAMPLES

ADDING

   2.451
  32.06
516.004

550.515

SUBTRACTING

305.06
  1.5724

303.4876

Rule 6

In multiplying by numbers with decimals, point off the total number of decimals in the *multiplicand* and *multiplier*.

EXAMPLE

54.2 — Multiplicand	1 decimal point
.08 — Multiplier	2 decimal points
4.336 — Product or sum	3 decimal points

3 decimal points (count from decimal each position to the left)

In using a decimal number in dividing, be sure to place the decimal properly by comparing decimals in the dividend with those in the divisor.

Rule 7

Move the decimal point in your imagination to the right in the divisor; in the dividend move it in your imagination the same number of positions, adding zeros to the dividend if necessary. Be sure to place the decimal point in the quotient directly above the new imaginary decimal position in the dividend.

EXAMPLE

```
                 4000.    quotient
Divisor   .08. |320.00.  dividend
                 32
                 000
```

INTEREST   Interest is the rent paid for the privilege of using another person's money.

The amount of money borrowed is known as the *principal*. A certain percentage of the principal is paid to the lender as *interest*. This percent or *rate* is quoted on an annual basis (yearly) unless otherwise specified.

The *time* is the period for which the money has been loaned, or borrowed, expressed in days, months, and/or years.

To facilitate computations, these symbols are used:

I = interest

P = principal

R = rate or percent

T = time

Follow this diagram.

Basic formula is $I = P \times R \times T$

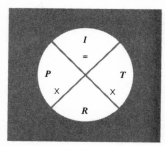

Other formulas derived from the basic formula are:

$$T = \frac{I}{PR} \qquad P = \frac{I}{RT} \qquad R = \frac{I}{PT}$$

Rule 8

Rate is expressed in percent or hundredths—commonly expressed in fractions or decimal fractions.

EXAMPLE

8% or .08 or $\frac{8}{100}$

Rule 9

In computing ordinary interest, (30 days per month and 360 days per year) days are usually expressed as a *fraction* of a year, if less than a year.

EXAMPLE

60 days or $^{60}/_{360}$ (if exact interest is used—exact days in month with 365 days per year)

SAMPLE PROBLEM   A note for $2000 at 8% for 60 days—find the ordinary interest.

$$\frac{\$2000}{1} \times \frac{8}{100} \times \frac{60}{360} = \$26.67$$

The 6%-60 day method is a shortcut to be used in computing interest.

SAMPLE PROBLEM   If the loan period is 60 days and the interest rate charged is 6%, the time and rate will cancel each other and the interest will always be .01 or 1/100 of the principal.

$$R \times T = \frac{\overset{1}{\cancel{6}}}{100} \times \frac{\cancel{60}}{\underset{6}{\cancel{360}}} = \frac{1}{100} \text{ or } .01 \text{ or } 1\%$$

EXAMPLE

A note for $300 at 6% interest for 60 days—find the ordinary interest.

$$\frac{\$300}{1} \times \frac{6}{100} \times \frac{60}{360} = \frac{300}{100} = \$3.00$$

Rule 10

In calculating the interest on a note for 60 days at 6%, move the decimal point in the *principal* two places to the left.

EXAMPLE

A note for $500 for 60 days at a 6% interest rate—find the ordinary interest using short cut method.

$500 = principal   interest = $5.00

Rule 11

If the product of the number of days specified in the note and the percent being charged is 360, the interest can be computed by moving the decimal in the *principal* two places to the left, the same as in Rule 10. The product of $6 \times 60 = 360$.

$300 at   2%—180 days =   3.00.

$1600 at   3%—120 days = 16.00.

$900 at   4%— 90 days =   9.00.

$2400 at   6%— 60 days = 24.00.

$2200 at   9%— 40 days = 22.00.

$1500 at 12%— 30 days = 15.00.

Rule 12

If the product of the number of days specified in the note and the percent being charged is close to 360—the exact amount can be computed by converting the *principal,* as in the 6%-60 day method, by first moving the decimal two places to the left and then adjusting the principal to meet the specified *time* and *rate,* in the problem.

SAMPLE PROBLEMS WITH SOLUTIONS

1. Find the interest on $300 at 3% for 60 days.

   2 |$3.00   2 |6%   for 60 days
      1.50   3%   for 60 days

2. Find the interest on $400 at 6% for 90 days.

   2 |$4.00   6%   2 |60 days
      2.00   6%   30 days
    $6.00   6%   90 days

3. Find the interest on $900 at 7% for 30 days.

   2 | 9.00   6%   2 |60 days
   6 | 4.50   6 |6%   30 days
      .75   1%   30 days
    $5.25   7%   30 days

If you either add, subtract, multiply, or divide the time or the rate as in problems 1, 2, and 3, you must do the same to the principal.

PERCENT   There are many problems using percent in their solutions, particularly in relation to real estate.

Problems related to the following are most common.

1 Commissions.

2 Depreciation of property.

3 Profit and loss.

4 Interest on loans.

CAUTION

Remember that the term *percent* is expressed in various ways. The figure 8% may be expressed as follows: 8 hundredths—8/100 or .08.

Rule 13

To change a fraction to a decimal, divide the numerator by the denominator.

EXAMPLE

$$\frac{2}{3} = 3 \overline{)2.00} \quad .66\tfrac{2}{3} \text{ or } 66\tfrac{2}{3}\%$$
$$\underline{1\ 8}$$
$$20$$
$$\underline{18}$$

Rule 14

To change a percent to a fraction, drop the percent sign and place the number over a denominator of 100. Then reduce the fraction to its lowest terms.

EXAMPLE

$$24\% = 24 \text{ hundredths} = \frac{24}{100}$$
$$\text{Reduced to lowest terms} = \frac{6}{25}$$

COMPUTING PERCENT PROBLEMS

In each percent problem there are three *variables* or quantities known as *percentage, base,* and *rate.*

Base is the beginning or the whole amount in the problem.

Percentage is a number representing part of the whole.

Rate or *percent* is a figure representing a ratio between *base* and *percentage,* in other words, percentage divided by the base.

NOTE

In any problem involving percent there will be two known values and one unknown variable.

To facilitate the solution of basic problems dealing with percent, follow this diagram.

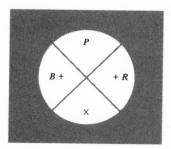

P = percentage B = base R = rate on percent

When the unknown variable is "*P*," cover the symbol "*P*." This will leave the symbols "*B*" and "*R*" uncovered.

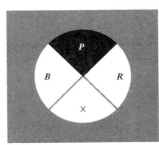

Multiplying the $B \times R$ will give the unknown (covered) symbol "*P*."

$$P = B \times R$$

EXAMPLE

John Jones owned $42,000 worth of stock. If he sold 25% of his stock last month, what was the value of the stock he sold?

$B = \$42,000$

$R = 25\%$

$P = \text{missing quantity}$

$$P = B \times R \text{ or } \$42,000 \times .25 = \$10,500$$

When the unknown variable is "*B*" cover the symbol "*B*." This will leave the symbols "*P*" and "*R*" uncovered.

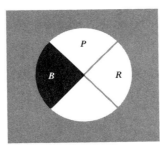

Dividing the P/R will give the unknown (covered) symbol "*B*."

$$B = \frac{P}{R}$$

EXAMPLE

James Philips sold $18,000 worth of equipment last week. If this was 37½% of the total company sales, what were the total company sales?

$P = \$18,000$

$R = 37\frac{1}{2}\%$

$B = \text{missing quantity}$

$B = \dfrac{P}{R} \text{ or } \$18,000 \div .375 = \$48,000$

When the unknown variable is "*R*," cover the symbol "*R*." This will leave the symbols "*P*" and "*B*" uncovered.

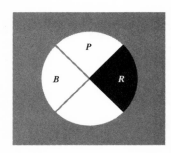

Dividing the *P/B* will give the unknown (covered) symbol *"B."*

$$R = \frac{P}{B}$$

EXAMPLE

John Brown sold $37,500 worth of merchandise last month. If the company sales were $125,000, what percent of the total sales did Brown make?

$B = \$125,000$

$P = \$37,500$

$R = $ missing quantity

$R = \frac{P}{B}$ or $\$37,500 \div \$125,000 = 30\%$

UNIT SUMMARY

This unit pointed out the importance of math in real estate transactions. A review of mathematical designations such as numbers, fractions, decimals, interest, and percent was given.

How to write and read fractions and decimal numbers was explained. Rules relating to use of fraction decimals and decimal fractions were reviewed with sample problems illustrating each rule.

Shortcuts and "memory joggers" related to the completion of problems concerning interest and percentage were represented by means of a wheel.

REVIEWING YOUR UNDERSTANDING

PROBLEMS INVOLVING INTEREST

1 Mr. Slade borrows $200 from the United California Bank, to be repaid in 6 months at 9% interest. What is the total amount of the note when due?

2 If Mr. Jones pays an annual rate of interest on a mortgage of 6%, the amount he pays is $360. What is the amount of the principal?

3 What is the annual interest rate on an $8000 loan with interest payments of $320 semiannually?

PROBLEMS INVOLVING COMMISSION

1 What amount will a salesman of a residential lot receive as commission if the lot sells for $14,000 and he receives 16% of a 6% commission paid to the broker?

2 A homeowner lists his home for sale. His asking price is $25,000 after paying a 6% commission to the broker. At what price would the broker have to sell the property in order to net $25,000 to the seller?

3 A salesman's commission on the sale of a house was $1800. The house sold for $26,500. What rate of commission did he receive?

PROBLEMS INVOLVING DEPRECIATION

1 Mr. Smith has owned his home for 5 years. He has depreciated it at the rate of 3% each year. When he bought the house, he paid $28,000. What is its present value?

2 A house is appraised at $22,000. The owner has been in possession for 6 years. The original price was $34,000. At what rate did the home depreciate each year?

PROBLEMS INVOLVING PROFIT AND LOSS

1 Mr. Snyder sold his home for $12,500. He made a profit of 25% on the sale. What was the original cost of the home?

2 Mr. James bought four pieces of property for $2000 each. He subdivided each piece into four lots and sold each lot for $1000. What was his gross profit?

PROBLEMS INVOLVING INTEREST

1 $209.00

2 $6000.00

3 8%

PROBLEMS INVOLVING COMMISSION

1 $134.40

2 $26,595.74

3 6.79%

PROBLEMS INVOLVING DEPRECIATION

1 $23,800.00

2 5.8%

PROBLEMS INVOLVING PROFIT AND LOSS

1 $10,000.00

2 $8000.00

29

In this unit we discuss the importance of deeds to home ownership. There are certain essentials that should be contained in the most common types of deeds. We will learn the various types of deeds and when each is used. We will also discuss some of the procedures involved in recording to safeguard your interests.

Read this study guide (pages 274–280).
View TV program, number 29.

At the conclusion of this unit, you will be able to:

1 List six essentials for a valid grant deed.

2 List the two implied warranties of a grant deed.

3 Compare a grant deed with a warranty deed.

4 List at least five different types of deeds and identify when you would use each.

acknowledgment   implied warranties
recordation   express warranties
delivery

BACKGROUND   When a property is sold, it is necessary to transfer ownership to the new buyer. This is usually done in California by executing a written instrument called a grant deed. The grant deed must be properly executed (completed), delivered, and accepted. The parties to the deed are the grantor (seller) and the grantee (buyer).

In order for the grant deed to be valid the following essentials must be present.

1 It must be in writing.

2 The parties must be properly described.

3 The parties must be competent to convey and capable of receiving the grant of the property.

4 The property conveyed must be adequately described.

5 There must be a granting clause.

6 The deed must be signed by the party or parties making the conveyance or grant.

Only the grantors' signatures are required. The deed must be delivered to the grantees. It is unwise for the grantors to sign a deed in blank (without the buyers' names), since the courts may later declare the deed void.

Witnesses or a seal are not required. The deed should be dated, but its validity is unaffected if it is undated. Below is an example of the form usually found in grant deeds.

"I Jerry Seller, grant to John Buyer, all that real property situated in Solano County, State of California, described as follows: Lot 13, Tract 47, recorded in Book 5 of Page 75 of maps of Solano County, Filed March 17, 1939. Witness my hand this sixth day of June, 1976.

(signed) Jerry Seller"

Although there is generally a consideration (something of value) given, this fact need not be mentioned in the deed. Nor is it necessary for a valid deed. In certain cases, the rights of the grantee relative to the rights of third parties may be affected by the lack of consideration. If a grantor is being sued and tries to dispose of his property to a friend or relative without a fair consideration, his creditors may have the deed set aside in some cases.

It is not legally required that a deed be acknowledged or recorded. As a practical matter, however, most deeds are both acknowledged and recorded for the protection of the parties.

ACKNOWLEDGMENT   An acknowledgment is a formal declaration before a duly authorized officer by a person who has executed an instrument that such execution is his act and deed. With certain exceptions, in order to be recorded, a deed must first be acknowledged. Once a deed is recorded, it is said to provide constructive notice (notice given by the public records) of its contents. This allows the document to be used as evidence without further proof.

Acknowledgments may be taken anywhere within the state. The parties who are authorized take acknowledgments are: a justice or a clerk of the Supreme Court or of the District Court of Appeal or the judge of a superior court. Others who are so authorized are: clerks of courts of record, county recorders, county clerks, court commissioners, notary publics, or judges of municipal or justice courts. Deputies of the above who are duly authorized by law may also make and take acknowledgments. Certain military officers may also fulfill this function for persons serving in the military.

If an individual has an acknowledgment taken outside of California he should have a certificate attached to the document stipulating that the document was taken in accordance with the laws of that state.

An omission of the date or an error in the date will not invalidate the document if it is correct in all other respects. An acknowledgment may not be taken by a party directly involved in the document. For example, a grantee to a deed or a mortgagee to a mortgage could not take their own acknowledgments. A husband or a wife should not acknowledge documents for each other. Acknowledgments may not be altered subsequent to delivery of the document. It is necessary to prepare new documents to be recorded.

California law is concerned with protecting property owners from having unauthorized persons record documents on their property. If this were not the case the owners might be subject to many unauthorized claims against the property that would appear on the public records. Therefore, many instruments must be acknowledged by the affected person. Most documents affecting or conveying property must be executed and acknowledged prior to being recorded. Examples are conveyances, mortgage and trust deeds, and agreements of sale.

RECORDATION   Although it is not a legal requirement, it is prudent to record a deed to protect the grantee's rights. One of the reasons for the creation of the recording laws was to show the priority of recordings relative to later recordings affecting property. If, for example, a buyer did not record his deed and the seller fraudulently sold the property again to another buyer, the original buyer's ownership would be in jeopardy.

Certain problems are involved in the possession of property. A buyer might assume that the individual living on the property is the owner when such might not be the case. Also, the person in possession might have a partially paid contract of sale or he might have a lease with an option to buy; this could affect the transfer of title.

If a buyer subsequently changes his name and later sells the property, he should sign the conveyance in the same name as when he acquired title or he should make reference to the prior name. As an example, a single woman who buys property as Mary Buyer and later marries should sign the deed as Mary Buyer Seller, formerly Mary Buyer, when selling.

DELIVERY   A deed must be delivered to be effective. However, delivery means more than merely turning over the document to another party. The intention of the grantor must be to pass title immediately. A father, for example, should not give his son a deed and tell him not to record it until his death, since the intention to pass title immediately would not be present. The law presumes a valid delivery when the deed is in the possession of the grantee or is recorded, but this is rebuttable. The deed itself cannot contain conditions for its delivery. Delivery to the grantee or his agent for him is absolute and takes effect as of its date. If undated, the deed takes effect as of the date of delivery.

TYPES OF DEEDS A grant deed (Figure 1) is the type of deed that we have been discussing. It is distinguishable because of a granting clause. A grant deed has certain implied warranties. These are that the grantor has not previously sold the property to another person and that he has not encumbered the property beyond that which he has disclosed to the buyer. Included are any easements and restrictions. These warranties are not expressly set forth in the deed. However, they are legally effective whether or not they are set forth.

FIGURE 1

RECORDING REQUESTED BY

AND WHEN RECORDED MAIL TO

Name
Street
Address
City &
State

SPACE ABOVE THIS LINE FOR RECORDER'S USE

GRANT DEED

DOCUMENTARY TRANSFER TAX $ _____
_____COMPUTED ON FULL VALUE OF PROPERTY CONVEYED,
_____OR COMPUTED ON FULL VALUE LESS LIENS AND
ENCUMBRANCES REMAINING AT TIME OF SALE.

Signature of Declarant or Agent determining tax. Firm Name.

THIS INDENTURE, made the _____day of_____,19____

BETWEEN

, the part_____of the first part

and

, the part_____, of the second part,
WITNESSETH: That the said part _____ of the first part, for and in
consideration of the sum of _____Dollars,
lawful money of the United States of America, to _____
in hand paid by said part _____ of the second part, the receipt whereof is hereby acknowledged, do_____by these presents, GRANT
_____unto the said
part_____ of the second part, and to_____heirs and assigns
forever, all th_____ certain lot_____, piece_____ or parcel_____ of land, situate,
lying and being in the _____, County of _____,
and State of _____, and bounded and particularly described as follows,
to-wit:

TOGETHER with all and singular the tenements, hereditaments and appurtenances thereunto belonging, or in anywise appertaining, and the reversion and reversions, remainder and remainders, rents, issues and profits thereof.
TO HAVE AND TO HOLD, all and singular the said premises, together with

Figure 1 (Continued)

the appurtenances, unto the said part_____ of the second part, and to _____heirs and assigns forever.

IN WITNESS WHEREOF, the said part_____ of the first part ha_____ hereunto set _____hand_____ and seal_____ the day and year first above written.

_____

_____

STATE OF CALIFORNIA,

County of_____ _____ }ss.

On _____, before me, the undersigned, a Notary Public in and for said State, personally appeared_____

_____

known to me to be the person____ whose name_____ subscribed to the within instrument and acknowledged that _____ executed the same. WITNESS my hand and official seal.

_____

Notary Public in and for said State.

MAIL TAX
STATEMENTS TO _____
        NAME   ADDRESS   ZIP

DEED—GRANT—WOLCOTTS FORM 778   This standard form covers most usual problems in the field indicated. Before
REV. 2-70   you sign, read it, fill in all blanks, and make changes proper to your
    transaction. Consult a lawyer if you doubt the form's fitness for your purpose.

FIGURE 2

RECORDING REQUESTED BY

WHEN RECORDED MAIL TO

┌─   ─┐
Name
Street
Address
City &
State
└─   ─┘

SPACE ABOVE THIS LINE FOR RECORDER'S USE

QUITCLAIM DEED

┌─────────────────────────────────────┐
DOCUMENTARY TRANSFER TAX $ _____
_____COMPUTED ON FULL VALUE OF PROPERTY CONVEYED,
_____OR COMPUTED ON FULL VALUE LESS LIENS AND
ENCUMBRANCES REMAINING AT TIME OF SALE.

Signature of Declarant or Agent determining tax. Firm Name
└─────────────────────────────────────┘

FOR A VALUABLE CONSIDERATION, receipt of which is hereby acknowledged

do hereby

Figure 2 (Continued)   REMISE, RELEASE AND FOREVER QUITCLAIM to

the real property in the   County of
State of California, described as:

Dated: _____

_____

_____

_____

State of California,

County of_____ } ss

On _____, before me, the undersigned,
a Notary Public in and for said State, personally appeared_____

_____

known to me to be the person____ whose name_____subscribed to the within
instrument and acknowledged that _____ executed the same.
Witness my hand and official seal.

(Seal) _____
Notary Public in and for said State.

Title Order No._____   Escrow or Loan No. _____

MAIL TAX
STATEMENTS TO _____
NAME   ADDRESS   ZIP

DEED—QUITCLAIM—Wolcotts Form 790   This standard form covers most usual problems in the field indicated.
Rev. 2-70   Before you sign, read it, fill in all blanks, and make changes proper to your
                                    transaction. Consult a lawyer if you doubt the form's fitness for your
                                    purpose.

A quitclaim deed (Figure 2) extinguishes any right or claim that a grantor felt he had. A quitclaim deed implies no warranties, nor does it guarantee anything. It is generally used to clear the title of a minor defect.

A warranty deed is seldom used in California because of the availability and reliance on title insurance. A warranty deed contains express covenants of title.

A reconveyance deed conveys the title to property from the trustee to the trustor when the trust is ended. This type of deed was discussed in Unit 11.

A sheriff's deed is given to the buyer as the result of a foreclosure sale. The title that is conveyed is only that acquired by the state or the sheriff under the foreclosure. It carries no warranties.

Sometimes an owner will make a gift of some or all of his property to another. He may do this with a grant deed, a quitclaim deed, or a gift deed. It is not required that the deed state love and affection as the consideration for the deed. A gift deed is void if it is made to defraud creditors.

UNIT SUMMARY

REVIEWING YOUR UNDERSTANDING

We discussed the importance of deeds to real estate transactions. We said that a grant deed was the most common type of deed used and that it had two important implied warranties. We learned the six essentials of a valid grant deed. We discussed the importance of acknowledgment, recordation, and delivery. We learned the basic characteristics of six different types of deeds and the characteristics of each.

TRUE OR FALSE

(   )   **1**   A grant deed has two important expressed warranties.

(   )   **2**   Warranty deeds are more frequently used in the eastern states than in California.

(   )   **3**   A deed may be given conditionally with instructions that it be recorded after a person's death.

(   )   **4**   Recording is necessary to provide public notice of property interests.

(   )   **5**   Recording establishes a list of priority between different interest and encumbrances.

FILL-INS

1 A _____ deed is frequently used to release a person's interest in property.

2 An instrument used to show that a deed of trust has been repaid is called a _____ deed.

3 An instrument given to the buyer at a foreclosure sale is a _____ deed.

REVIEWING YOUR UNDERSTANDING— ANSWERS

TRUE OR FALSE

1 False

2 True

3 False

4 True

5 True

FILL-INS

1 quitclaim

2 reconveyance

3 sheriff's

30

You have probably heard about homesteads in the past. In this unit you learn specifically what a homestead is and the theory behind the homestead laws. The exemption amounts, the selection of homesteads, the requirements for a valid homestead, and the termination of a homestead are discussed.

Read this study guide (pages 282–286).
View TV program, number 30.

At the conclusion of this unit you will be able to:

1 State the amount of a homestead exemption for a single person, the head of a household, and a person over 65 years.

2 List the order in which funds are distributed as the result of a forced sale of the homestead property.

3 List at least three important points involved with the selection of a homestead.

4 List at least three requirements for a valid declaration of a homestead.

5 Give a written explanation as to how a homestead may be terminated.

declaration of homestead
selection of homestead
declaration of abandonment

HOMESTEAD EXEMPTION

The word homestead refers to the personal residence of the owner. It consists of the residence itself, including outbuildings and the land on which they exist. The dwelling may be a home, a condominium, a planned development, a stock cooperative, or a community apartment project. It may exist on land that is leased for a period of 30 years or more. The law does not stipulate the amount of land that may be included in the homestead property. The determining factors are the use and occupation of the property.

The homestead with which we are concerned here should not be confused with the acquisition of title to federal lands by establishing residence or making improvements on them. Our discussion concerns the California law that permits a homeowner to protect his home from sale to satisfy his debts, within certain limitations. The homestead serves as a shield that enables an owner to save his home from certain creditors whom he is unable to pay. It is an example of the social policy of upholding the family.

EXEMPTION AMOUNT The amount of the homestead exemption is $20,000 for the head of the family or for any person over 65 years of age. The exemption is $10,000 for any other person. The head of the family is further defined as follows.

1 The husband or wife when the claimant is a married person.

2 Every person who has resided on the premises with him or her, and under his or her care and maintenance, either:

a His or her minor child, or minor grandchild, or the minor child of his or her deceased wife or husband.

b A minor brother or sister, or a minor child of a deceased brother or sister.

c A father, mother, grandfather, or grandmother either of himself or herself or of a deceased husband or wife.

d An unmarried sister.

e Or any other relatives above mentioned who have reached majority and are unable to take care of or support themselves.

The declaration of homestead protects the owner against seizure from unsecured judgments only. Examples of unsecured judgments are damages judgments, doctors' fees, and business debts. A homestead does not protect against secured judgments such as mechanic's liens or mortgages. Nor does a homestead protect against prior judgments that become liens before the declaration is recorded.

The homestead declaration can be recorded on property subject to a mortgage, and it will protect the property above the mortgage amount. In the example below if a homestead for $20,000 was recorded the property could not be subject to a forced sale because the equity is less than the homestead amount.

EXAMPLE

$ 40,000 value of home
−25,000 first deed of trust

$ 15,000 equity (equity is protected up to $20,000)

In the following example the home could be sold to satisfy the creditors because the equity exceeds the $20,000 homestead.

EXAMPLE

$ 40,000 value of home
−10,000 first deed of trust

$ 30,000 equity
−20,000 homestead exemption

$ 10,000 available to creditors

After receiving a judgment, the judgment creditor may apply to the superior court in which the homestead is located for an appointment of appraisers. He would do so to determine if the property value exceeds the total of the homestead exemption plus all liens and encumbrances. If this is true, the court may order the sale.

Whenever possible, the court may order a division of the land if practicable, and may order that only a portion be sold if that is sufficient to satisfy creditors. If a division is not possible, the court may order that all the real property be sold. At the sale the minimum bid must exceed the value of all liens and encumbrances on the property.

The proceeds from the sale are distributed in the following manner.

1 To the discharge of all liens and encumbrances, if any, on the property.

2 To the homestead claim and to the amount of the homestead exemption.

3 To the satisfaction of the execution.

4 To the homestead claimant if there is a balance.

If the owner sells the homestead property himself, the homestead exemption portion is protected for a 6-month period to allow him to reinvest in another dwelling and to declare a homestead on the new dwelling.

SELECTION OF HOMESTEAD

Only one homestead at a time is permitted. If a person has several properties, he may select only the property in which he resides.

If the homestead claimant is married, the property may be selected from community property, separate property, or from property held by the spouses as tenants in common, joint tenants, or separate property.

If the claimant is not married, or is the head of a family, any of his or her property may be selected.

REQUIREMENTS FOR A VALID DECLARATION

Each of the following requirements must be observed to have a valid declaration.

1 A statement showing that the claimant is the head of a family.

2 A statement that the claimant is residing on the premises and claims them as a homestead.

3 A description of the premises.

The law further provides that the declaration of homestead may but need not necessarily contain, in addition to the requirements above mentioned:

4 A statement of the character of the property sought to be homesteaded with sufficient detail to show it to be a proper subject of homestead, and that no former declaration had been made or, if made, that it had been abandoned or that the present claim of homestead is an augmentation of value of a former claim and is within the limits prescribed by law.

Even though the declaration may be sufficient in that it conforms to the statutory requirements, the homestead may be invalid in fact because the statements contained in the declaration are not true. From the records alone the validity of a homestead cannot be finally determined. As against attaching or judgment creditors, it is necessary to obtain a judicial determination as to the truth of the statements contained in the declaration.

Although the claimant must reside on the premises as of the date the declaration is recorded, he may later move from the premises and retain the homestead protection as long as he continues to own the property.

TERMINATION OF HOMESTEAD

A homestead may be abandoned by recording a document known as a declaration of abandonment. The date of recording is the termination date of the homestead. A deed does not destroy the homestead except as to innocent purchasers for value relying on the record. A reconveyance to one of the spouses under a trust deed does not destroy the homestead.

You should be cautioned against recording a homestead declaration on your property as a matter of course. The homestead is designed to protect your home from sale when you are being sued. A declaration can be recorded quickly any time before the case is heard and a judgment is recorded. Premature filing of the declaration when it is unnecessary may have a bearing on your credit rating; a potential lender may think you are being sued when, in fact, a law suit may not be in progress.

UNIT SUMMARY

In this unit we learned about the theory behind the homestead laws and the amount of the exemptions. We discussed the selection of a homestead, the requirements for a valid homestead, and the termination of a homestead. We stated that you should not necessarily file a declaration of homestead automatically when you buy your home as it may affect your credit rating. There is usually plenty of time to file if and when you are sued.

REVIEWING YOUR UNDERSTANDING

TRUE OR FALSE

(   )   **1**   A person over 65 years of age is entitled to a $20,000 homestead exemption.

(   )   **2**   If you have a homestead recorded on your home and you buy a new home, you may also file a declaration of homestead on the new property and be protected on both properties.

(   )   **3**   In a forced sale, the owner receives his money first.

(   )   **4**   A homestead claimant may subsequently move from his property and the homestead is still good, provided that another declaration is not made on another property.

( ) **5** A homestead may be terminated by recording an abandonment of homestead.

FILL-INS

1 If an owner had several properties he is entitled to _____ the property in which he lives on which to record his homestead.

2 The document used to protect the owner's equity from a forced sale up to a certain amount is called a _____.

3 An _____ would be recorded to dissolve a homestead.

TRUE OR FALSE

1 True	**4** True
2 False	**5** True
3 False	

FILL-INS

1 select

2 declaration of homestead

3 abandonment of homestead

GLOSSARY

Abatement   A method of termination of a nuisance.

Abstract   Recorded history of a property (copies of all recorded documents).

Abstract of judgment   A condensation of a court judgment which, when recorded in county where property of debtor is located, becomes a lien on said property.

Abstract of title   A summary or digest of the conveyances, transfers, and any other facts relied on as evidence of title, together with any other elements of record which may impair the title.

Acceleration clause   A clause in a trust deed or mortgage giving the lender the right to call all sums owing him to be immediately due and payable upon the happening of a certain event.

Acceptance   When the seller or agent's principal agrees to the terms of the agreement of sale, approves the negotiation on the part of the agent, and acknowledges receipt of the deposit in subscribing to the agreement of sale, that act is termed an acceptance.

Access right   The right of the owner to have ingress and egress to and from his property.

Accession   Acquiring property because it has become joined with other property (example: fixtures).

Accretion   An addition to land from natural causes as, for example, from gradual action of the ocean or river waters.

Accrued depreciation   The difference between the cost of replacement new as of the date of the appraisal and the present appraised value.

Acknowledgment   A formal declaration before a duly authorized officer by a person who has executed an instrument that such execution is his act or deed.

Acquisition   The act or process by which a person procures property.

Acre   A measure of land equaling 160 square rods, or 4840 square yards, or 43,560 square feet, or a square tract about 208.71 feet on a side.

Adaptability   One of the tests of a fixture.

Adjusted cost basis   For accounting purposes, the value of property equal to original cost plus improvements less depreciation.

Administrator   A person appointed by probate court to administer the estate of a deceased.

Administratrix   Woman administrator.

Ad valorem   According to valuation.

Adverse possession   The open and notorious possession and occupancy under an evident claim or right, in denial or, opposition to the title of another claimant.

Affidavit   A written statement sworn to under oath.

Affirm   To ratify or verify.

Affirmation   A solemn statement before a court by a person whose religion prohibits him from taking an oath.

Agency   The relationship between principal and agent which arises out of a contract, either expressed or implied, written or oral, wherein the agent is employed by the principal to do certain acts dealing with a third party.

Agent   One who represents another from whom he has derived authority.

Agreement of sale   A written agreement or contract between seller and purchaser in which they reach a meeting of minds on the terms and conditions of the sale.

Alienation   The transferring of property to another; the transfer of property and possession of lands, or other things, from one person to another.

Alienation clause   A form of acceleration clause usually to be found only in notes involving junior loans stipulating that all monies become due and payable immediately should there be a transfer of title.

Alluvion   Soil or silt deposited by water, as by the flow of a river or by tides. Also called illuviation.

Amenities   Satisfaction of enjoyable living to be derived from a home; conditions of agreeable living or a beneficial influence arising from the location or improvements.

A.L.T.A.   American Land Title Association   An extended coverage policy of title insurance to protect the lender.

Amortization   The liquidation of a financial obligation on an installment basis; also recovery, over a period, of cost or value.

Appraisal   An estimate and opinion of value; a conclusion resulting from the analysis of facts.

Appurtenance   Something annexed to another thing which may be transferred incident to it. That which belongs to another thing, as a barn, dwelling, garage, or orchard is incident to the land to which it is attached.

Assessed value   Value placed on property as a basis for taxation.

Assessment   The valuation of property for the purpose of levying a tax, or the amount of tax levied.

Asset   Anything of value, expressed in terms of money. Tangible or intangible.

Assignment   The transfer or making over to another of the whole, or any part of any property or any right therein. Assignor transfers to assignee.

Assignor   One who assigns to another.

Assumption   Taking over an obligation of another and agreeing to pay.

Assumption agreement   An undertaking or adoption of a debt or obligation primarily resting upon another person.

Assumption of mortgage   The taking of title to property by a grantee, wherein he assumes liability for payment of an existing note secured by a mortgage or deed of trust against the property, becoming a coguarantor for the payment of a mortgage or deed of trust note.

Attachment   Seizure of property by court order, usually done to have it available in the event that a judgment is obtained in a pending suit.

Attest   To affirm to be true or genuine, an official act establishing authenticity.

Attorney in fact   One who is authorized to perform certain acts for another under a power of attorney; power of attorney may be limited to a specific act or acts, or be general.

Auditor   One who examines and verifies accounts.

Avulsion   The sudden detachment or tearing away of land by action of water flowing over or through it.

Balance sheet   A statement of financial condition as of a given date, showing assets, liabilities and capital.

Balloon payment   A final payment, ordinarily the unpaid balance, which is much greater than preceding installments.

Bankruptcy   A situation in which one cannot pay his debts as they become due or in which his liabilities exceed his assets.

Base line   The arbitrary and imaginary east-west line used by surveyors under the Rectangular Survey system from which all north-south locations commence. Also see **Meridians.**

Basis   The beginning point for computing the amount of gain or loss on the sale.

Bench marks   A location indicated on a durable marker by surveyors.

Beneficiary   (1) One entitled to the benefit of a trust. (2) One who receives profit from an estate, the title of which is vested in a trustee. (3) The lender on the security of a note and deed of trust.

Bequeath   To give or hand down by will; to leave by will.

Bequest   That which is given by will.

Bilateral contract   A promise made for a promise.

Bill of sale   A written instrument given to pass title or personal property from vendor to vendee.

Blanket mortgage   A single mortgage which covers more than one piece of real estate.

Blighted area   A declining area in which real property values are seriously affected by destructive economic forces, such as encroaching inharmonious property usages, infiltration of lower social and economic classes of inhabitants, and/or rapidly depreciating buildings.

Board of equalization   Sits as an appeal board when one believes his property taxes are too high.

Book value   A value at which a firm carries an asset on its books. Its cost plus improvement expense less depreciation.

Bona fide   In good faith. Without fraud or intent to defraud.

Breach   To break. The violation of law, contract, right, or duty by omission or comission.

Broker   One employed as an agent for real estate dealings. Only a broker can employ a salesman.

Bundle of rights   Beneficial interests or rights.

Buyer's instructions   Instructions agreed upon by the buyer and filed in escrow.

C's of Credit, Three   In judging a credit risk, most lenders will adhere to this test—capacity, character, and capital.

Capacity   Refers to the borrower's ability to pay.

Capital   The difference between assets and liabilities of a business, showing owner(s) liabilities. Also expressed as net worth.

Capital assets   Physical assets (land, buildings, and equipment).

Capital gain   Profit from the sale of a capital asset (tax advantage).

Capital loss   Loss from the sale of a capital asset.

Capitalization method   An appraisal method based on income of a property.

Capitalization rate   A percentage of return which is divided into net income to arrive at value.

C.A.R.   California Association of Realtors.

Cash flow   Amount of cash left over from gross receipts after cash expenses (does not consider paper expenses such as depreciation).

Caveat emptor   "Let the Buyer Beware." The old rule now being replaced with duties on the seller.

CC&R's   Covenants, conditions and restrictions.

Certificate of title   An opinion of title showing liens.

Chain of title   A history of the actual conveyances from the original patent to the present owner.

Chattel   Archaic term for personal property.

Chattel mortgage   A mortgage on personal property.

Chattel real   An interest in real property (a lease).

Choses   Legal term for "things," relating solely to personal property. Two forms: choses in action and choses in possession.

Closing costs   A statement made at the close of escrow including: appraisal fees, escrow fees, costs of investigating or guaranteeing title, notary fees, recording fees, and prepaid items such as insurance or taxes.

Closing statement   Final accounting statement for a real estate transaction.

Cloud on title   Anything of record which may create any possible doubt as to marketability of the title.

C.L.T.A.   California Land Title Association. A C.L.T.A. policy is a policy of title insurance for the buyer.

Codicil   An addition or change to a will.

Collateral   Property given as security for a loan.

Color of title   An appearance of having title but actually not having title at all.

Commercial acre   A term applied to the remainder of an acre of newly subdivided land after the area devoted to streets, sidewalks and curbs, etc., has been deducted from the acre.

Commingling   Failure to properly segregate funds of licensee from funds entrusted to licensee as an agent.

Commission   An agent's percentage for successfully completing a sale, lease, and the like.

Community property   Property acquired during marriage owned equally by husband and wife.

Compaction   Packing soil to support a building load. Important where fill material has been used.

Comparables   Properties used in the market comparison approach in appraising.

Complete escrow   Escrow in which everything required to be done has been completed.

Compound interest Interest paid on original principal and also on the accrued and unpaid interest which has accumulated.

Condemnation The exercise of the power of eminent domain.

Condominium A system of individual fee ownership of units in a multifamily structure, combined with joint ownership of common areas of the structure and the land. (Sometimes referred to as a vertical subdivision.)

Consideration Anything of value given to induce entering into a contract; it may be money, goods or personal services.

Constructive eviction Any act by a landlord that renders property temporarily unfit for its intended use.

Constructive notice The notice given by recording. While parties are not actually notified it serves as notice.

Constructive severance When crops are sold they are considered to be personal property even though they have not been physically severed.

Contiguous In actual contact, near, adjoining.

Contract An agreement between two or more persons, upon sufficient consideration, either written or oral, to do or not to do a particular thing.

Contract of sale A document which is drawn to enable a buyer to purchase property.

Conventional loan A loan neither guaranteed nor insured by the government. Made by a lending institution.

Conversion Taking property of others and converting it to your own use.

Conveyance A transfer of property.

Corporation A fictional person, created according to law, which possesses many of the same rights as individuals in doing business.

Correlation The process wherein the results of the different appraisal approaches are analyzed.

Cosmetic changes This term refers to the appearance, the beautification of your home, inside and outside.

Cost basis A valuation of property for accounting purposes, equal to the original price plus acquisition expenses.

Counteroffer An offer made by the seller to the buyer.

Covenant An agreement written into a deed and other legal documents promising performance or nonperformance of certain acts or certain uses of the property.

C.P.M. Certified Property Manager A member of the Institute of Real Property Management of the National Association of Real Estate Boards.

Creditor One to whom money is due.

C.R.V. Certificate of Reasonable Value Required for VA loans.

Cul de sac A dead-end street ending in a circle. Desirable for homes as subject to little sound.

Curtesy The right a husband has in a wife's estate at her death. Abolished in most states and not applicable in any state recognizing community property.

Custom built home One designed to the owner's needs and specifications.

Damages Financial indemnification for injuries sustained by tort, following a successful court trial. The usual end result of a judgment. Also known as liquidation damages if a forfeit is involved.

Debtor A person owing a debt.

Declaration of homestead A recorded document giving person an exemption from unsecured liens. Filed on home by owner at time he is living in it.

Declaration of restrictions Restrictions recorded by the subdivider to cover all the parcels.

Dedication Giving real property free of charge to a public body.

Deed An instrument which, when properly executed and delivered, transfers the title to real estate.

Deed of reconveyance The transfer of a legal title from the trustee to the trustor after a trust deed debt has been paid.

Default Failure to perform a duty or promise. Failure to discharge an obligation incurred by agreement.

Defeasance clause Wording in a note or contract stipulating that the extra security held as collateral shall be returned intact, upon fulfillment of the contract.

Deferred maintenance Needed maintenance which has not been performed.

Deficiency judgment A judgment obtained when foreclosure sale of the loan security does not satisfy the entire debt.

Delivery Delivery means more than merely turning over the document to another party, the intention, time and recording are valid considerations.

Demand One of the four essential elements of value. Others are utility, scarcity, and transferability.

Demise To transfer a right in real property. Lessor demises to lessee the right of occupancy under a lease when lessee meets his obligations.

Deposit receipt A form used to accept earnest money to bind an offer for the purchase of real property.

Depreciation Decline in value of a fixed asset.

Devisee A person who receives under a will.

Devisor One who gives by will.

Discharge of contract Contracts can be discharged by full performance or by a breach by either party.

Discount loan A loan in which the interest is deducted in advance from the proceeds.

Discount points Interest rate lower than the rate charged by conventional lenders.

Discounting a loan Selling a loan for less than value owed.

Documentary transfer tax Tax amount for transfer of property, appearing on either the deed or an accompanying document.

Dominant tenement The property held by a tenant benefiting by an easement appurtenant.

Donee A person to whom a gift is made.

Donor A person who makes a gift.

Dower A wife's right in her husband's estate under common law (not in California).

Duress Unlawfully forcing a person to do some act which is against his will. If threat of physical violence is involved it becomes menace.

Easement A right or interest held by one person in property belonging to another, such as the right to maintain a road across it, or to install and maintain public utility services.

Economic life The useful life of an improvement. The period of time during which improvements are useful enough to justify their maintenance.

Egress Exit. Reference is usually to easements.

Emblements Cultivated crops (tenant has right to take crops after tenancy had ended if the product of his labor).

Eminent domain Right of government to acquire private property for public or quasi-public use. Owner is compensated.

Encroachment This is a trespass where a building or improvement is placed on or over the land of another.

Encumbrance Anything affecting title or use, such as liens, easements, covenants, and the like.

Endorsement Signing your name on the back of a negotiable instrument.

Enforceable The objects and considerations of a contract that can be enforced by law.

Equity The value of real estate less the sum of the liens against it. In law, it refers to natural justice, taking into consideration reason, natural rights, and ethics, rather than written law.

Equity investment The amount invested in property.

Equity of redemption The right to buy back property during foreclosure.

Erosion The wearing away of land by the action of water, wind, or glacial ice.

Escalator clause A clause in a contract or lease proving for adjustments in costs upward or downward.

Escheat The reversion of property to the state when a person dies with neither a will nor heirs.

Escrow A neutral depository for documents and funds to carry out instructions in a real estate transaction.

Estate An interest in property.

Estate for life A freehold interest that a person has in property for the duration of his life or someone else's life. His interest is not inherited by his heirs but either reverts to grantor or goes to someone having a remainder interest.

Estate for years An interest for a definite period of time (example: a lease for a specified period).

Estate of inheritance An interest that may be inherited.

Estate of will An estate which can be terminated without notice by either party (not in California).

Estoppel A doctrine whereby a person is barred from raising defenses when, by previous statements, he induced another to act to his detriment.

Et al. And others.

Et ux. And wife.

Exchange Trade for "like property."

Exclusive right to sell listing A written agreement between the owner and the agent giving the agent the right to collect a commission if the property is sold by anyone during the term of the agreement.

Execute To sign or to complete.

Executed contract A contract which has been performed.

Execution of judgment Having sheriff collect on a judgment by going against property or debtor.

Executor Person named in a will to carry out wishes of deceased.

Executrix Woman executor.

Exposure The directional position of a building with respect to sunlight and wind.

Express warranty A deed which contains express covenants of title.

Extended lease When a lease is extended, it is a continuation in possession under the old or original lease, after due notice has been given under its provisions.

Fee An estate of inheritance.

Fee simple Highest possible ownership. No time limit and it can be transferred or inherited.

Fiduciary The relationship of trust an agent has with the principal whom he represents by appointment.

Financing statement An instrument filed with a county clerk to give public notice of a security interest, in order to protect the interest of the secured parties in the collateral.

Fixture Anything of an accessory nature and which was personal property and which is attached to the land or any appurtenance in such a manner as to become a part thereof. Plumbing and electrical "fixtures" are examples.

Foreclosure The legal procedure by which a lender forces the sale of real property, after default by the borrower, to recover the monies advanced. Can be either by court action or public auction.

Forfeiture Liquidated damages. Loss of money or anything of value given as deposit due to failure to perform in accordance with an agreement or contract.

Fraud Intentional trickery or deceit to induce another to act to his detriment.

Freehold An interest in land either for life or in **Fee simple.**

F.T.C. Federal Trade Commission.

Gift deed A deed where the only consideration is love and affection.

G.N.M.A. Government National Mortgage Association (Ginny May) A government-owned corporation of the Department of Housing and Urban Development which assists federally aided housing programs and carries out the management and liquidating functions of the old Federal National Mortgage Association. The Government National Mortgage Association also guarantees securities issued by private lenders backed by the federal association, the Federal Housing Administration, the Veterans Administration, and some Farm Home Administration mortages or loans.

Government survey   A method of describing property measuring from base lines and meridians.

Grant   A transfer of real property.

Grant deed   The most usual instrument used to transfer the title to property in California. The deed carries implied warranties.

Grantee   One who acquires the title to property by deed.

Granting clause   A section in a deed stating "I grant" or "I convey" and essential to a valid deed.

Grantor   One who conveys the title to property by deed.

Ground lease   A lease of land only.

Ground rent   That portion of the rent attributable to the land alone.

Guarantee of title   A guarantee based entirely upon recorded documents (by abstractor).

Habendum   The granting clause of a deed. Defines extent of ownership transferred and sets forth any exceptions or reservations.

Holder in due course   A person who, in good faith and for value, obtains a promissory note or check before it is overdue, without knowledge of any defects.

Holographic will   A handwritten, dated and signed will (no witnesses required).

Homestead   A home on which a Declaration of Homestead has been filed.

Hypothecate   To give or offer a thing as security for a loan without surrendering possession. The opposite of pledging.

Identification test   To determine whether or not a given piece of personal property is a fixture.

Implied warranty   A guarantee assumed by law to exist in an instrument, although it is not specifically stated, as in a grant deed.

Impound   A trust account established by lenders for the accumulation of funds to meet taxes, Federal Housing Administration mortgage insurance premiums, and future insurance policy premiums required to protect their security. Impounds are usually collected with note payments.

Increment   An increase, such as the increase in the value of land that accompanies population growth and increasing wealth in a community. The term unearned increment is used in this connection, since values are supposed to have increased without effort on the part of the owner.

Initial investment   Amount invested in the beginning by the buyer.

Injunction   A court order prohibiting or compelling an act.

Installment sale   A sale in which, for income tax purposes, the seller spreads the receipt of the proceeds over two or more tax years and does not receive more than 30 percent in the first year of sale.

Intention   One of the tests of a fixture.

Intestate   Having died without a will. Estate passes to heirs on the basis of relationship.

Intestate succession   When a person dies without leaving a will, the decadent's share of the estate automatically passes to the surviving spouse by intestate succession.

Involuntary lien   A lien imposed without the agreement of the property owner, such as a tax lien.

Joint and several   A term meaning "together or individually." Commonly used in a note which has two, or more signers authorizing lender to collect from any one or combination of the signers. Often referred to as a "joint" note.

Joint tenancy   Joint ownership by two or more persons with right of survivorship, all joint tenants own equal interest and have equal rights in the property.

Judgment   The final order of a court.

Junior lien   A subordinate lien.

Jurisdiction   The area in which a court or officer has authority.

Laches   Delay or negligence in asserting one's legal right.

Land contract   An agreement whereby land is sold, usually on an installment basis, and the buyer does not receive a deed until the contract is paid in full.

Landlord An owner or manager of real property who leases property to someone else.

Latitude Latitude lines are imaginary lines circling the globe running parallel at a given distance north or south of the equator.

Lease A contract between owner and tenant, setting forth conditions upon which the tenant may occupy and use the property, and the term of the occupancy.

Lessee One who contracts to rent property under a lease contract.

Lessor An owner who enters into a lease with a tenant.

Leverage Purchasing raw land with the express purpose of selling some of the property and developing the balance is known as leverage.

Liabilities Amounts owed by an individual or company.

Lien A form of encumbrance which usually makes property security for the payment of a debt or discharge of an obligation (examples: judgments, taxes, mortgages, deeds of trust, and the like).

Life estate The right to use property for one's lifetime only.

Liquidated damages The extent of monetary compensation agreed upon in a contract in the event of default.

Liquidity The ability to quickly convert assets to cash.

Lis pendens A notice of a pending lawsuit.

Listing A contract between owner and broker authorizing broker to procure buyer or tenant for an agreed compensation.

Loan correspondent A person who acts as a servicing agency for blocks of money made available by savings and loan organizations, insurance companies, individuals and other groups.

Longitude Imaginary lines circling the globe. They are located east or west of the prime meridian at Greenwich, England.

Lot and block system A system used most frequently for identifying and registering residential and business property.

M.A.I. Designation of a member of American Institute of Appraisers of the National Association of Realtors.

Maker Person who signs a note or instrument and is primarily liable.

Map Act The act which gives local control of the general layout of streets, lot size, and other physical aspects of a subdivision.

Margin of security Difference between amount of mortgage and appraised value.

Marginal land Land where financial return barely pays for the effort expended.

Market price Price paid regardless of circumstances of the sale.

Market value Price a willing buyer would pay to a willing seller.

Marketable title Merchantable title, free from objectionable liens and encumbrances.

Meridians Imaginary north-south lines intersecting the base lines. In locating land from government survey we measure from these intersections.

Metes and bounds Measuring land by distances and directions, setting forth all of the boundary lines.

Method A means used to determine whether or not personal property is a fixture. (The method by which it is fastened down.)

M.L.S. **Multiple listing service** Used in listing property for sale.

M.M.I. Mutual Mortgage Insurance.

Mobile home Living accomodations, when on wheels considered as personal property, when permanently established in mobile home park considered real property.

Model A home prepared for viewing by prospective buyers.

Moisture control A type of preventative maintenance to prevent moisture damage or water seepage.

Monument A fixed surveyor's marker from which property is located.

Moratorium A delay in the performance of a legal obligation or payment of a debt, usually authorized by law.

Mortgage A security device whereby the borrower retains title but gives a lien and a note to the lender (property is hypothecated).

Mortgage guaranty insurance Private insurance which guarantees the lender against loss caused by buyer's default.

Mortgagee The lender of money under a mortgage.

Mortgagor One who gives a mortgage on his property to secure a loan or assure performance of an obligation; a borrower.

Multiple listing Usually an exclusive right to sell listing which is given out to a group of brokers with rights to sell (a cooperative listing).

Mutual consent The parties to a contract must mutually agree to be bound to the terms of the contract.

Mutual water company A water company organized by users to supply water at reasonable rates. Stock is issued to users.

N.A.R. National Association of Realtors.

N.A.R.E.B. National Association of Real Estate Boards.

National Home Improvement Council A national association of quality contractors whose main function is that of raising the professional standards in the business.

Net listing A listing which provides that the broker may retain as his commission that part of the sale price above a specified amount.

Nonfreehold estate An estate for years or a leasehold interest.

Note Signed instrument acknowledging a debt and promising to pay.

Notice of abandonment Formal way to end homestead declaration. Homestead is also abandoned by its sale.

Notice of cessation Notice filed when construction is halted. It sets period for filing mechanics liens.

Notice of completion Filed by owner for purpose of setting time for filing of mechanics liens.

Notice of default Issued under a deed of trust and sets three-month period for trustor to make his payments.

Notice of nonresponsibility Recorded and posted by owner within 10 days of discovering unauthorized work on his property to avoid liability.

Notice of sale A notice from an owner or broker that a specific real property has been sold and is no longer available.

Notice to quit Notice to tenant to vacate rented premises.

Novation The substitution of a new agreement for an old one.

Nuncupative will An oral deathbed will which must be reduced to writing by the witnesses.

Obsolescence Loss in value due to reduced desireability.

Offer A proposal to make a contract. Also called offer to buy.

Offeree One who receives an offer.

Offeror One who makes the offer.

Offset statement Statement by holder of lien (amount owed).

Open listing An authorization by the owner to the broker where the broker has a nonexclusive right to sell. More than one open listing can, therefore, be given at the same time.

Option A right given for a consideration to enter into a purchase or contract (a contract to make a contract).

Optionee Person receiving the right to form a contract.

Optionor Person giving the option.

Owner One who holds title to property.

Ownership in severalty When title to property is held by one person or a corporation.

Par value Market value; nominal value.

Party wall A wall built on the dividing line of property for use of both owners. Also called common wall.

Patent Conveyance of title to government land.

Percentage lease For business purposes, lessee pays as rent a percentage of his gross sales.

Perfect escrow One in which all the terms of the escrow have been met.

Periodic tenancy Ownership rights are established over an indeterminable period of time.

Personal property Material or things of a movable nature; any property which is not real property.

Planning commission A local government agency which determines the proper physical growth of a community and recommends zoning ordinances and other laws for that purpose.

Pledge The making of personal property security for payment of a debt, including the transfer of possession to the lender.

Plottage increment The appreciation in unit value created by joining smaller ownerships into one large single ownership.

Points In loan transactions, 1 point is 1 percent of the amount of the loan. Bonuses and commissions are often expressed in points.

Police power The right of the state to enact laws and enforce them for the order, safety, health, morals, and general welfare of the public.

Potable Drinkable.

Power of attorney A written authorization given by an individual to another to act for him. It may be for specific purposes or in general.

Power of sale Legal method of disposing of property after default at a trustee's sale.

Prepayment penalty Penalty for paying off a note prior to its maturity.

Prescription Obtaining an easement by adverse use.

Principal Employer of an agent.

Probate A period during which the superior court has jurisdiction over the administration of the estate of a deceased person.

Progression, principle of The rule that the worth of a residence of lower value tends to be enhanced by association with many higher-valued residences in the same area.

Promissory note A written contract containing a promise to pay a definite amount of money at a definite future time.

Property Either real or personal—termed "material wealth."

Proration To apportion based on actual time to the date of sale (taxes, rents, and the like).

Quiet title A court action brought to establish title; to remove a cloud on a title.

Quitclaim deed A deed to relinquish any interest in property which the grantor may have.

Range A strip of land six miles wide determined by a government survey, running in a north-south direction.

Real estate board An organization whose members consist primarily of real estate brokers and salesmen.

Real property Land and that which is attached to and goes with land.

Real property securities dealer A broker who sells notes secured by real estate for which there is a guaranteed rate of return.

Realtist A black broker organization composed of members of N.A.R.E.B., formed in 1947.

Realtor A broker member of N.A.R.E.B.

Reconveyance The deed from the trustee back to the trustor when the debt has been satisfied.

Recordation Giving notice by recording with county recorder.

Regression, principle of The rule that in a neighborhood of differing values a more valuable home will seek the level of the less valuable homes.

Release clause An agreement in a blanket encumbrance to release individual properties from the encumbrance upon payment of an agreed sum.

Rental agreement Whether written or oral it is to state when rent is to be paid along with other items of mutual agreement.

Request for notice of default   An acknowledged request filed with the county recorder by the holder of a junior lien so he may be notified of the actions of prior lien holders.

Restriction   An encumbrance which limits the use of real estate in some way.

Right of survivorship   The right of a joint tenant to acquire the interest of a deceased joint tenant automatically.

Right of way   Privilege to pass over land of another.

Riparian right   Right of a landowner to reasonable use of water on, under, or adjacent to his property.

Risk   The chance that the investor takes that he may lose all investments.

Rumford Act   A California fair housing act.

Satisfaction   Discharge of mortgage or trust deed lien from the records upon payment of the evidenced debt.

Scarcity   A condition of inadequate supply which creates value.

Security   Something posted as a guarantee for the full and faithful performance of an agreed upon act.

Secondary financing   A loan secured by a second mortgage or trust deed on real property.

Section   A one mile square parcel of land containing 640 acres. There are 36 sections in a township.

Security agreement   Agreement between debtor and lender or seller whereby the latter retains a security interest in personal property of the debtor (under Uniform Commercial Code).

Seller's instructions   Instructions agreed upon by the seller and filed in escrow.

Selection of homestead   If a person has several properties, he may select one property on which to file his declaration of homestead.

Separate property   Property which is separately owned and not community property. Acquired prior to marriage or by gift or inheritance.

Settlement sheet   Before close of escrow a distribution of cost items between buyer and seller.

Severalty ownership   Ownership by one person.

Sheriff's deed   Deed by sheriff after a sale to satisfy a judgment.

Specific performance   An action to compel performance of an agreement (example: sale of land).

S.R.A.   One who is a member of the Society of Real Estate Appraisers.

S.R.E.A.   Senior real estate appraiser.

Stamp sale   If delinquent taxes remain unpaid by June 30 the property is sold to the state. It is called a stamp sale because the tax bill is marked with a rubber stamp.

Statute of frauds   State law which provides that certain contracts must be in writing in order to be enforceable at law (examples: real property lease for more than one year; agent's authorization to sell real estate).

Statute of limitations   Sets forth the time in which legal action must be started or the right will extinguish (for contracts, four years).

Straight lease   A lease for a fixed, agreed-upon price for a certain period, with regular periodic payments of equal amounts. Also known as a flat lease.

Straight note   An instrument which acknowledges a debt and promises payment, in which the principal is payable in one sum.

Subject property   Property being appraised.

Sublease   Lease given by a lessee to another.

Subordinate   To be junior to another encumbrance.

Subrogation   Substitution of one party for another. In an accident, a victim's insurance company, after paying him, can sue party causing injury in his place.

Surety   One who guarantees performance of another.

Surrender   Mutual agreement of parties to terminate lease.

Survivorship   Right of joint tenants to interests of other joint tenants upon their death.

Tax deed   Given by tax collector at auction.

Tax rate Amount assessed real property, based on 25 percent of the market value.

Tax shelter An income property or other investment that offers considerable tax savings.

Tenancy at sufferance Tenant holding over after expiration of his lease.

Tenancy at will Tenancy where no advance notice is required to end tenancy. In California 30 days notice is required to evict.

Tenancy for years The most commonly used leasehold, specifically states a mutually agreeable time period.

Tenancy in common Ownership by two or more of an undivided interest without the right of survivorship. Interests do not need to be equal.

Tenant One who resides on the property of a landlord.

Tenements Rights which pass with the land.

Termination statement Statement filed with secretary of state by lender to remove personal property lien of the financing statement.

Termites Insects which feed on wood. Most dangerous are subterranean termites.

Termite report A report made to the licencee on the condition of the home, dealing with all forms of pests and infestations.

Testate Having died leaving a will.

Testator Person who made a will.

Tier East-west rows of townships.

Title Evidence of ownership. Passed by deed.

Title insurance Insurance written by title company to owner guaranteeing ownership.

Topography Changing surface elevations of land.

Township A territorial subdivision 6 miles long and 6 miles wide, containing 36 sections, each 1 mile square.

Trade fixture Personal property annexed to real estate for purpose of carrying on a business or trade. It may be removed by owner prior to expiration of lease.

Traffic pattern Most convenient route of passage from room to room.

Transferability One of the four essential elements of value.

Trespass Wrongful entry on the land of another.

Trust deed Deed given by trustor to trustee as security for loan.

Trustee Party who holds trust property for another.

Trustor One who gives the trust deed (the buyer or borrower).

Uniform Commercial Code Since January, 1965 in California. Sets standard commercial laws.

Unilateral contract A promise in exchange for an act. It is accepted by the performance of the act.

Unity of interest In joint tenancy, each tenant has the same interest in the property.

Unity of possession In joint tenancy, each tenant has an equal right to possession over the whole of the property.

Unity of time In joint tenancy, each owner possesses his interest and his title at one and the same time.

Unity of title In joint tenancy, joint tenants must own in the same manner evidenced by the same conveyance or means of title transfer and have equal rights to the property.

Utility value Related to an appraisal concept known as the "highest and best use."

Unlawful detainer The legal eviction proceeding in which tenant is ordered to appear in court.

Unruh Act An act which prohibits a broker from discrimination based on race.

Valuation The estimated worth or price of something; the act of valuing by appraisal.

Vara A measurement of approximately 33 inches used in early surveying days.

Variable interest rate An interest rate that can go up or down, pegged to an economic indicator.

Vendee A purchaser; buyer.

Vendor   A seller; one who disposes of a thing in consideration of money.

Verification   Sworn statement before a duly qualified office to the correctness of the contents of an instrument.

Veterans Administration (VA)   A federal agency which insures or guarantees the repayment of home loans taken out by veterans of the armed forces.

Void   To have no force or effect; that which is unenforceable.

Voidable   That which is capable of being adjudged void, but is not void unless action is taken to make it so.

Voluntary lien   Any lien placed on property with consent of, or as a result of, the voluntary act of the owner.

Warranty deed   A deed used to convey real property which contains warranties of title and quiet possession; the grantor thus agrees to defend the premises against the lawful claims of third persons. It is commonly used in other states, but not in California, where the grant deed has supplanted it. The modern practice of securing title insurance policies has reduced the importance of express and implied warranty in deeds.

Witnessed will   A formal written document signed by the one who is making it, wherein he declares in the presence of at least two witnesses that it is his will.

Yield   The interest earned by an investor on his investment. Also called return.

Zoning   The act of city or county authorities specifying the type of use to which property may be put in specific areas.